Energy in
Orthodox Theology
and Physics

The publication of this book is part of the activities of the
International Center for Theological and Scientific Culture (ICTSC)
Faculty of Theology, Sofia University "St Kliment Ohridski," Bulgaria

Energy in Orthodox Theology and Physics

From Controversy to Encounter

Stoyan Tanev

WITH A FOREWORD BY
David Bradshaw

PICKWICK *Publications* · Eugene, Oregon

ENERGY IN ORTHODOX THEOLOGY AND PHYSICS
From Controversy to Encounter

Pickwick Publications
An Imprint of Wipf and Stock Publishers
199 W. 8th Ave., Suite 3
Eugene, OR 97401

www.wipfandstock.com

PAPERBACK ISBN: 978-1-5326-1486-6
HARDCOVER ISBN: 978-1-5326-1488-0
EBOOK ISBN: 978-1-5326-1487-3

Cataloguing-in-Publication data:

Names: Tanev, Stoyan | Bradshaw, David, 1960–, foreword writer

Title: Energy in Orthodox theology and physics : from controversy to encounter / Stoyan Tanev, with a foreword by David Bradshaw.

Description: Eugene, OR: Pickwick Publications, 2017 | Includes bibliographical references.

Identifiers: ISBN 978-1-5326-1486-6 (paperback) | ISBN 978-1-5326-1488-0 (hardcover) | ISBN 978-1-5326-1487-3 (ebook)

Subjects: LCSH: Religion and science—Christianity | Orthodox Eastern Church—Doctrines | Physics—Religious aspects—Christianity | Gregory Palamas, Saint, 1296–1359

Classification: BL240.3 T152 2017 (print) | BL240.3 (ebook)

Manufactured in the U.S.A.   08/28/17

To Mateo Tanev—my newly born grandson,
the son of my son George and Mary

Contents

Part II: The Encounter between Theology and Physics

Foreword _____

The Distinction between Divine
Essence and Energies

I t has now been more than half a century since a number of pioneers such as Fr. Georges Florovsky, Vladimir Lossky, Fr. Dumitru Staniloae, and Fr. John Meyendorff began to draw the attention of the Western world to St. Gregory Palamas (1296–1359). Broadly speaking, their claims on his behalf fell under three headings: ecclesiastical, historical, and theological. At the ecclesiastical level they maintained that Palamas's thought was not merely a piece of late Byzantine arcana of interest only to scholars, but represents the authentic and authoritatively affirmed teaching of the Eastern Orthodox Church. From a historical standpoint, they maintained that Palamas's thought is in full continuity with that of the Greek Fathers, including St. Athanasius, the Cappadocian Fathers, St. Dionysius the Areopagite (although Fr. Meyendorff had reservations at this point), St. Cyril of Alexandria, St. Maximus the Confessor, St. John of Damascus, and St. Symeon the New Theologian. Finally, at the theological level they maintained that Palamas's teaching is of essential value today, representing the best and most cogent way of understanding the relationship between God, Man, and the World.

These three claims have had widely different fates. The first has won virtually unanimous acceptance; the second has won widespread, although far from unanimous, acceptance, and remains an object of scholarly debate; and the third has received not even much attention, to say nothing of agreement, beyond the bounds of Eastern Orthodoxy. In English-speaking countries, at any rate, one rarely finds Palamas mentioned within popular or semi-popular discussions of Christianity, nor in scholarly works outside of academic theology. Within my own two fields, the history of philosophy and the philosophy of religion, he remains virtually unknown. This is not because philosophers are uninterested in the Christian tradition; the same period has seen lavish philosophical analyses of the thought of Augustine, Anselm, Aquinas, Scotus, and others. It is because, for most Western scholars, the Christian tradition remains almost exclusively the *Western* Christian tradition. Unfortunately, despite its considerable value, the work of the pioneers I have mentioned has failed to make much of a dent upon this wide-standing predilection.

I believe that this is due to two primary causes. First, the advocates of Palamas have failed to situate his thought within the history of Western philosophy in the way that Augustine, Aquinas, and other such luminaries can be placed within it. Second, they have failed to explain it directly in relation to its biblical sources. Much of my own work has been directed toward correcting these two deficiencies. A number of other scholars have also been engaged in this effort, so much so that one may legitimately speak of a renewal of interest in the Orthodox teaching on the divine essence and energies.[1] Among other topics, this new wave of scholarship has addressed the reception of the teaching of St. Gregory Palamas among both the Orthodox and non-Orthodox.

It is within this context that we should consider the present book by Dr. Stoyan Tanev, a Bulgarian-born physicist, theologian, and interdisciplinary scholar with a vigorous interest in Orthodox theology. The majority of existing works on this topic tend to address it from a polemical interconfessional perspective. The work of Dr. Tanev is not less polemical, but focuses on two specific main aspects—the initial reception of the teaching within twentieth-century Eastern Christian theological thought and the exploration of its interdisciplinary potential, with an emphasis on the interplay between theology and physics. To my knowledge this is by far the most thorough analysis yet made of the structural isomorphism in the diverse roles of the concept of energy in these two widely disparate fields. Readers of this volume will have no difficulty in familiarizing themselves with the insights and value of Dr. Tanev's work. In the remainder of this Foreword I will provide a brief introduction to the concept of the divine energies, focusing particularly on its biblical sources and its use by the early Church Fathers.[2]

1. In addition to my own works I would mention some of the most relevant the recent publications such as: Larchet, *La théologie des energies divines*; Tollefsen, *Activity and Participation in Late Antique and Early Christian Thought*; and the papers collected in Athanasopoulos and Schneider, *Divine Essences and Divine Energies*, as well as the recent works by Bulgarian authors such as: Каприев, *Византийската философия*; Стоядинов, *Божията благодат*; Христов, *Византийското богословие през XIV век*.

2. A longer version of this text has been published as: Bradshaw, "The Concept of the Divine Energies," 93–120; and republished in Athanasopoulos and Schneider, *Divine Essence and Divine Energies*, 27–49.

I.

Energeia is a term coined by Aristotle and of great importance for Greek philosophy. The role it plays in Aristotle's works is complex. Without attempting to probe all of its complexities, a brief summary of some key points will help to indicate the resonances it had already acquired prior to its use by St. Paul.

In Aristotle's earliest works *energeia* means the active exercise of a capacity, such as that for sight or thought, as distinct from the mere possession of the capacity. From this beginning it soon acquired two further, seemingly unrelated senses: that of "activity" and that of "actuality." (Its correlative term *dunamis* likewise has two meanings, capacity and potentiality.) These two senses, which seem to us quite distinct, sometimes reconverge. In *Metaphysics* IX.6 Aristotle distinguishes *energeia* from motion or change (*kinēsis*) on the grounds that a motion or change is ordered toward some extrinsic end—as housebuilding aims at a house—whereas an *energeia* is its own end. The examples given are seeing, thinking, understanding, living well, and flourishing. Plainly these are activities, but they are *activities that are fully actual* in the sense that they contain their own end and thus are fully complete at each moment of their existence, rather than requiring a stretch of time for their completion. Aristotle illustrates this difference with the so-called "tense test," namely that at each moment that one sees (or thinks, or so on) one also "has seen," whereas at each moment that one builds a house one has not also built a house.

During the Hellenistic era the term's meaning most often is simply "activity," although the association with actuality is often not far beneath the surface. The most important development is that in some works of Hellenistic Judaism, as well as in the Greek historian Diodorus Siculus, there is a new focus on the *energeia* of God or the gods, where these are understood now as personal agents. In such contexts it can sometimes be appropriate to translate *energeia* as "energy."[3] However, there is not yet a developed concept of divine energy, something that began to emerge only in early Christian literature.

In addressing this development it is helpful first to note the range of meaning of the English term "energy" (shared by cognate terms in other modern European languages). Here is the entry for "energy" in the *American Heritage Dictionary*:

> 1. a. Vigor or power in action. b. Vitality and intensity of expression. 2. The capacity for action or accomplishment: *lacked*

---

3. Bradshaw, *Aristotle East and West*, 54–56.

energy to finish the job. 3. (Usually plural) Power exercised with vigor and determination: *devotes one's energies to a worthy cause.* 4. (Physics) The work that a physical system is capable of doing in changing from its actual state to a specified reference state.

We can set aside sense 4 as irrelevant to the ancient period. In order to show that *energeia* means energy in an ancient author, one must show that its sense corresponds to one of the senses 1–3.

When one turns to St. Paul against this Hellenistic background, the first point which leaps to attention is that Paul reserves *energeia* and *energein* (the active form of the corresponding verb) for the action of spiritual agents—God, Satan, or demons.[4] This was quite unprecedented. Earlier sources had used both terms freely in a variety of ways, including for the action of material objects, human beings, and the natural elements, as well as of spiritual beings. This is true even of two sources that in other respects often provide important precedents for Pauline usage, the Septuagint and Philo of Alexandria.[5] Paul's restriction of *energeia* and *energein* to supernatural action was so striking that it apparently established a precedent for subsequent Christian literature. All occurrences of the two terms in the Apostolic Fathers refer to the action of God, Christ, angels, or demons. This association between *energeia/energein* and supernatural agency was not without an effect upon the meaning of the two terms. The *energeia* of a supernatural agent, when it is present in a human being, is most readily understood as a power or capacity for certain kinds of action. We accordingly find *energeia* shifting toward the meaning of "a capacity for action or accomplishment" ('energy' in sense 2), and *energein* shifting toward that of "to be active in a way that imparts an energy."

To what extent does St. Paul's own usage fit this pattern? This question does not admit of a simple answer, for Paul's usage is subtle and varied. One reason why most scholars have been reluctant to see in it anything more than the traditional meanings of the two terms is that (unlike the Apostolic Fathers and Greek Apologists) he apparently does not reserve the middle/passive form of *energein*, *energeisthai*, for spiritual agents. Taking this verb as middle, as it is standardly rendered, the subjects of whom it is used include "the motions of sin," comfort, death, faith, power, the divine

---

4. See 1 Cor 12:6, 10–11; Gal 2:8; Eph. 1:11, 19–20; 2:2; 3:7; 4:16, Phil 2:12–13; 3:21; Col 1:29; 2:12; 2 Thess 2:9, 11. I shall assume for the sake of simplicity that Paul was in fact the author of all the Pauline writings. Those who doubt this may, if they wish, substitute for my references to Paul a circumlocution such as "Paul and his imitators."

5. Bradshaw, *Aristotle East and West*, 51–60; Bradshaw, "The Divine Energies in the New Testament," 198.

energeia, the word of God, and the "mystery of iniquity."[6] It is certainly strange that Paul would use the noun and the active form of the verb with programmatic consistency, while using the middle form in such an apparently random fashion.

In fact, it can be shown that *energeisthai* in antiquity is never middle, but only passive, and furthermore that Paul's use of the term was uniformly taken as passive by the Church Fathers. So understood the meaning of *energeisthai* falls into place as correlative to *energein*, meaning either (depending on the context) "to be acted upon" or "to be made effective, to be energized." That *energeisthai* is passive was already recognized around the turn of the last century by two eminent New Testament scholars, Joseph B. Mayor and J. Armitage Robinson.[7] Unfortunately their work was ignored by most subsequent translators and lexicographers. I will not repeat here the evidence that *energeisthai* is passive, merely remarking that it seems to me about as solid as such a case could be.[8] Once the true meaning of this word is recognized, Paul's usage in the anomalous verses turns out to fit the predominant pattern, for the unexpressed agent in virtually every case is God or Satan. I have elsewhere reviewed all the relevant passages in detail.[9] Here I will mention just a few that seem especially significant. One is Colossians 1:29, where Paul refers to himself as "striving according to Christ's working (or energy, *energeia*), which is being made effective (or energized, *energoumenēn*) in me" (Col 1:29). This verse brings out well the synergistic tendency of Paul's thought. On the one hand, the divine energy is at work within Paul, transforming him, so that from this standpoint he is the object of God's activity; on the other, it finds expression in Paul's own activity, so that Paul's free agency and that of God coincide. Indeed, not only do the actions Paul alludes to in this passage exhibit full engagement and self-control, they do so more than did his actions prior to his conversion. As the story is told in Acts, Saul was trapped in self-deception until God set him free on the road to Damascus. Now the divine energy which works in him is also his own, more truly than anything he did was his own before he ceased to "kick against the pricks" (Acts 9:5).

Other passages also bring out what I believe we may call, without exaggeration, Paul's synergistic ontology. One of particular clarity is Philippians 2:12–13: "Wherefore, my beloved, as ye have always obeyed, not as in my

6. See Rom 7:5; 2 Cor 1:6; 4:12; Gal 5:6; Eph 3:20; Col 1:29; 1 Thess 2:13; and 2 Thess

7. Mayor, *The Epistle of St. James*, 177–79; Robinson, *St. Paul's Epistle to the Ephesians*, 244–47. Both works have been frequently reprinted.

8. Bradshaw, "The Divine Energies in the New Testament," 201–8.

9. Ibid.; see also Bradshaw, *Aristotle East and West*, 121–22, from which I borrow in this and the next few paragraphs.

presence only, but now much more in my absence, work out (*katergazesthe*) your own salvation with fear and trembling. For it is God which worketh in you (*ho energōn en humin*) both to will and to do (*energein*) of his good pleasure." Here the exhortation to act is coupled with a reminder that it is God who is acting. Neither negates the other; the Philippians are both free agents responsible for their own salvation, and the arena in which God works to bring about that salvation. Bearing this duality in mind, one could legitimately translate, "it is God who *imparts energy* in you both to will and to do of his good pleasure," where "to do" refers *both* to the Philippians' action *and* to God's action as it is expressed in them. This rendering helps bring out why for Paul there is no contradiction in urging the Philippians to do something that he also sees as the work of God. The peculiar nature of God's activity is that it imparts the energy to do His will, although this energy must be freely expressed or "worked out" to be effective.

Finally let us note a passage that was of the utmost importance for the Greek Fathers, the description of the gifts of the Spirit in 1 Corinthians 12.

> Wherefore I give you to understand, that no man speaking by the Spirit of God calleth Jesus accursed: and that no man can say that Jesus is the Lord, but by the Holy Ghost. Now there are diversities of gifts, but the same Spirit. And there are diversities of administrations, but the same Lord. And there are diversities of operation (*energēmatōn*), but it is the same God which worketh (*ho energōn*) all in all. . . . For to one is given by the Spirit the word of wisdom; to another the word of knowledge by the same Spirit; to another faith by the same Spirit; to another the gifts of healing by the same Spirit; to another the working of miracles; to another prophecy; to another discerning of spirits; to another divers kinds of tongues; to another the interpretation of tongues; but all these worketh (*energei*) that one and the selfsame Spirit, dividing to every man severally as he will. (12:3–11, A.V.)

This passage begins by asserting that even such an ordinary and voluntary action as calling Jesus lord requires the cooperation of the Spirit. It goes on to list a variety of spiritual gifts, each one an *energēma* (something performed) of the Spirit. They include not only extraordinary gifts like the working of miracles, but also more ordinary qualities such as faith and the "word of wisdom." Again there is no dividing line between the natural and the divine. Any believer is called to a life of continual cooperation with the Spirit, a cooperation that can manifest itself in any number of ways, both exceptional and mundane.

To speak of synergy could be misleading if it suggested a picture of two equal agents who simply choose to work together. Plainly, since in these cases one is the Creator and the other a creature, the action of the latter depends for its reality upon the active support of the former. I take it that Paul interprets this notion in light of the common experience (which he had vividly shared) of feeling that one's actions were not truly one's own while one was mired in sin and self-deception. On his view, synergy, the cooperation of God and man, is neither a symmetrical relation nor one in which the divine overpowers and replaces the human. It is rather one in which the human *becomes fully human* by embracing the divine. This is not a radically new idea; indeed, it is a prominent theme in the Old Testament.[10] What is new is the use of the vocabulary of *energeia* to express it.

II.

We are now are in a position to see what use the Greek Fathers made of these ideas. For brevity I will focus on the Eunomian controversy of the mid-fourth century. Eunomius was a philosophically sophisticated Arian who had a simple argument that the Son is not God. It was that God is ingenerate or unbegotten, and furthermore this is not merely a privative attribute or human conception, but the divine essence (*ousia*) itself. Plainly such an *ousia* cannot be shared with another by begetting; hence the Son, who is begotten of the Father, cannot be of one essence (*homoousion*) with the Father. As for terms such as "life," "light," and "power," which in the New Testament are used of both the Father and the Son, Eunomius argued that they must be taken differently in the two cases. Since the divine essence is utterly simple, "every word used to signify the essence of the Father is equivalent in force of meaning to 'the unbegotten' (*to agennēton*)."[11] Said of the Father such words signify the divine essence; said of the Son they signify a creature.

The task of replying to Eunomius fell to St. Basil of Caesarea. Basil objected both to the assumption that the divine *ousia* can be known and to assumption that, because of divine simplicity, all non-privative terms said of God are identical in meaning. He writes:

> We say that we know the greatness of God, His power, His wis-
> dom, His goodness, His providence over us, and the justness of
> His judgment, but not His very essence (*ousia*). . . . But God,

10. For example, in Psalm 1, and in the psalms of repentance such as Psalm 51.
11. Eunomius, "Apology 19," in *Extant Works*, 59.

he [Eunomius] says, is simple, and whatever attribute of Him you have reckoned as knowable is of His essence. The absurdities involved in this sophism are innumerable. When all these high attributes have been enumerated, are they all names of one essence? And is there the same mutual force in His awfulness and His loving-kindness, His justice and His creative power, His foreknowledge and His requital, His majesty and His providence? In mentioning any of these, do we declare His essence?

The question, then, is how to characterize the distinction between that in God which cannot be known (the divine *ousia*) and that which can be known, such as the divine power, wisdom, and goodness. Basil's answer emerges in the continuation of the passage:

The energies are various, and the essence simple, but we say that we know our God from His energies, but do not undertake to approach near to His essence. His energies come down to us, but His essence remains beyond our reach.[12]

As I understand him, Basil is here applying to the Christian God the distinction between *ousia* and *energeia* found in the philosophical tradition, and particularly in Plotinus.

His doing so raises at least two distinct questions. One is that of the ontological relationship between the essence and the energies. The other question is that of divine freedom, or, more precisely, the capacity to do otherwise. In the Christian tradition God is thought of as sufficiently like a person that in at least some cases, such as the creation of the world, He could do otherwise. Should we say, then, that His energies could be different than they are?

As regards the first question, plainly for Basil the energies are not a separate hypostasis or series of hypostases; rather, they are acts that God performs. Many scholars would in fact prefer to translate *energeia* in the passage which I have quoted as "operation," and to take Basil as saying only that God's *operations* come down to us. I believe that the entire history of the distinction between the divine *ousia* and *energeia*, both in pagan and Christian thought, argues against such a view. I find support at this point in an interesting semantic argument presented by Basil's brother, St. Gregory of Nyssa. Gregory adopts the view, which was widespread in antiquity, that a name is in some way indicative of the form or intrinsic characteristics of the thing named. Since God has no form, He has no name in the proper sense. Instead, terms such as "god" (*theos*) name the divine *energeia* of oversight

---

12. Basil, "Epistle 234," in *Nicene and Post-Nicene Fathers*, Vol. 8, 274 (modified).

or governance.[13] (Gregory derives *theos* from *theaomai*, behold.) Now it is plain that by *energeia* here Gregory has in mind an operation. However, it cannot be *only* an operation, for then in speaking of God we would be speaking of an operation of God—that is, an operation of an operation, and so on in an infinite regress. Somehow by *energeia* Gregory and Basil would appear to understand *both* that which God is *and* that which God performs. For them there is a distinction is between God *as He exists within Himself and is known only to Himself*, and God *as He manifests Himself to others*. The former is the divine *ousia*, the latter the divine energies. It is important to note that both are God, but differently conceived: God as unknowable and as knowable, as wholly beyond us and as within our reach.

In putting the distinction this way, however, we must not suppose that the essence and energies are separated by a fixed and permanent boundary. The Cappadocians think instead of that which is unknowable in God as a kind of receding horizon. Precisely the fact that we cannot know God as He knows Himself draws us forward to seek to know Him ever more deeply. St. Gregory Nazianzen expresses vividly this sense of a longing that is always both being satisfied and seeking satisfaction:

> In Himself [God] sums up and contains all being, having neither beginning in the past nor end in the future; like some great sea of being, limitless and unbounded, transcending all conception of time and nature, only adumbrated by the mind, and that very dimly and scantily—not from the things directly concerning Him, but from the things around Him; one image (*phantasias*) being got from one source and another from another, and combined into some sort of presentation (*indalma*) of the truth, which escapes us when we have caught it, and takes to flight when we have conceived it, blazing forth upon our master-part, even when that is cleansed, as the lightning flash which will not stay its course does upon our sight—in order as I conceive by that part of it which we can comprehend to draw us to itself . . . and by that part of it which we cannot comprehend to move our wonder, and as an object of wonder to become more an object of desire, and being desired to purify, and by purifying to make us like God.[14]

---

13. Bradshaw, *Aristotle East and West*, 161–64; Le Grys, "Names for the Ineffable God," 333–54.

14. Gregory Nazianzen, "Orations 38.7," in *Nicene and Post-Nicene Fathers*, Vol. 7, 346–47.

The "things around God" are, I take it, another name for the divine energies.[15] This fundamental distinction between God as He is known to Himself and as He is known to us was derived by the Cappadocians not from philosophical sources, but from the Bible. Most obviously, it was inspired by the encounter of Moses with God on Mount Sinai (Exodus 33). There God warns Moses that "thou canst not see my face: for there shall no man see me, and live." Nonetheless he continues: "it shall come to pass, while my glory passeth by, that I will put thee in a clift of the rock, and will cover thee with my hand while I pass by: And I will take away mine hand, and thou shalt see my back parts: but my face shall not be seen" (33:22–23, A.V.). Gregory Nazianzen takes this passage as a model for understanding his own experience. In doing so he draws a distinction much like that we have seen in Basil between God as He is known to Himself and as He "reaches to us":

> What is this that has happened to me, O friends and initiates and fellow lovers of the truth? I was running up to lay hold on God, and thus I went up into the mount, and drew aside the curtain of the cloud, and entered away from matter and material things, and as far as I could I withdrew within myself. And then when I looked up I scarce saw the back parts of God, although I was sheltered by the rock, the Word that was made flesh for us. And when I looked a little closer I saw, not the first and unmingled nature, known to itself—to the Trinity, I mean; not that which abides within the first veil and is hidden by the Cherubim, but only that nature which at last even reaches to us. And that is, so far as I can tell, the majesty, or as holy David calls it, the glory which is manifested among the creatures, which it has produced and governs. For these [i.e., the majesty and glory] are the back parts of God, which He leaves behind Him as tokens of Himself like the shadows and reflections of the sun in the water, which show the sun to our weak eyes because we cannot look at the sun itself.[16]

More broadly, the Cappadocians took all the biblical theophanies—including, most famously, the burning bush of Exodus 3—as pointing to a similar distinction. In such events God is known *precisely as unknowable*; it is the very extremity of His condescension in appearing and making Himself known which underscores the deep chasm between His mode of being and our own.[17]

15. Bradshaw, *Aristotle East and West*, 166–67.

16. Gregory Nazianzen, "Orations 28.3," in *Nicene and Post-Nicene Fathers*, Vol. 7, 289.

17. See further Bradshaw, "The Divine Glory and the Divine Energies".

In light of this biblical background, the notion of *theōsis* or deification may seem like a foreign importation. It is at this point that the Pauline usage of the concept of *energeia* becomes crucially important. As I mentioned earlier, an especially important passage was 1 Corinthians 12. Basil in *On the Holy Spirit* builds upon this passage to develop an understanding of the gifts of the Spirit as a form of divine energy. He writes:

> As is the power of seeing in the healthy eye, so is the energy (*energeia*) of the Spirit in the purified soul. . . . And as the skill in him who has acquired it, so is the grace of the Spirit ever present in the recipient, though not continuously active (*energousa*). For as the skill is potentially in the artisan, but only in operation when he is working in accordance with it, so also the Spirit is present with those who are worthy, but works (*energei*) as need requires, in prophecies, or in healings, or in some other carrying into effect (*energēmasin*) of His powers.[18]

This passage is almost Aristotelian in its distinction between an enduring state of the soul (in Aristotelian terms, first actuality) and its active expression (second actuality). But for Basil these are two different forms of energy, the one latent and the other active. Basil understands participation in the divine energy as an ongoing state of the soul that finds expression, as need be, in particular acts. This is what is meant by deification in the Greek patristic tradition: an ongoing and progressively growing participation in the divine energies.[19]

From all of this it is clear how the second of our two questions, that of whether the divine energies could be different than they are, is to be answered. If they are the sphere of personal action in the way that I have described, then at least some of them could be different; otherwise they would be a kind of emanation rather than the free acts of a free Creator. However, the same constraint means that there are limits to the ways that they could be different. The range of acts which would constitute a legitimate expression my character is quite large, yet I trust that at least some acts, such as murder, adultery, or treason, fall beyond it. In the same way, if the divine energies are to manifest the divine *ousia*, then although they can vary enormously they must fall within the range that is properly related to the divine *ousia* (whatever it might be!) as expression to source. For example, God need not have created, and given that He did create He might have created the world differently than He did; furthermore, even given that He created this world He might act within it differently, for example, by distributing

18. Basil, "On the Holy Spirit XXVI.61," in *Nicene and Post-Nicene Fathers*, Vol. 8, 38.

19. See further Bradshaw, *Aristotle East and West*, 172–78, 193–201; Russell, *The Doctrine of Deification*.

different spiritual gifts. Thus, many of the divine energies, including those of creation, providence, and foreknowledge, as well as the gifts of the Spirit, could be different or could not exist at all. On the other hand, if He acts at all His action cannot fail to be good. Hence, if there are any energies at all, goodness is among them. The same would seem to be true of wisdom, being, power, life, love, holiness, beauty, virtue, immortality, eternity, infinity, and simplicity, all of which the Cappadocians, or other Church Fathers after them, list among the divine energies.

To know whether these energies are necessary, then, we must ask whether it is possible that God not act at all—that is, whether He could be wholly without energy (*anenergēton*). So far as I know this question was not raised in such terms. However, a question very close to it—that of whether there would be divine energies even apart from creation—was at the center of the celebrated hesychast controversy in the fourteenth century which provoked the work of Gregory Palamas. The hesychast monks claimed to have been granted a vision of what they called the uncreated light. Whether it is possible that there be such a light, and if so what its nature is, became the focus of intense debate. Ultimately it was decided that there *is* an uncreated light and that it is simply the visible form of the divine energy.[20]

This means that the divine energy is present in some form with the Godhead from all eternity, quite independently of the act of creation. And that in turn implies that the divine energy is not (as one might otherwise be tempted to suppose) simply the way in which God manifests Himself to creatures. It is that, to be sure, but even without creatures there would still be an eternal self-manifestation within the Godhead. Within a Christian context it is natural to understand this as the mutual love and self-revelation of the persons of the Trinity. There are hints of such a view among the earlier Greek Fathers, beginning with Gregory of Nyssa, but unfortunately the debate over the divine energies in the fourteenth century failed to make these connections explicit.[21] Once they are made it becomes clear how there can be *uncreated* divine energies which are not "emanations," as was charged by Palamas's critics.

David Bradshaw

University of Kentucky

20. See Meyendorff, *A Study of Gregory Palamas*; Bradshaw, *Aristotle East and West*, 229–42.

21. See Bradshaw, *Aristotle East and West*, 214–20, 242, 273–74.

Preface

I have never been satisfied with textbook definitions of energy in physics—neither during the time of my Masters and PhD studies, nor during my years as a professor of physics. Most of these definitions tend to adopt an instrumentalist approach to its meaning, thus avoiding the discussion of any physical reality behind the concept. As it appears, many physicists, including many great ones, do not seem to appreciate what would they call "philosophical" questions. Yet the concept of energy has a fundamental place in physics. I found some comfort in the fact that other physicists have also struggled with its definition. According to Eugene Hecht the concept of energy "influences our thinking about every branch of physics, indeed, about every aspect of our existence. Yet there is no completely satisfactory definition of energy. Even so," continues Hecht, "we will quantify its various manifestations as we struggle to define it."[1] And that is what I have been doing—struggling to find a more meaningful definition of energy and continuously looking for ideas and contexts that could help for a better articulation of the concept.

The opportunity to explore further the concept of energy came from within the realm of Christian theology and, more specifically, Eastern Christian or Orthodox theology. It was exactly twenty years ago when I realized that the concept has had a fundamental role in Byzantine and contemporary Orthodox theology. It goes right to the heart of Orthodox theology and affects the whole body of Christian doctrine. According to Vladimir Lossky, "Wholly unknowable in His essence, God wholly reveals Himself in His energies. . . . The doctrine of the energies, ineffably distinct from the essence, is the dogmatic basis of the real character of all mystical experience."[2] This was a striking message for me. *First*, it makes a whole lot of sense for a

---

1. Hecht, *Physics*, Vol. 1, 222.

2. See Lossky, "Uncreated Energies," Ch. 4 in *The Mystical Theology of the Eastern Church*.

physicist who was systematically trained that the only way to explore invisible physical realities is by enabling the energetic manifestations of their inner structures. *Second*, it turns upside down the dominant understanding of religion as the adoption of a coherent system of obligatory beliefs associated with specific institutions and rituals, concerning a supernatural God who governs the world as a kind of natural law, having little to do with relating to human beings in a personal manner. *Third*, it puts the question of God into an epistemological context by emphasizing that He can actually be known.

"God wholly reveals Himself in His energies." I felt that this is a critically important message but what were the Holy Fathers telling me? What type of knowledge were they talking about? How does this knowledge relate to the words of the Lord in the Gospel of John (17:3) "And this is eternal life, that they know you, the only true God, and Jesus Christ whom you have sent." What do I need to do in order to become part of such revelation? What did the Fathers mean by using the term energy and what does it mean in the context of Orthodox theology? How do others understand the above statement? Having struggled for a long time with the meaning of energy in physics, do I have an advantage in understanding the message of the Church Fathers?

Searching for answers to the questions above was the reason for me to start a parallel study of the concept of energy in Orthodox theology and physics. And I have been greatly encouraged by my spiritual father and first theology teacher at St. Paul University in Ottawa, Canada,—Fr. Maxym Lysack, the parish priest of Christ the Saviour Orthodox Cathedral in Ottawa: "You are a physicist and you should search for these answers by studying theology and exploring the theological insights of the Church Fathers!" I must emphasize therefore that this exploration for me has been, before everything, theo-logical. The comparison with physics was not what I have been looking for, but part of the way I have been looking. I have not tried to use physics to explain theology or the other way around. I have tried to see how theology and physics struggle in articulating the challenges of knowing in their own way. In articulating and comparing these challenges I did find my own way to the dialogue between theology and physics. In both cases the challenges have been associated with controversies. It is the similarity of the challenges and the controversies that offers a way to the encounter of theology and physics, and hence the subtitle of the present book.

I am grateful to Fr. Maxym Lysack as well as to Fr. George Dragas—Fr. Maxym's theology professor and teacher from the Holy Cross Greek Orthodox School of Theology in Boston, USA, whom I had the blessing of having as a teacher myself at the University of Sherbrooke, Québec, Canada, for their guidance, encouragement and wisdom. My deepest gratitude goes also to Dr. John Hadjinicolaou, the Director of the Orthodox Theology Program at the Montreal Campus of the University of Sherbrooke (now at Laval

University), who encouraged me to join the program and focus on research at the interface of theology and science. It has been a rewarding journey. I am also grateful for the encouragement and help by Georgi Kapriev, Jean-Claude Larchet, and David Bradshaw. My interaction with their works and with each one of them personally turned into friendships that have been most valuable to me over the years. Kapriev's books *Byzantine Philosophy*[3] and *Maximus the Confessor*[4] helped me seeing the teaching on the distinction between Divine essence and energies as a key to a deeper understanding of Orthodox theology. Bradshaw's *Aristotle East and West*[5] and the debates it has initiated[6] just confirmed my initial insights and let me go deeper into the substance of the different theological issues. I am grateful to him for the Foreword of this book, which I find to be a great and necessary introduction to the topic. Larchet's *La divinisation de l'homme selon saint Maxime le Confesseur*,[7] *La théologie des* énergies *divines*[8] and *Personne et nature*,[9] have become a great source of insights and inspiration for me. I first met Larchet face-to-face in a miraculously unexpected way in 2007, in the main Church of the Vatopedi monastery on Mount Athos. I have particularly appreciated his friendly insistence that the subject of my work is highly relevant and that I should focus on transforming my initial excitement into a completed published work. He was also the one who encouraged me to present a first version of it at the Colloquium "The Theology of the Divine Energies" of the Orthodox Theology Program of the University of Sherbrooke in Montreal, 2008.[10] Last but not least, I would like to express my gratitude to Fr. Nicholas Loudovikos whose works, theological contributions, and style have become a great inspiration for me. I have greatly enjoyed our fruitful discussions and look forward to our future copperation in both theological and interdisciplinary projects.

My colleagues at the Faculty of Theology at Sofia University, Bulgaria—Pavel Pavlov, Ivan Christov, Alexander Omarchevski and Svetoslav Ribolov—deserve a special gratitude. The reference to the works of Ivan Christov was an important part of my work. His newly published book

3. Каприев, *Византийска философия*.

4. Каприев, *Максим Изповедник—Въведение в мисловната му система*.

5. Bradshaw, *Aristotle East and West*.

6. Athanasopoulos and Schneider, *Divine Essence and Divine Energies: Ecumenical Reflections on the Presence of God in Eastern Orthodoxy*.

7. Larchet, *La divinisation de l'homme selon saint Maxime le Confesseur*.

8. Larchet, *La théologie des énergies divines*.

9. Larchet, *Personne et nature*.

10. It was included in: Ladouceur, Paul, ed. *The Wedding Feast—Proceedings of the Colloquia of Orthodox Theology of the Univeristé de Sherbrooke 2007–2009*. Montreal: Alexander, 2010.

Byzantine Theology in the XIV Century[11] is a serious and highly valuable contribution to the field. I hope that his and Kapriev's works will be soon translated into English. On a personal level, I should say that my colleagues in Sofia have accepted me as one of their own and encouraged me to write a PhD dissertation in theology that was published in Bulgarian by Sofia University Press as *Thou, Who art everywhere and fillest all things: Essence and energy in Orthodox theology and physics.*[12] I am particularly grateful to my friend Pavel Pavlov, who first suggested that I should engage into a formal PhD study in theology and guided me through the process. Our friendship emerged in parallel to our discussions of the ideas articulated in the first part of this book. The Faculty of Theology in Sofia was also open enough to engage in exploring the interface between Orthodox theology and contemporary physics by letting me teach a first course on this subject and drive the organization of the International Conference "Orthodox Theology and the Sciences" in April 2010.[13] I must say that my adjunct professorship at the Faculty of Theology in Sofia has been a great honor for me.

I am grateful to my wife Maia, my son George, my parents and closest relatives, for their continuous support over the years. It is my real pleasure and joy to let them join me in dedicating this book to my newly born grandson Mateo, the son of my son and his lovely wife Mary.

The present book is not an extended version of my PhD dissertation in theology. It includes modified and further elaborated versions of two chapters from my PhD dissertation, but its main purpose is to go further and offer newly published material with a stronger focus on interdisciplinarity and the interface between theology and physics. It is, however, a book on theology that could be seen as a collection of essays that I have published in English. There will be therefore some overlaps across the different chapters for which I apologize in advance. I tried to minimize them as much as possible but it was impossible to remove them entirely without destroying the integrity of the individual chapters. I hope that the reader will appreciate the coherency of the different themes, theological opinions and potential insights.

Stoyan Tanev

January 19, 2017, Odense, Denmark
Feast of the Theophany of our Lord God and Savior Jesus Christ

---

11. Христов, *Византийското богословие през XIV век.*

12. Танев, *Ти, Който си навсякъде и всичко изпълваш.*

13. See Dragas et al., *Orthodox Theology and the Sciences.*

Introduction[1]

The teaching of the Church Fathers focusing on the distinction between Divine essence and energies constitutes a fundamental part of Orthodox theology. It was explicitly articulated by the Cappadocian Fathers—St. Basil the Great, St. Gregory of Nazianzus and St. Gregory of Nyssa, and later by St. Maximus the Confessor, and by the Fathers of the Sixth Ecumenical Council (Constantinople, 680–81). It was further refined theologically by St. Gregory Palamas[2] and by the Church Councils that took place in Constantinople in

1. Part of the introduction was published in: Tanev, "ΕΝΕΡΓΕΙΑ vs. ΣΟΦΙΑ," 15–71. The text was substantially refined and extended.

2. Saint Gregory Palamas (1296–1357) is acknowledged as the most systematic representative of Hesychasm and the latest of the Church Fathers who could be qualified as "the theologian." Gregory Palamas was born in Constantinople in the family of the senator Constantine Palamas. He received classical education with the intention of pursuing a public career but in 1314 chose the monastic life and went to Mount Athos. During a Turkish invasion of Athos, he went back to Thessaloniki (1322), where he was ordained to the priesthood. In 1331 he returned to Mount Athos and from 1333 to 1935 became the abbot of the Esphigmenu monastery. In the second half of the 30s he engaged into a theological debate with Barlaam the Calabrian (c. 1290–1348)—a theologian, philosopher and mathematician, born in a Greek Orthodox community in Calabria, South Italy, who came to Byzantium to explore the wisdom of his Greek ancestors. Barlaam was involved by the Byzantine Emperor in the theological discussions with the representatives of the Latin Church where he overemphasized the unknowability of God in order to find ways for potential agreement. Later on he attacked the spiritual practices of the Hesychasts. In the course of this theological controversy St. Gregory began to articulate his teaching in a written form as a polemic defense of Hesychasm. The first part of the debate (1335–37) concerned the possibility of using logical proofs about the Divinity and applying Aristotle's logic to theology. The central question was about the experience of the Apostles of the light of Tabor and, respectively, whether or not the vision experienced by the Hesychasts was created or not. This phase of the Hesychast controversy ended in 1341 with the acceptance of the Palamite teaching and the condemnation of Barlaam. The second phase was marked by another controversy involving Gregory Akindynos and developed during the period of the Civil War in the Byzantine Empire (1341–47). St. Gregory Palamas and his

1

1341, 1347, 1351, and 1368.[3] The Council of 1351 was the most important one from a doctrinal point of view.[4] At this Council St. Gregory Palamas pointed out that his argumentation was based on the doctrinal formulations of the Sixth Ecumenical Council.[5] In its final decisions the participants in the Council made a clear distinction between four interrelated theological concepts by giving reference to St. John of Damascus:

> We hold, further, that there are two energies in our Lord Jesus Christ. For He possesses on the one hand, as God and being of like essence with the Father, the divine energy, and, likewise, since He became man and of like essence to us, the energy proper to human nature. But observe that energy and capacity for energy, and the product of energy, and the agent of energy, are all different. Energy is the efficient and essential activity of nature; the capacity for energy is the nature from which pro-ceeds energy; the product of energy is that which is effected by energy; and the agent of energy is the person or subsistence which uses the energy. Further, sometimes energy is used in the sense of the product of energy, and the product of energy in that of energy, just as the terms creation and creature are sometimes transposed. For we say "all creation," meaning creatures.[6]

For the Byzantine Church Fathers the distinction between essence and energy had a universal meaning, i.e., it was applied to both God and creation. For example, St. John of Damascus defines energy as "the natural force and activity of each essence" or the activity innate in every essence, "for no essence can be devoid of natural energy. Natural energy again is the

---

followers supported John Kantakouzenos (c. 1292–1383) and, as a result, St. Gregory was temporarily imprisoned. In addition, a Synod called by the patriarch John XIV Kalekas excommunicated him on November 4, 1344. After Kantakouzenos ascended the Byzantine Emperor's throne (1347), Palamas was ordained as a Bishop of Thes-saloniki. At that time a new controversy began because of the attacks of Nikephoros Gregoras against Palamas. The Synod of 1351 anathematized Barlaam and Akindynos, accused Gregoras and his followers, and proclaimed Palamas' teaching as a doctrine of the Eastern Christian Church. The last years of St. Gregory Palamas were devoted to his duties as a bishop. He died on November 4, 1357. A Council of 1368 declared him a saint. Palamas is considered as the last teacher of Orthodoxy, and his teach-ing is accepted as an official doctrine of the Orthodox Church. (See Kapriev, "Gregory Palamas," 520–30.)

3. Dragas, Book review of Koutsourēs, *Synods and Theology,* 631–46.

4. Meyendorff, *Byzantine Hesychasm.*

5. Larchet, "Hesychasm and the Sixth Ecumenical Council," 66–80.

6. John of Damascus, *Orthodox Faith,* III, XV, "Concerning the Energies in Our Lord Jesus Christ," 685.

force in each essence by which its nature is made manifest."[7] In his *Triads*
St. Gregory Palamas also points out that, "As Basil the Great says, 'The guarantee of the existence of every essence is its natural energy which leads the
mind to the nature.' And according to St. Gregory of Nyssa and all the other
Fathers, the natural energy is the power which manifests every essence, and
only nonbeing is deprived of this power; for the being which participates in
an essence will also surely participate in the power which naturally manifests that essence."[8]

In other words, it is the essence that is manifested through the energies
and not vice versa. Thus, the Church Fathers, and more specifically the Cappadocian Fathers, adopted the energetic terminology in the way it was articulated in book IX of Aristotle's *Metaphysics* and semantically adapted it to
the service of Christian theology by moving it away from its impersonalistic
Aristotelian connotation. The Divine energy is what manifests *that* God is,
while the essence is *what* He is. This is why St. Gregory Palamas emphasizes
that if there was no distinction between Divine essence and Divine energy,
the fact that "God is" would have remained unknown:

> With respect to the fact of its existence but not as to what it is,
> the substance is known from the energy, not the energy from the
> substance. And so, according to the theologians, God is known
> with respect to the fact of his existence not from his substance
> but from his providence. In this the energy is distinct from the
> substance, because the energy is what reveals, whereas the sub-
> stance is that which is thereby revealed with respect to the fact
> of existence.[9]

St. Gregory Palamas did not define in great detail the nature of the
distinction between essence and energy. For him the distinction is real
and not just semantic or conceptual. At the same time, it is not real in the
terms of scholastic terminology, where *distinctio realis* means a difference
in substance.[10] The Divine energy is not an independent substance. The
word reality (*realitas* originating from the Latin word *res*) presupposes a
difference in substance and it is difficult to express it in the Greek language.
The Greek word πράγμα means "something existing," but not necessarily an
independent substance or essence. It belongs to the same group as the concept πρᾶξις and also means "something actual."[11] St. Gregory Palamas dis-

7. John of Damascus, *Orthodox Faith*, II, XXIII, "Concerning Energy," 635.

8. Gregory Palamas, *The Triads*, III, 2.7, 94.

9. Gregory Palamas, *One Hundred and Fifty Chapters*, chs. 141, 247.

10. Georgi Kapriev, *Philosophie in Byzanz*, 344.

11. Ibid.

tinguishes the energies from the essence and calls them sometimes "things."
He talks about an "actual distinction" (πραγματικὴ διάκρισις), opposing
it, on the one hand, to the "actual division" that would destroy the Divine
unity and simplicity and, on the other hand, to a merely mental distinction
(διάκρισις κατ᾽ἐπίνοιαν).[12] The energies do not refer to something other in
God than His essence but to the Divine activities *ad extra*.[13] These activities
ad extra include God's works such as creating, sustaining, providing, deifying, etc. "When the activity is spoken 'objectively' as a divine work (ἔργον)
or being . . . we are not to imagine a something existing between the divine
essence and creatures. The terms 'work' and 'being' denote . . . the reality of
God's activity as a powerful presence."[14] God's works represent His activity
or energies in respect to His creatures and God, as He is in Himself, should
be distinguished from God as He relates to something other than Himself.
The Divine energies, however, are proper to God's essence even before God
relates through them to anything or anyone other than Himself. It is the
Divine will that actualizes the energies and actively manifests them ad extra
in relation to everything other than Himself.[15]

For St. Gregory Palamas the Aristotelian dyad nature-energy was
insufficient to express the being of God in an adequate way "because the
Divine action, or energy, is not simply 'caused' by the Divine essence, but is
also a *personal act*. Thus, the being of God is expressed in Palamite theology
by the triad essence-hypostasis-energy."[16] According to St. John of Damascus, "the holy Fathers used the term hypostasis and person, and individual
for the same thing,"[17] but also distinguished between the hypostases of animate and inanimate, rational and irrational beings. For them the essential
differences are actualized in the hypostases and "are one thing in inanimate
substances and another in animate, one thing in rational and another in
irrational, and, similarly, one thing in mortal and another in immortal."[18]
The terms 'person' and hypostasis are both used in reference to Divine and
human persons and, in this case, refer to someone who "by reason of his
own operations and properties exhibits an appearance which is distinct and
set off from those having the same nature."[19]

12. Кривошеин, *Аскетическое и богословское учение*, 132.

13. Tollefsen, *The Christocentric Cosmology*, 141.

14. Ibid.

15. Ibid., 144–45.

16. Meyendorff, "The Holy Trinity in Palamite Theology," 25–43.

17. John of Damascus, *Writings*, 66–67.

18. Ibid., 68.

19. Ibid., 67.

It is impossible however to reduce the hypostatic order to the natural (essential) one.[20] Every actually subsisting being, living or inanimate, has a hypostasis which is related to an essence and manifests its natural energies. The hypostasis does not possess the natural energy but only manifests it according to its specific mode of existence which is expressed in specific hypostatic properties. The specific manner and the intensity of this manifestation depend on the way the hypostasis exists and not on the principle of existence of its nature. The hypostatic characteristics shape out and provide the particular mode of the manifestation of the energies.[21] In this sense, it is incorrect to speak about the manifestation of the natural energies of a particular being out of the context of its hypostatic existence—the energies are always the energies of a hypostasis, i.e., there are energies of something or of someone (a person).[22] The Divine energies are therefore described as originating in the Divine nature but the Divine nature is tri-hypostatic and the energy manifests itself always personally:

> God is identical within Himself, since the three divine hypostases mutually co-inhere and inter-penetrate naturally, totally, eternally, inseparably, and yet without mingling or confusion, so that their energy is also one. This could never be the case among creatures. There are similarities among creatures of the same genus, but since each independent existence, or hypostasis, operates by itself, its energy is uniquely its own. The situation is different with the three divine hypostases that we worship, for there the energy is truly one and the same. For the activity of the divine will is one, originating from the Father, the primal Cause, issuing through the Son, and made manifest in the Holy Spirit.[23]

God manifests Himself to creatures not as an impersonal God, but through the acts of the three Divine persons in their co-inherence and mutual co-existence. It is the total and transcendentally perfect co-inherence and mutual co-existence, that make the three Divine persons indeed One God, so that "through each of His energies one shares in the whole of God . . . the Father, the Son and the Holy Spirit."[24] A careful reading of the works

---

20. Maxime le Confesseur, *Opuscules théologiques et polémiques*, XVI, 214.

21. Tchalakov and Kapriev, "The Limits of Causal Action," 389–433.

22. The Cappadocian Fathers were the first to identify hypostasis with person—person is the hypostasis of being and it is the personal existence that makes being a reality. For more details see Yannaras, *Elements of Faith*, 33.

23. Gregory Palamas, *The One Hundred and Fifty Chapters*, Ch. 112.

24. Meyendorff, "The Holy Trinity in Palamite Theology," 39; Matti Kotiranta, "The Palamite Idea of Perichoresis," 59–69.

of St. Gregory Palamas will clearly demonstrate that the teaching on the distinction between Divine essence and energies is deeply rooted in Trinitarian theology. In this sense, "A discussion of Palamism which would ignore the fact that the God of Palamas is personal, *Trinitarian* God is bound to lead into a dead end."[25] For St. Gregory Palamas the distinction between essence and energies did not serve any particular philosophical purpose. For him the emphasis on this distinction emerged from the necessity to articulate his theological point of departure—the confession of the real possibility for the knowledge of God *Himself* and the deification of humans in this present life.[26] Deification and knowledge of God imply the participation of human beings in the uncreated life of God, but God's essence remains transcendent and unparticipable.[27]

Today, in the same way as before, the teaching on the distinction between Divine essence and energies goes right through the heart of Orthodox theology and affects the whole body of Christian doctrine.[28] One could point out a number of Orthodox theologians who have provided a synthesis that makes them theologians of the Divine energies *par excellence*. For example, Fr. John Meyendorff is well known for translating the *Triads* of St. Gregory Palamas[29] in French and providing the details of the historical background of the fourteenth-century Councils dealing with the distinction between Divine essence and energies.[30] In all of his works Fr. Dumitru Staniloae underlined the organic synthesis between God's transcendence and his reality in creation, history, and humanity. He provided an integral approach to spirituality by integrating St. Maximus' doctrine of the λόγοι, St. Dionysius' concept of σύμβολον/λόγος and participation, and the Palamite doctrine of the uncreated energies.[31] Fr. John Romanides has also emphasized the relevance of this teaching by pointing out that "The teaching of the Church Fathers on God's relation to the world can be understood if one knows: a) the difference between 'created' and 'uncreated'; b) the distinction between 'essence' (οὐσία) and 'energy' (ἐνέργεια) in God; and c) the teaching of the Fathers concerning the world."[32] According to Christos

25. Ibid., 31.

26. Tollefsen, *The Christocentric Cosmology*, 140.

27. Meyendorff, *Byzantine Theology*, 186.

28. Florovsky, "St. Gregory Palamas and the Tradition of the Fathers," 165–76; Yannaras, "The Distinction between Essence and Energies," 242–43.

29. Grégoire Palamas, *Défense des saints hésychastes.*

30. Meyendorff, *A Study of Gregory Palamas.*

31. Berger, "An Integral Approach to Spirituality," 125.

32. Romanides, *An Outline of Orthodox Patristic Dogmatics*, 3.

Yannaras "the Theology of the Church interprets the reality of existence, the appearance and disclosure of being, starting from these two fundamental distinctions: It distinguishes essence or nature from the person or hypostasis, as it distinguishes the energies both from the nature and from the hypostasis. In these three basic categories, nature–hypostasis–energies, theology summarizes the mode of existence of God, the world, and man."[33] Finally, Fr. Georges Florovsky, one of the theologians discussed in this book, had a first key role in articulating the relevance of the teaching in contemporary Orthodox theology. His position was expressed in the following resounding statement:

> This basic distinction (i.e., between divine essence and energies) has been formally accepted and elaborated at the Great Councils of Constantinople in 1341 and 1351. Those who would deny this distinction were anathematized and excommunicated. The anathematisms of the council of 1351 were included in the rite for the Sunday Orthodoxy, in the Triodion. Orthodox theologians are bound by this decision.[34]

33. Yannaras, *Elements of Faith*, 43.
34. Florovsky, *Bible, Church, Tradition*, 105–20.

Part I

Divine Essence, Energy, and the Sophiological Controversy

Chapter 1

Fr. Georges Florovsky and the Rediscovery of the Distinction between Divine Essence and Energies in Modern Orthodoxy

Fr. Georges Florovsky was one of the most prominent Orthodox theologians of the twentieth century.[1] Fr. Sergius Bulgakov was the Dean of the St. Sergius Orthodox Theological Institute in Paris and was the one who invited the young Florovsky to teach Patristics at the Institute.[2] He became known for his teaching on the Divine Sophia and in 1930 some of his works were found to be non-Orthodox by the newly formed Synod of the Russian Church abroad and by the Metropolitan Sergius of Moscow. The following developments led to the need for Bulgakov to provide a formal theological clarification. Florovsky was unwillingly involved in these developments and was forced to express his criticism. Going through this experience was painful for both Bulgakov and Florovsky, but the two men remained highly respectful to each other.[3] It is, however, evident from their letters to each other that there was a profound disagreement and divergence between their views on the legacy of Soloviev's philosophy, and specifically, on its inherent sophiological component.

The influence of Soloviev's philosophy on Bulgakov's thought seems to have been inspired by his close friendship

---

1. For a recent discussion of Florovsky's life and theological vision see Павлов, Богословието като Биография.

2. For a most recent discussion of the relationship and the debate between Florovsky and Bulgakov see the multiple contributions in: Павлов, Протойерей Георги Флоровски (1893–1979)—*IN MEMORIAM*; as well as Ch. 8 "The Sophiological Subtext of Neopatristic Theology" in Gavrilyuk, *George Florovsky and the Russian Religious Renaissance*, 132–58. The most recent and thorough discussion of sophiology could found in Loudovikos, *Church in the Making*, 179–211.

3. Geffert, "The Charges of Heresy against Sergius Bulgakov," 47–66.

with Pavel Florensky.[4] Florensky was clearly influential in Bulgakov's return to the faith as well as in his adoption of a specific concept of Sophia, the Wisdom of God.[5] It was as a result of Florensky's influence that Bulgakov took a renewed interest in Soloviev's theoretical constructions[6] and it was in the *Unfading Light* (1917)[7] that Sophia started to emerge as a theological construction somehow in parallel to the three hypostases of the Holy Trinity to become a cornerstone in his philosophical worldview and theology.[8]

According to A. Klimoff, Florovsky viewed Soloviev's influence on Russian intellectual history as "unequivocally pernicious."[9] This statement however should not be interpreted in a simplistic one-sided way. Florovsky was fully aware of the evolution of Soloviev's thought and had perhaps his own evolution in interpreting Soloviev's works and role as a Russian religious thinker.[10] For example, in his early publications, Florovsky defended Soloviev as a genuine voice of Orthodox catholicity promoting a genuine synthesis of faith and understanding.[11] He significantly revised however his judgment by the early 1920s, distinguishing sharply his own conception of synthesis from Soloviev's synthesis of All-Unity.[12] Florovsky pointed out that while Soloviev's earlier philosophy of All-Unity was marked by a certain pantheism and Gnosticism, his *Tale of the Antichrist*[13] represented a second metaphysic in Soloviev's thought, which could be considered as a philosophy of miracle and struggle. According to Fr. Matthew Baker, "Florovsky contrasts two syntheses: the pan-logism of Soloviev's syn-

4. Rosenthal, "The Nature and Function of Sophia," 157.

5. As described in the last four chapters of Florensky, *The Pillar and Ground of the Truth*. These chapters were additionally added to the text of Florensky's dissertation that was earlier deposited in fulfillment of the requirements of a Masters degree from the Moscow Theological Academy.

6. Zenkovsky, *A History of Russian Philosophy*, 897.

7. Булгаков, Свет невечерний.

8. Evtuhov, *The Cross and the Sickle*, 138, referring to Булгаков, "Природа в философии Владимира Соловьева."

9. Klimoff, "Georges Florovsky and the sophiological controversy," 67–100.

10. I am grateful to Fr. Matthew Baker, of blessed memory, for personally sharing with me his thoughts on this matter. See also Baker, "Neo-patristic Synthesis and Ecumenism."

11. Ibid.

12. Ibid.

13. Соловьёв, Краткая повесть об антихристе.

thesis of All-Unity, and the new synthesis suggested by the 'Tale of the Anti-Christ,' grounded on the vision of the historic Christ."[14] For Fr. Matthew this is a clear indication that Florovsky's own neo-patristic synthesis took its starting point precisely where he thought Soloviev's last vision left off.

In spite of Florovsky's subtlety in interpreting the works of Soloviev, he considered Bulgakov's sophiology (which he saw as strongly influenced by Soloviev's philosophy of All-Unity) as an unnecessary and, actually, a dangerous attempt to develop a philosophically-driven, non-patristic alternative of the Christian teaching on creation *ex nihilo* and the Trinitarian relationship between God, man, and the world. He remained deeply respectful towards Bulgakov, but passionately, although not personally, rejected his most fundamental ideas as wrong and harmful to the Church.[15] Interestingly, in this indirect debate with Bulgakov it was not the understanding of Sophia but its implication for the Christian dogma on creation out of nothing that emerged as the real stumbling block. Bulgakov addressed the doctrine of creation from a sophiological point of view. Florovsky, addressed the doctrine of creation within the context of his "neo-patristic" synthesis by focusing on the distinction between Divine essence and will and, respectively, between Divine essence and energies. By doing so he contributed to the rediscovery of the teaching on the Divine essence and energies and provided a theological reflection that became the source of the key Orthodox theological themes in the twentieth century. In this sense, "one cannot really understand Florovsky's 'neo-patristic' synthesis without understanding that in the background lurks Bulgakov,"[16] i.e., Florovsky's theology, including his first emphasis on the relevance of the distinction between Divine essence and energy, was articulated in opposition to Bulgakov's thought.

It should be pointed out therefore that the key reason for the rediscovery of the teaching of the Divine essence and energies was (as it was in the middle of the fourteenth century) deeply theological. This fact seems to be currently diluted by arguments about the existence of special personal motives of the Russian émigré theologians in Paris in the 1920s who were trying to build a unique theological identity within the context

14. Private communication by Fr. Matthew Baker associated of his panel presentation of the book by Gavrilyuk, Paul. *George Florovsky and the Russian Religious Renaissance*, Oxford University Press, 2014, during the Orthodox Studies Group panel discussion at the Annual Meeting of the American Academy of Religion, San Diego, November 2014.

15. Meyendorff, "Creation in the History of Orthodox Theology," 27–37.

16. Papanikolaou, "Sophia, Apophasis, and Communion," 243–58. I am grateful to Dr. Papanikolaou for sharing with me the manuscript of his unpublished paper "*Sophia! Orthoi!* The Trinitarian Theology of Sergius Bulgakov," presented at the Catholic Theological Soceity of America Conference, June 5, 2009.

of their new non-Orthodox cultural environment. Without any doubt, such motives might have had some relevance. However, as we shall see, the theological issues were the key reason for the need to recapture the theology of St. Gregory Palamas.

In fact, it was Bulgakov's specific (non-patristic) interpretation that forced Fr. George Florovsky to engage in reaffirming the place of St. Gregory "within mainline patristic tradition, in this sense refuting Bulgakov's claim that St. Gregory can be seen as one of the originators of Sophiology."[17] Bulgakov's reading of St. Gregory Palamas was driven by a very specific context— his commitment to provide a theological defense for the Name-Worshipers at the Russian Church Council of 1917–18. The Name-Worshipers were Russian monks on Mount Athos that were associated with a controversy (1912–13) due to their claim that the name of God was God Himself. The monks believed that they follow the theology of St. Gregory Palamas. This belief was expressed for the first time by Hieromonk Anthony Bulatovich (1870–1919), who wrote an *Apology of Faith in the Name of God and the Name Jesus*,[18] which was distributed at first in lithographic form and later printed in St. Petersburg (1913) with the help of Fr. Pavel Florensky and M. A. Novoselov. As it appears, it was Fr. Pavel Florensky who was the first among Russian clergymen and intellectuals to pay a closer attention (through the discussions with Anthony Bulatovich) to the theology of St. Gregory Palamas.[19] According to T. Sénina, Anthony Bulatovich learned about the theology of St. Gregory Palamas most probably from the Russian scholar of Byzantine studies Ivan Ivanovich Sokolov[20] who in 1911 published a review of the recently published book by G. Papamichael dedicated to St. Gregory Palamas: Ὁ ἅγιος Γρηγόριος Παλαμᾶς ἀρχιεπίσκοπος Θεσσαλονίκης.[21] According to N. Pavlyuchenkov however, the rediscovery of Palamite theology and the teaching on the distinction between essence and energies should be clearly attributed to Fr. Pavel Florensky,[22] and it was from him that Fr. S. Bulgakov adopted ideas from the theology of the Divine energies and tried to introduce them into sophiology.[23] It was most probably Florensky who

17. Klimoff, "Georges Florovsky and the Sophiological Controversy," 96.

18. Булатович, *Апология веры во Имя Божие.*

19. Медведев и Лурье, "Послесловие," 340.

20. Соколов, „Святой Григорий Палама," № 4, 378–93; № 5, 159–86; № 6, 409–29; № 7, 114–39; Sénina, "Un palamite russe," 400–405.

21. Παπαμιχαήλ, Ὁ ἅγιος Γρηγόριος ὁ Παλαμᾶς.

22. Павлюченков, "Философия имени священика Павла Флоренского," 79.

23. One should be however very careful in attributing too much to Fr. P. Florensky in terms of a patristic interpretation of St. Gregory Palamas. It is worth mentioning a detailed comment by I. Medvedev and V. Lurier in their Postcript to the Russian

wrote an anonymous Foreword to the book of Bulatovich, but did not want to go in public with an open defense of the Name-worshipers (until 1921) because of his status as an Orthodox priest.[24] Interestingly, Vladimir Lossky and Fr. John Meyendorff would later use the theology of St. Gregory Palamas as a way of refuting Bulgakov's sophiology. We shall see however that it was Fr. George Florovsky who, in reply to Bulgakov's sophiological inspirations, was the first to articulate a patristic interpretation of the theology of St. Gregory Palamas, offering some of the key anti-sophiological arguments that were to be used later by Lossky and Meyendorff. The observation of N. Pavlyuchenkov is quite important since it positions the rediscovery of the theology of St. Gregory Palamas between 1913 (the publication of the *Apology of Faith in the Name of God and the Name Jesus* by Anthony Bulatovich) and 1917 (the publication of *The Unfading Light* by Fr. Sergius Bulgakov, where he offered a more detailed discussion of the theology of St. Gregory Palamas).[25] What is much more important here is the fact that the teaching of St. Gregory Palamas was rediscovered within the context of the discussion of the spiritual practices of the Athonite monks and not just as part of the speculative theological efforts of Russian émigré theologians in France.

The Russian Church Council of 1917–18 appointed a special commission in order to address the Name-Worshiper heresy and it was Bulgakov who provided the most systematic dogmatic elaboration in support of the Name-worshipers by trying to read the theology of St. Gregory Palamas within an entirely sophiological perspective.[26] He interpreted the adoption of Palamism during the Council of 1351 as Church's first serious commitment

translation of Meyendorff, *Introduction à l'étude de Grégoire Palamas* (Медведев и Лурье, Жизнь и труды святителя Григория Паламы, 327–73). According to Medvedev and Lurier "Florensky had a genuine interest not simply in the history of the theological controversy of the fourteenth century but specifically in promoting the teaching on the energies which was for him a true discovery. In the years after 1913 he incorporated it as part of the occultistic foundations of his natural science and philosophical studies and, more specifically, in the part of his studies that could be called today semiotics. Florensky was a conscious occultist even though he stayed apart of the theosophical and occult circles of his time. In spite of that, he was using (not only in his early works but also during the Name-worshiper controversy) all the achievements of the occult sciences by accepting the existence of special occult forces (which, according to him, were neither the commonly accepted physical forces, neither the angelic powers, nor the Divine energies, but, at the same time, they were not demonic powers either) developing his own theory of the symbol (including Church symbols and icons) on the basis of the energies inherent in the symbol which are not only the physical ones but also the occult ones."

24. Павлюченков, "Философия имени священика Павла Флоренского," 79.

25. Булгаков, *Свет невечерний*.

26. Evtuhov, *The Cross and the Sickle*, 210.

to a sophiological agenda but also found it in need of further sophiologocial development. Fr. G. Florovsky expressed an alternative interpretation the articulation of which could be seen as part of the initiation of his "neo-patristic synthesis" focusing on organizing some of the key resources of patristic theology from St. Athanasius the Great to St. Gregory Palamas and beyond. The confrontation between these two approaches materialized in different understandings of the doctrine of creation *ex nihilo*:

> The debate on the doctrine of creation, as found in Soloviev, Florensky, Bulgakov, and Berdyaev, was probably the most interesting episode in the history of Orthodox theology in the twentieth century. Their most brilliant and constant critics were Georges Florovsky and, on a slightly different level, Vladimir Lossky. Florovsky gave a critique of the metaphysics of Vladimir Soloviev in his well-known book *The Ways of Russian Theology* (Paris, 1937), but it can be said that practically the entire œuvre of Florovsky dealing with Greek patristic thought and published in the prewar period was directed against the sophiological postulates of Sergius Bulgokov, Florovsky's older colleague at the Theological Institute in Paris. However, the name of Bulgakov is nowhere directly mentioned in these works. Lossky, on the other hand, criticized sophiology directly, agreeing with the main positive points of FIorovsky's "neo-patristic synthesis." On the idea of creation, both Florovsky and Lossky simply reaffirmed the position of St. Athanasius . . . as opposed to the views of Origen.[27]

Many non-orthodox theologians believe that the rediscovery of the theology of the Divine energies was the result of the works of Vladimir Lossky and Fr. John Meyendorff, which appeared in response to polemical articles by Catholic theologians arguing against the orthodoxy of the theology St. Gregory Palamas.[28] There are even Orthodox theologians who argue that the rediscovery of St. Gregory Palamas

27. Meyendorff, "Creation in the History of Orthodox Theology," 27–37.

28. See for example, Finch, "Neo-Palamism," 233–49. Finch shares a relatively common opinion (see p. 233) that it was a polemical article by Martin Jugie on St. Gregory Palamas (although Finch wrongly refers to 1925 instead of 1931 as year of publication) that "prompted Vladimir Lossky, whose own Parisian teacher, Etienne Gilson, had instructed him in the importance of St. Thomas's 'real distinction' within creatures between *esse* and *essentia*, to begin a spirited and protracted defense of Palamas's theology—one that would come quickly, with the help of John Meyendorff and many other Orthodox theologians. . . . For this reason, Lossky is generally regarded as the founder of the neo-Palamite school of thought, which is properly called *neo*-Palamism because Palamas had been almost forgotten within Eastern Orthodoxy until Lossky

was occasioned by the publication in 1931 of an article on St. Gregory by Martin Jugie in the authoritative *Dictionnaire de théologie catholique*.[29] Jugie, a member of an Augustinian religious congregation and a great expert on Byzantine theology, declared Palamas' distinction between the essence and the energies of God to be fundamentally wrong and his notion of deifying uncreated grace to be 'near to heresy'. This provoked a vigorous response from the Russian community which had established itself in Paris after the Bolshevik revolution of 1917 and Lenin's expulsion of prominent intellectuals in 1922. Their defense of Palamas soon led to exposition of theosis, which was perceived to rest primarily on the essence-energies distinction. If this debate had been conducted in Russian it would have attracted relatively little attention. The fact that it was conducted in French was to have far-reaching consequences.[30]

The above paragraph comes from Norman Russell's book *Fellow Workers with God: Orthodox Thinking of Thesosis* (2009), where he identified the rediscovery of the teaching of St. Gregory Palamas as one of the key factors behind *theosis* (or deification) becoming today a common expression summarizing the whole economy of salvation. The paragraph represents an opinion that offers a questionable historical interpretation of one of the key insights of twentieth-century Orthodox theology and in Eastern Christian theology in general. Although it makes a valuable point, the opinion of Norman Russell should be taken only as far as it goes since it overlooks the fact that the rediscovery of the theology of St. Gregory Palamas was initiated almost twenty years earlier than the 1930s and in a completely different context—the theological controversy which emerged in 1911–12, focusing on the spiritual practices of the Russian monks on mount Athos. Interestingly, Russell's interpretation aligns very well with a recent remark by Fr. Matthew Baker in which he shared his recent experience of witnessing an Orthodox seminary professor who has sarcastically suggested that "Orthodox theology was invented in a 1930's Paris salon."[31]

In his book Norman Russell emphasizes that the first books published in Paris by the exiled Russian scholars were in their native language and that the influential titles in French only began to appear in the 1930s. As an example of authors whose publications in French were found to be most influential, Russell refers to a series of articles on the doctrine of deification

and Meyendorff revived interest in his thought."

29. Jugie, "Palamas Grégoire," 1735–76; "Palamite (Controverse)," 1777–1818.
30. Russell, *Fellow Workers with God*, 14.
31. Baker, "Neopatristic Synthesis and Ecumenism," 235–60.

published in 1932 and 1933 by Myrrha Lot-Borodine,[32] the book of Vladimir Lossky the *Mystical Theology of the Eastern Church*[33] published in 1944, and John Meyendorff's work, *A Study of Gregory Palamas*, published in 1959.[34] Other scholars have also pointed out the influential role of the earlier works on St. Gregory Palamas by Archimandrite Basil Krivoshein (1936) and Fr. Dumitru Staniloae (1938).[35] What is most interesting here is that Russell, in addition to focusing only on publications in French, does not mention Florovsky at all. It is important however to realize that in some of his letters to Bulgakov written as early as 1925 Florovsky had already argued against Bulgakov's sophiological ideas by using arguments from the theology of St. Gregory Palamas.[36] Last but not least, his paper "Creature and Creaturehood" was published as early as 1927 or 1928[37] and was perceived by his Russian compatriots in Paris as a direct reaction against Bulgakov's sophiology. "Creature and Creaturehood" offers a discussion of the distinction between Divine essence and energies within the context of creation and deification, with a specific reference to the theological insights of St. Athanasius, St. Basil the Great, St. Gregory the Theologian, St. Gregory of Nyssa, St. John Chrysostom, St. Cyril of Alexandria, St. Dionysius Areopagite, St. Maximus the Confessor, St. John of Damascus, St. Symeon the New Theologian, St. Gregory Palamas, and St. Mark of Ephesus. The theological line of thought linking these Church Fathers (and the decisions of the Ecumenical Councils they participated in) is quite remarkable and could be associated with the distinction between theology and economy, between nature and will, and between Divine essence and energies. According to Florovsky this distinction was first clearly articulated by the Fathers of the fourth century, starting with the Great Athanasius.[38] In the final part of his paper "The Concept of

32. Lot-Borodine, "La doctrine de la deification dans l'Eglise grecque."

33. Lossky, *Essai sur la théologie mystique de l'Église d'Orient*.

34. Meyendorff, *Introduction à l'étude de Grégoire Palamas*.

35. Krivoshein, "The Ascetic and Theological Teaching of Gregory Palamas"; Staniloae, *Life and Teachings of Gregory Palamas*.

36. Пентковский, "Письма Г. Флоровского С. Булгакову и С. Тышкевичу," 205.

37. Флоровский, "Тварь и тварьность," 176–212; Florovsky, "Creation and Creaturehood," 43–78.

38. Fr. G. Florovsky discussed explicitly the distinction between Divine essence and energies in two other texts that were republished in several versions in the period between 1959 and 1975: Florovsky, "St. Gregory Palamas," (1959) 119–31; "St. Gregory Palamas," (1961) 165–76; "St. Gregory Palamas," (1972) 105–20; "The Concept of Creation in Saint Athanasius" (1962) 36–57; "St. Athanasius' Concept of Creation," (1975) 39–62. He has another brief publication which was dedicated to the Light of Tabor and St. Gregory Palamas which appears to be published only in Russian: Флоровский, "Тайна Фаворского Света," (1935) 2–7.

Creation in Saint Athanasius," which was published thirty years later than "Creature and Creaturehood," he emphasized that the distinction between Divine nature or generation and creation or will

> is one of the main distinctive marks, of Eastern theology. It was systematically elaborated once more in late Byzantine theology, especially in the theology of St. Gregory Palamas (1296–1359). St. Gregory contended that unless a clear distinction had been made between the "essence" and "energy" in God, one could not distinguish also between "generation" and "creation." And once again this was emphasized, somewhat later, by St. Mark of Ephesus. It was a true Athanasian motive, and his arguments again came to the fore.

What is even more interesting is that Florovsky addresses directly the question:

> Is the distinction between "Being" and "Acting" in God, or, in other terms, between the Divine "Essence" and "Energy," a genuine and ontological distinction—*in re ipsa*; or is it merely a mental or logical distinction, as it were, κατ' ἐπίνοιαν, which should not be interpreted objectively, lest the Simplicity of the Divine Being is compromised. There cannot be the slightest doubt that for St. Athanasius it was a real and ontological difference. Otherwise his main argument against the Arians would have been invalidated and destroyed. Indeed, the mystery remains. The very Being of God is "incomprehensible" for the human intellect: this was the common conviction of the Greek Fathers in the Fourth century—the Cappadocians, St. John Chrysostom, and others. And yet there is always ample room for understanding. Not only do we distinguish between "Being" and "Will"; but it is not the same thing, even for God, "to be" and "to act." This was the deepest conviction of St. Athanasius.[39]

The link between St. Gregory Palamas and St. Athanasius is very important. It provides the right perspective for the appreciation of the theological contribution of Fr. G. Florovsky with respect to both the emphasis on the distinction between Divine essence and energies, and the rediscovery of the theology of St. Gregory Palamas. For Florovsky the theological significance of the distinction between Divine essence and energy was not a question about *pro* or *contra* some kind of *Neo-Palamism*, as some

---

39. Florovsky, "St. Athanasius' Concept of Creation," 60–62.

modern theologians might be willing to believe; it was about following the
consensus partum:[40]

> The Fathers were true inspirers of the Councils, while being
> present and *in absentia*, and also often after they have gone to
> Eternal Rest. For that reason, and in this sense, the Councils
> used to emphasize that they were "following the Holy Fathers"—
> επόμενοι τοις άγίοις ιτατράσιν, as Chalcedon has said. *Secondly*,
> it was precisely the *consensus patrum* which was authoritative
> and binding, and not their private opinions or views, although
> even they should not be hastily dismissed. Again, this *consensus*
> was much more than just an empirical agreement of individuals.
> The true and authentic *consensus* was that which reflected the
> mind of the Catholic and Universal Church—τό έκκλησιαστικόν
> φρόνημα. It was that kind of *consensus* to which St. Irenaeus was
> referring when he contended that neither a special "ability," nor
> a "deficiency" in speech of individual leaders in the Churches
> could affect the identity of their witness, since the "power of
> tradition"—*virtus traditionis*—was always and everywhere the
> same (*Adv. haeres.* I.10.2). The preaching of the Church is al-
> ways identical: *constans et aequaliter perseverans* (ibid., III.24.1).
> The true *consensus* is that which manifests and discloses this pe-
> rennial identity of the Church's faith—*aequaliter perseverans*.[41]

It is surprising therefore why some contemporary Orthodox theologians would keep insisting that "Palamite theology did not play in Florovsky's retrieval of the Fathers the prominent role accorded to Palamism by
Vladimir Lossky, John Meyendorff, Christos Yannaras, and other neopatristic theologians."[42] Such statements are historically misleading and unjust; they simply diminish Florovsky's pioneering role in rediscovering the
authentic value of Palamite theology as part of Orthodoxy in general. For
any theologian who tends to question or underestimate Florovsky's engagement with and high respect towards the theology of St. Gregory Palamas
and his teaching on the distinction between Divine essence and energies,
it would be good to have a closer look at "Creature and Creaturehood."[43] It

40. See the recent book by Jean-Claude Larchet for a comprehensive review and
analysis of the theology of the Divine energies since Aristotle to St. John of Damascus:
Larchet, *La théologie des énergies divines*.

41. Florovsky, "The Authority of the Ancient Councils," 103.

42. Gavrilyuk, *George Florovsky and the Russian Religious Renaissance*, 143.

43. In an unpublished address written in response to an honor that was bestowed
upon him, the eighty-years-old Florovsky pointed out that he considered his two theological essays, on the Doctrine of Creation and the Doctrine of Redemption, to be his
best and, probably, only theological achievements. See: Blane, *Georges Florovsky*, 153–55.

is worth referring to some of Florovsky's own comments and references in the paper.[44] According to him the part of Byzantine theology concerning the powers and energies of God still awaits monographic treatment since at that time the greater part of the works of St. Gregory Palamas existed only in library manuscripts (MSS). This was a clear call for regaining the theology of St. Gregory Palamas its proper place within twentieth century Orthodox theology, a call that was obviously heard by the younger generation of Orthodox theologians such as Dumitru Staniloae, Basil Krivoshein, Vladimir Lossky, John Meyendorf, and John Romanides. In his text Florovsky refers also to Bulgakov's book *The Unfading Light* (p. 103) where Fr. S. Bulgakov briefly discusses the negative theology of St. Gregory Palamas.[45] Interestingly, Florovsky points out that "the Eastern distinction between essence and energy met with severe censure from Roman Catholic theology" and refers to a work of Petavius[46] published in 1864 where the author "speaks of it at great length and most harshly." Florovsky does not refer to the paper by M. Jugie simply because it was not published yet. In this sense, it might be actually more truthful to assume, unlike Norman Russell, that Martin Jugie's paper in the *Dictionnaire de théologie catholique* was motivated by the ongoing rediscovery of St. Gregory Palamas in Orthodox theology and not the other way around.

It appears then that the rediscovery of the theology of St. Gregory Palamas, and the Orthodox teaching on the Divine essence and energies in particular, were predominantly driven by deeply theological reasons, namely, by the attempt to provide a theological justification of the spiritual practices of the Name-worshiping Russian monks, and the necessity to provide an Orthodox theological response to the sophiological tendencies in Russian religious philosophy. It is true that the inter-confessional theological polemic might have played some role in accelerating this process but its role might have been secondary and complementary in nature. Florovsky's key role in shaping the tone of Orthodox theology in the twentieth century could be illustrated by referring to a comment in a letter to him by Archimandrite *Sophrony* (Saharov) written on Pascha, 1958:

> Dear Fr. George, while reading again Lossky's *Mystical Theology* just before my presentation about him on the event dedicated to his memory, I was amazed to realize for the first time

---

44. See note 86 in Florovsky, "Creation and Creaturehood," 276. Interestingly, Florovsky refers to Соколов, "Святой Григорий Палама," and Παπαμιχαήλ, Ὁ ἅγιος Γρηγόριος ὁ Παλαμᾶς.

45. Булгаков, Свет невечерний.

46. Petavius, *Opus de theologicis dogmatibus*, I, 145–60; III, 273–76.

to what extent the greater majority of the positions expressed in his work were articulated some fifteen years earlier by you in your paper "Creature and Creaturehood." Of course nobody works alone and independently of the others: in terms of language, references etc., and the entire structure of the treatise itself,—everything is so much influenced by the specific times of author's life but, despite all of that, the entire book of Lossky was so much prepared by you, that I found it really striking. Before, I was not noticing that, since I read first and long time ago your paper, and then afterward Lossky's book. But now I read them both at once, starting first with Lossky, then reading you, and again going back to Lossky.[47]

The Elder Sophrony continues by asking Fr. Georges for a permission to translate his paper "Creature and Creaturehood" in French so that the French-speaking public could become aware of his early contribution to and influence on Lossky's work. In his reply (April 8, 1958) Florovsky provided some valuable details about the context of its first publication:

> Dear Fr. Sophrony! . . . Your impression is absolutely correct. At that time my paper *"Creature and Creaturehood"* was accepted *with silence*, because it was seen (not without a reason) as an opposition to sophiology and, at that time in Paris, that was considered to be an unforgivable tenacity. Even now the professors at the theological institute do not mention it, even when they write about "creaturehood" (for example, Fr. Zenkovsky). In some circles the independence in thinking and the commitment to the Church Fathers is not much tolerated. . . . My paper was published in French, in a somewhat uncompleted form and before its publication in Russian, in an edition that was practically inaccessible and even unknown, even though in the same issue there were papers by Berdyaev and Karsavin (as early as 1927). It was in the *Logos*, a journal that was published in Romania but

47. Софроний (Сахаров), Переписка с протоиереем Георгием Флоровским, Письмо № 10: "Дорогой отец Георгий, читая снова книгу Лосского « *Théologie mystique*» перед докладом о нем на собрании в память его, я на сей раз был удивлен, до какой степени подавляющее большинство высказанных им в его труде положений за пятнадцать лет до того были изложены Вами в Вашей статье «Тварь и тварность.» Конечно, никто не работает так, чтобы все создать самому: и язык, и цитаты, и прочее, и самую структуру своего трактата,—так как все это обусловлено временем, в которое живет автор, но все же работа Лосского была настолько подготовлена во всем Вами, что я просто поражен. Раньше я этого не замечал, читая сначала и давно Вашу статью, а затем уже книгу Лосского. А теперь это совпало по времени: сначала я прочитал немного Лосского, затем читал Вас, затем снова Лосского . . ."

its publication was interrupted after the first two issues and they were not sent to any library.[48]

Fr. Florovsky continues his letter by pointing out that based on the Russian text[49] he prepared an English version of his paper that was published much later in 1948 in Eastern Churches Quarterly. He also mentions that he has no problem with the translation of its Russian version in French and, more importantly, that if it was going to be translated, it would need only an update of its references. It appears then that more than thirty years after the first publication of "Creature and Creaturehood," Fr. Georges did not have anything to add to its content, i.e., he stayed behind all the theological positions expressed in it.

48. Ibid., Florovsky's reply to letter № 10: "Дорогой отец Софроний! . . . Ваше впечатление совершенно справедливо. Моя статья «Тварь и тварность» была в свое время замолчана, так как в ней (не без основания) усмотрели оппозицию софианству, и в то время это считалось в Париже непростительной дерзостью. И теперь профессора Богословского института её не упоминают, даже когда пишут как раз на тему о «тварности» (например, отец В. Зеньковский). Независимость мысли и верность отеческому преданию в некоторых кругах мало поощряется. ... Моя статья была напечатана по французски, в неразработанном виде, прежде ее появления по-русски, но в издании практически недоступном, даже мало известном, хотя в том же номере появились статьи Бердяева и Карсавина (еще в 1927 году). Это был «Logos," который начали издавать в Румынии, издание оборвалось на втором номере, и его не достать ни в какой библиотеке. Я сам сделал экстракт из русской статьи, с небольшими дополнениями по-английски для нашей конференции в Англии, на которую не попал из-за отъезда в Соединенные Штаты, но статья появилась в The Eastern Churches Quarterly (Supplement) в 1948 году. Против перевода русской статьи на французский ничего не имею и буду очень рад, если это сделаете. В случае, что найдется, где ее напечатать, нужно будет сделать небольшие дополнения - указания к литературе и кое-где добавить отеческие тексты, да и проверить еще раз ссылки."

49. Here Fr. G. Florovsky refers to the version of the paper that was published in Russian: Флоровский, "Тварь и тварьность."

Chapter 2 _____

Energeia vs. *Sophia* in the Works
of Fr. Sergius Bulgakov

The Concept of Sophia and the Holy Trinity

The key to understanding Bulgakov's sophiology is to unfold what he means by "Sophia" as well as to answer the question why the concept of Sophia is necessary for his theology at all. In fact, as it has been recently pointed out by Mikhail Sergeev[1] and A. Papanikolaou,[2] this question should be asked within the context of Trinitarian theology since Bulgakov's sophiological problematics emerges within an entirely Trinitarian perspective.[3] According to Sergeev, it is the logic of his religious-philosophical evolution that leads him to extend his sophiology to the Trinitarian problem and "[w]ithout betraying his 'first love,' Sophia, he turns to the eternal love of Christianity, the Holy Trinity."[4] Interestingly, it is precisely the implications from the adoption of this logic that were criticized even by his own colleagues at the theological institute St. Sergius in Paris. His critics at St. Sergius include not only G. Florovsky and V. Lossky. For example, Vasilli Zenkovsky, an authority of the history of Russian thought, criticizes him for reconstructing his system theologically by applying the metaphysics of All-Unity along with sophiology to Trinitarian dogmas, thus, adopting a position of sophiological monism that was doomed to fail.[5] The introduction of Sophia into the Trinity manifested the "highly provocative dualism existing

1. Sergeev, "Divine Wisdom and Trinity"; *Sophiology in Russian Orthodoxy*, 103.

2. Papanikolaou, "Sophia, Apophasis, and Communion," 244.

3. For a most recent and insightful analysis of Bulakov's sophiology in terms of its Trinitarian and Christological aspects, see Loudovikos, *Church in the Making*, 196–211.

4. Sergeev, *Sophiology in Russian Orthodoxy*, 103.

5. Zenkovsky, *A History of Russian Philosophy*, 908 (referenced by Sergeev, *Sophiology in Russian Orthodoxy*, 104).

in the concept of Sophia itself which consisted in combining both good and evil principles and making God responsible for the origin of evil . . . ."[6]

Papanikolaou summarizes Bulgakov's Trinitarian theology in two key points: first, the "formal acceptance of the categories of ὑπόστασις and οὐσία that were hammered out during the trinitarian controversies of the fourth century" and, second, the adoption of "an Augustine-inspired interpretation of the Trinity as the Father's self-revelation in the Son, with the Holy Spirit being the love that unites the Father and the Son, and, as such, completes the self-revelation of the Father in the Son."[7] Bulgakov sees Augustine's identification of the Holy Spirit as the love that binds the Father and the Son as an advancement on the Trinitarian theology of the Cappadocian Fathers, arguing at the same time that neither Augustine nor the Cappadocians did "elaborate on the doctrine of the Trinity in such a way as to make sense of how God can be in communion with what is not God."[8] For him the proper meaning of Sophia can be found in a proper understanding of the term substance (οὐσία) or nature (φύσις), but as a category it was not fully developed in Trinitarian theology. It was taken from ancient Greek philosophy and applied by the early Christian theologians to the concept of the Trinity. In his own words "the doctrine of the consubstantiality of the Holy Trinity, as well as the actual conception of substance or nature, has been . . . apparently, almost overlooked"[9] and was entirely neglected in respect to the Creator as related to creation. The concept of Sophia emerges therefore out of the necessity to further elaborate on the implications of the ὁμοούσιος, or the consubstantiality that exists in the Father, Son, and Holy Spirit, especially in terms of God's self-revelation and in terms of the God-world relation as Trinity.[10] "Sophia, then, for Bulgakov is God's being as the self-revelation of the Father in the Son and the Holy Spirit. As Bulgakov himself states, 'Sophia is Ousia as revealed,' or 'Sophia is the revelation of the Son and the Holy Spirit, without separation and without confusion,' or 'Divine Sophia is God's *exhaustive* self-revelation, the fullness of divinity, and therefore has absolute content.'"[11] Thus, Divine self-revelation is a key aspect of Bulgakov's sophiology. Papanikolaou sees its relevance in providing Bulgakov the opportunity to engage in a theological deduction of the Trinitarian dogma

6. Sergeev, *Sophiology in Russian Orthodoxy*, 93.

7. Papanikolaou, "Sophia, Apophasis, and Communion," 244.

8. Ibid.

9. Bulgakov, *The Wisdom of God*, 44.

10. Ibid.

11. Ibid., 8.

since for Bulgakov there is a need to "show" and "prove" the ontological necessity of God, as Trinity, to be in precisely three hypostases:[12]

> the trinity in Divinity in unity, as well as in the distinction of the three concrete hypostases, must be shown not only as a divinely revealed *fact*, valid by virtue of its facticity, but also as a *principle* owing to which Divinity is not a dyad, tetrad, etc., . . . but precisely a trinity, exhausting itself in its fullness and self-enclosedness. . . . Of course, deduction is incapable of establishing the fact of divine Trinity, which is given by Revelation; but thought is called to fathom this revealed fact to the extent this is possible for human knowledge.[13]

Papanikolaou sees the biggest problem with Bulgakov's Trinitarian sophianic vision in the inconsistency it creates in his own system by defining God as an absolutely free Spirit or Subject and then subjecting Him to the necessity of the logic of His self-revelation: "In the Divine Spirit's self-positing of self, that is, in the divine self-revelation, God's knowledge of God's self, i.e., God's οὐσία as Sophia is fully transparent to God's personal consciousness, and lived as the very being of God. This knowledge of God's self, this self-revelation, is the revelation of God's οὐσία in the Son, meaning that such a self-revelation is οὐσία as Sophia."[14] It appears therefore that for Bulgakov "in order for God to know Godself, God must reveal God to Godself." In this way he could not escape the use of necessity language, appearing to subject God to a principle of necessity of self-revelation, i.e., to a principle other than God's own being.[15] In doing so, continues Papanikolaou, "he saw that the categories of οὐσία and ὑπόστασις could not by themselves do the work of conceptualizing God's being as one of communion with the not-God" and Sophia "emerges from the insight that a third term is needed in order to account God's communion with the world."

The reason to provide a more detailed reference to Papanikolaou's insightful paper was to use the opportunity of pointing out some of the key aspects of Bulgakov's sophianic vision. *First*, this is the Trinitarian context of its theological articulation, or rather its peculiar positioning on the borderline between the Trinity and the Divine Unity. One could even

12. Ibid., 12.

13. Bulgakov, *The Comforter*, 8.

14. Papanikolaou, "*Sophia! Orthoi!* The Trinitarian theology of Sergius Bulgakov," 14. See also Papanikolaou, "Sophia, Apophasis, and Communion," 245: "For Bulgakov, if the self-positing of the subject is the condition for the possibility of relating to what is other than the 'I,' God is free to commune with what is not God because God's life is one of self-positing as self-revelation."

15. Ibid., 15.

say that Bulgakov's approach dilutes itself by getting trapped between the articulations of the two different modes of Divine being. *Second*, this is the commitment to a systematic theological agenda that is called to fathom the facts of Divine revelation to the extent that this is possible for human knowledge (an agenda that goes against the patristic theological attitude which usually operates "on demand," driven by the necessity to deal with specific deviations from "the faith once delivered to the Saints," Jude 1:3). *Third*, this is the commitment to a "necessity language" by subjecting God to a principle of necessity of self-revelation other than God's own being. *Fourth*, this is Bulgakov's forced terminological restriction to the categories of οὐσία and ὑπόστασις and the persistent avoidance of the patristic term ἐνέργεια which, as shown in the introduction to this essay, is fundamentally important for the articulation of God's communion with the world. Interestingly enough, he shows a clear awareness of the energetic terminology in the theology of St. Gregory Palamas, but consistently tries to work out his own way without it by opening up the possibility for Sophia to emerge as kind of replacement of the Divine energies. It is worth highlighting a key passage at the end of the patristic section of Bulgakov's discussion of the creation *ex nihilo* in his *The Bride of the Lamb*:

> In Eastern theology, the development of theology after St. John of Damascus is broken off in connection with a general stagnation of thought. Thought is squandered on a fruitless, scholastically schismatic polemic with Rome concerning the procession of the Holy Spirit. The sophianic-cosmological problematic lies dormant for six centuries. Byzantine theology once again approaches this question in St. Gregory Palamas's doctrine of energies, which is essentially an unfinished Sophiology. The fundamental idea of Palamism is that, alongside God's transcendent "essence," there exists His manifold revelation in the world, His radiation in "energies," as it were. But Palamas' doctrine of essence and energies is not brought into connection with the dogma of the Trinity, in particular with the doctrine of the three hypostases as separate persons and of the Holy Trinity in unity. The fundamental idea of Palamism concerning the multiplicity and equi-divinity of the energies in God discloses *polypoikilos sophia tou theou*, "the manifold wisdom of God" (Eph. 3:10). Palamas considers the energies primarily in the aspect of grace, the supracreaturely "light of Tabor" in the creaturely world. But these energies have, first of all, a world-creating and world-sustaining power which is a property of Sophia, the Wisdom of God, in both of her forms: the Divine Sophia, the eternal proto-ground of the world, and the creaturely Sophia, the divine force

of the life of creation. The sophianic interpretation and application of Palamism are yet to come in the future. By accepting
Palamism, the Church has definitely entered onto the path of
recognizing the sophianic dogma. But the theological realization of this recognition still requires a long path of intellectual
labor. Essential here is the connection with onomadoxy, which
has recognized the divine reality and power of the divine-human
name of Jesus and, in general, the power of the name of God in
the world. It is not by chance that onomadoxy is linked with
Palamism. However, these particular applications of Sophiology
do not yet go to the root of the sophianic problem.[16]

This passage provides important details about the nature of Bulgakov's
sophiological inspirations: his desire to provide a sophiological correction
to patristic theology; his appreciation for the relevance of the theology of St.
Gregory Palamas which he considers as an unfinished sophiology; and the
relationship of the whole problematic to the theological issues associated
with the Name-Worship controversy (Onomatodoxy). For anyone versed in
the writing of St. Gregory Palamas, the point about the lack of connection
between the Trinitarian dogma and the distinction between Divine essence
and energies would not be understandable. The fact that for Bulgakov the
doctrine of essence and energies is not brought into connection with the
dogma of the Trinity shows that he may have not been familiar with the entirety of the works of St. Gregory Palamas.[17] Interestingly, in the foreword to
his major work on St. Gregory Palamas,[18] Fr. John Meyendorff expresses his
hope that his study will help those Orthodox writers who have previously
analyzed the Palamite system and "have had at their disposal only a relatively limited selection of Palamas' works, all dating from a time when the
Palamite formulation was established, and in which his thought could no
longer be seen in its whole Christological and Biblical context." These words
of Fr. John Meyendorff could be considered as an anonymous reference to
Fr. Sergius Bulgakov. Fr. John Meyendorff was also one of the theologians
who have contributed to a better understanding of the Trinitarian aspects of
St. Gregory's teaching.[19]

16. Bulgakov, *The Bride of the Lamb*, 18.

17. For a discussion of the relationship between the teaching of St. Gregory Palamas on the distinction between Divine essence and energies, and his Trinitarian theology, see Amphiloque (Radović), *Le Mystère de la Saint Trinité*; Kapriev, *Philosophie in
Byzanz*, Section 6.3, 282; Kotiranta, "The Palamite Idea of Perichoresis," 59–69; Meyendorff, "The Holy Trinity in Palamite Theology," 25–43.

18. Meyendorff, *A study of Gregory Palamas*, 202.

19. Meyendorff, "The Holy Trinity in Palamite Theology," 25–43.

In seems therefore that Bulgakov's sophianic constructions are not based on any insight about the need of a third term in articulating the relationship between God the Trinity and the world, but rather on a terminological commitment to the spirit of Soloviev's Sophia and philosophy of All-Unity. The categories of οὐσία and ὑπόστασις are clearly insufficient in the articulation of the Divine-human communion and the Church Fathers have never restricted themselves to them alone by adopting the concept of ἐνέργεια.[20] This concept of ἐνέργεια has properly served Christian theologians for centuries and the claim about the need for another (third) term that comes somehow on top of it as a terminological replacement appears to be highly questionable.

Bulgakov and the Theology of St. Gregory Palamas

Bulgakov was obviously aware of the Palamite way of dealing with the God's communion with the world.[21] Why is it then that he did not follow that way? A possible answer to this question could be found in the historical context of his involvement as a theologian in the Onomatodoxy controversy. Bulgakov's participation as a key lay theologian at the Council required him to immerse himself in some of the works of St. Gregory Palamas. However, it should be pointed out that the discussion of the theological issues associated with the Onomatodoxy controversy had already began in 1912, right after the emergence of the controversy. From 1912 on, some of the followers of Soloviev's philosophy of All-Unity and Divine-Humanity, including Florensky, Bulgakov, Ern and Losev, grouped around the publishing house "Put'" and started studying the Name-Worshiping problem by focusing on the Hesychast sources of Orthodox spirituality.[22] Most of them, including Bulgakov himself, turned into active advocates of the teaching of the Name-Worshipers and came to the conclusion that

> the metaphysics of All-Unity should be complemented with the Palamite concept of Divine energy and, after being modified in this way, it will be able to provide the philosophical base for this teaching. . . . All the approaches by the Muscovite philosophers

---

20. Bradshaw, *Aristotle East and West.*

21. In Bulgakov's *Hypostasis and Hypostaticity* (1925) one can find one of his first claims that in his approach he is adapting the theology of St. Gregory Palamas (see Gallaher and Kukota, "Protopresbyter Sergii Bulgakov," 7).

22. Horujy, "The idea of energy in the Moscow school of Christian neo-Platonism."

share the same basic ontological structure, the Platonic ontology of All-Unity complemented by the concept of Divine energy.[23]

This ontological structure could be characterized as a type of "panentheism," according to which the world and all its phenomena are imbued with the essence which is in God.[24] Providing a philosophical and theological support to defend the Name-Worshipers was seen as a refreshing opportunity for Russian religious philosophy since at that time it had already become clear that the metaphysics of All-Unity did not evolve to the degree of incorporating some of the vital aspects of Orthodox spirituality and, more specifically, of Orthodox anthropology with its understanding of man in relation to God.[25] There was a growing awareness of the insufficiency of the theological resources of the metaphysics of All-Unity which made its adherents agree that both the dogmatic and philosophical support of the Name-Worshipers could only be provided by St. Gregory Palamas' fourteenth-century teaching on the Divine Energies. "Newly armed with Palamas' ideas, Russian philosophers tried to expand the existing base of Russian metaphysics."[26] One could say now that from the very beginning such an approach was doomed to fail since "[t]he important new elements contained in Hesychasm and Palamism could not be brought into philosophy as mere complements to the basis of the metaphysics of All-Unity (nor could they justify Name-Worshipers). The advancement of Russian thought required the rejection of this basis."[27] And this is exactly what G. Florovsky and V. Lossky did by taking another road in theology and completely cutting off the metaphysics of All-Unity, by abandoning claims to any philosophy or philosophical movement, and by focusing on the patristic emphasis on the experience of Orthodox mystical and ascetic life. The turn to this theological road was initiated in Florovsky's work "Creature and Creaturehood"[28] and later in the work of an Athonite monk Basil (Krivoshein)—*The Ascetic and Theological Teaching of St. Gregory Palamas* (1936).[29] It was at the First Congress of Orthodox Theology in Athens where Florovsky presented his programmatic lecture "Patristics and Modern Theology" proclaiming the need of a neo-patristic theological synthesis and pointing out that in Orthodox

23. Ibid., 2.

24. Horuzhy, "Neo-Patristic Synthesis and Russian Philosophy," 6.

25. Ibid.

26. Ibid., 7.

27. Ibid., 8.

28. Флоровский, "Тварь и тварьность," 176–212.

29. Кривошеин, "Аскетическое и богословское учение святого Григория Паламы."

theology the "Patristic mind is too often completely lost or forgotten . . .
Palamite teaching on the divine ἐνέργειαι is hardly mentioned in most of
our text-books. The peculiarity of our Eastern tradition in the doctrine of
God and His attributes has been forgotten and completely misunderstood
. . . ."[30] The new turn resulted in the rediscovery of the Orthodox teaching
on the distinction between Divine essence and energies and the articulation
of its theological implications. The dogmatic formulations of the Orthodox
Council of 1351 stated that it is possible for man to be united with God not
by essence but by energy only. According to *Sergey Horuzhy* the mere foundations of such "energetic" communion between God and man represent a
certain type of ontology which is radically different from the neo-Platonic
ontology of the metaphysics of All-Unity.[31] These foundations also imply
an active Divine realism and epistemology based on both Divine and human freedom which was simply missing in the metaphysics of All-Unity.
Interestingly, Mikhail Sergeev has recently made a point about the indepen-
dence of the sophiological theme from any particular epistemological or
ontological positions.[32] According to Valliere, "this actually is a discovery on
Sergeev's part; or at the very least a power corrective to mainstream interpretation" since most scholarly interpreters of Sophia have felt compelled to
treat the subject as an exercise in systematic philosophy or ontology.[33] One
would easily agree with Sergeev about the lack of any specific epistemological vision in sophiology. This is an important point that could clarify one of
the key differences between sophiology and the theological insights of St.
Gregory Palamas which emerged within a predominantly epistemological
context in an attempt to deal with both agnosticism and pantheism.[34]

There is a growing awareness about the relationship between the
sophiology of Fr. S. Bulgakov and the theology of St. Gregory Palamas. For

30. Florovsky, "Patristics and Modern Theology," 239.

31. Horuzhy, *"Neo-Patristic Synthesis and Russian Philosophy,"* 11.

32. Sergeev, *Sophiology in Russian Orthodoxy*, ii.

33. Ibid.

34. Hierotheos, *Saint Gregory as a Hagiorite*, 23: "We can see clearly the great
significance of his [of St. Gregory Palamas] teaching for Orthodoxy on the important question of epistemology. When se say epistemology we mean the knowledge
of God and, to be more precise, we mean the way which we pursue in order to attain
knowledge of God. The situation in St. Gregory's time was that Orthodoxy was being
debased; it was becoming worldly and being changed into either pantheism or agnosticism. Pantheism believed and taught that God in his essence was to be found in all
nature, and so when we look at nature we can acquire knowledge of God. Agnosticism
believed and taught that it was utterly impossible for us to know God, just because He
is God and man is limited, and therefore man was completely incapable of attaining a
real knowledge of God."

example, Bishop H. Alfeev has shown that most of the discussions during the Name-Worshiper controversy were anchored around the Palamite theology of the Divine energies by pointing out the key role of the philosophical circle around Florensky, Bulgakov, Ern, and Losev, who were the first to seriously uncover it to their opponents who did not know very much about it.[35] According to him, the appropriation of the Palamite insights in Fr. Bulgakov's *Philosophy of the Name*,[36] unlike his teaching on the Divine and creaturely Sophia, for which he was rightly critiqued, has made it one of his finest theological works, and probably the greatest contribution to Orthodox theology in the twentieth century, one that needs to be further studied. Fr. Sergius completed his *Philosophy of the Name* in 1920, but it was not published until 1953, after his death, with just one change—the addition of a short *Post scriptum* chapter that was (most interestingly) titled: "A Sophiological Interpretation of the Teaching on the Name of Jesus."[37] One must agree with Bishop Alfeev for the need to further study the *Philosophy of the Name* of Fr. Sergius. It would be important for example to see how, on one hand, he could be a sophiologist in his theology and, on the other hand, completely Orthodox in his philosophy of the name.

Antoine Arjakovsky has also pointed out the relationship between Bulgakov's sophiology and the theology of St. Gregory Palamas[38] by admitting that in Bulgakov's theology there were certain innovations with respect to patristic theology. However, he sees these innovations, somewhat uncritically, as a necessary development of and not as mere deviations from patristic tradition. According to him, Palamite theology focuses on answering the question "How?" in the relation between Divine essence and energies, while the question "Who?" remains unanswered. Most interestingly, Arjakovsky positions the theological contribution of Fr. Sergius exactly within the context of its relation to Palamite theology: "Bulgakov reconsidered the relationship between essence, energy and hypostasis . . ."[39] and, six centuries after the Palamite Councils in the fourteenth century, went "beyond their restriction on employing logic in theologizing about the relationship between essence, energies and the hypostases of the Trinity, thus enabling the emergence of a creative momentum for an entire generation of intellectuals, including those who believed to have been protecting the tradition

35. Alfeev, *Le Mystère sacré de l'Église*, 393.

36. Bulgakov, *La philosophie du Verbe*.

37. Ibid., 207: "Interprétation sophiologique du dogme relatif au nom de Jésus."

38. Аржаковски, Журнал Путь, 424; See also: Arjakovsky, "The Sophiology of Father Sergius Bulgakov," 219–35.; Arjakovsky, *Essai sur le père Serge Boulgakov*.

39. Аржаковски, Журнал Путь, 425.

of the Church."[40] Arjakovsky's works provide a passionate apology for the philosophical theology of Fr. Sergius. His contributions made a difference in the scholarship focusing on Bulgakov's intellectual legacy. It should be pointed out however that the theological motivation for Arjakovsky's advocating approach to the sophiology of Fr. Sergius remains unconvincing. In some cases his elaborations on Bulgakov's theology turn into mere reiterations of his opinions. In other cases, Bulgakov's deviations from mainstream Orthodox theology are uncritically considered as contributions to its body. For example, Arjakovsky refers to Olivier Clément, who "insisted on the importance of the theme of created Wisdom in Father Sergius Bulgakov as an indisputable continuation of the theology of uncreated energies begun by St. Gregory Palamas."[41] At the same time, right after that, he refers to Paul Evdokimov, who wrote that "the Wisdom of God is even the common energy of the three [Divine] persons"[42]—a statement which undermines the necessity of introducing the concept of Sophia in general. It seems that in his attempt to acknowledge the unique personality, the contributions, and the intellectual capacity of Fr. Sergius, Arjakovsky is actually blurring out the main point about his dialogical role in opening up the opportunity for a theological response to his own theology that would provide some of the key Orthodox theological insights in the twentieth century.[43]

More recently, Paul Gavrilyuk provided a comprehensive comparison of the theological approaches of Florovsky and Bulgakov in a book titled *George Florovsky and the Russian Religious Renaissance*. He pointed out that, in order to reinforce his argument from tradition, Bulgakov claimed that "sophiology was a creative contemporary reworking of the teaching of Gregory Palamas. More specifically, the divine Sophia was a repository of uncreated divine energies."[44] Gavrilyuk offers an interesting interpretation of Lossky's and Florovsky's reactions to such claim. According to Gavrilyuk, "Lossky argued that Bulgakov misinterpreted Palamas by identifying Sophia both with the divine essence and with the divine energies,"[45] while Florovsky

---

40. Ibid.

41. Arjakovsky, "The Sophiology of Father Sergius Bulgakov," 226.

42. Evdokimov, *The Art of the Icon*, 348.

43. For example, it is well known that in 1924 it was Bulgakov who convinced the young Florovsky that he should turn to patristics: "Why don't you turn to Patristics, no one else is doing it." It was him again who invited Florovsky to teach at St. Sergius and "[b]y the time he assumed his post at St. Sergius in 1926, Florovsky was well versed in patristics, but his mastery of the field came through teaching a required course of four years duration, with two lectures per week each term." See Blane, *Georges Florovsky*, 49.

44. Gavrilyuk, *George Florovsky and the Russian Religious Renaissance*, 143.

45. Gavrilyuk refers to: Лосский, "Спор о Софии."

"did not take issue with Bulgakov directly on this point."[46] This was the basis for Gavrilyuk to conclude that Palamite theology did not play a prominent role in Florovsky's retrieval of the Fathers. I have already pointed out earlier that such conclusion is factually incorrect and historically misleading. The letters between Bulgakov and Florovsky show that the theology of St. Gregory Palamas was key part of their discussions, and it might have been actually Florovsky who helped Lossky in familiarizing himself with the patristic interpretation of the theology of St. Gregory Palamas. In another publication Gavrilyuk compared Florovsky's and Bulgakov's readings of the theological insights of St. Maximus the Confessor, concluding that "Florovsky's interpretation of Maximus tended to take a direction against Bulgakov's sophiology."[47] At the same time he emphasized that

> Bulgakov's panentheism attempted to do justice to the best insights of the *creatio ex nihilo* doctrine, although ultimately Bulgakov modified this doctrine considerably. According to Bulgakov, God creates the temporal world out of the sophianic world already existing "in" God. For Maximus, God creates by means of his volitional thoughts, that is, by means of uncreated entities containing information, so to speak, about created beings.[48]

It appears that Gavrilyuk, in the same way as Arjakovsky, tries to locate the sources of Bulgakov's theological contributions in his ability to move beyond or against tradition. At the same time he shows certain disrespect towards Florovsky.[49] For example, Gavrilyuk suggests without any evidence that, in his understanding of the theological synthesis of St. Maximus the Confessor, Florovsky "closely followed Epifanovich's presentation of Maximus without acknowledging the fact directly."[50] Earlier on the same page he remarks that "it is difficult to judge how well Florovsky knew Maximus' works in the original." At another place, Gavrilyuk refers to Florovsky's statement that it was Florensky who directed his thought to the problem of creation as a result of which he became radically opposed to any "sophianism."[51] This statement was the basis for Gavrilyuk to solemnly conclude that "it was reading Florensky's *The Pillar and Ground of the Truth*, not the works of the Church Fathers, that prompted Florovsky to produce what he later recognized as one of his most significant theological works,"

---

46. Gavrilyuk, *George Florovsky and the Russian Religious Renaissance*, 143.

47. Gavrilyuk, *Georges Florovsky's Reading of Maximus*, 415.

48. Ibid., 414.

49. Ibid., 411.

50. Ibid., 411.

51. Gavrilyuk, *George Florovsky and the Russian Religious Renaissance*, 146.

i.e., "Creature and Craturehood," and that "the creative stimulus came from one of the Renaissance 'fathers,' not the Church Fathers."[52] Here it is worth noting that "Creature and Creaturehood" contains 116 footnotes full of references to the Church Fathers without a single reference to Florensky! The point is that Fr. Pavel Florensky might have indicated that the doctrine of creation is highly relevant for sophiology, but that does not mean that he had a well-articulated and acceptable doctrine of creation that was going to be adopted by Fr. Georges Florovsky. In addition, right after making the above point about Florensky, Florovsky emphasizes that it was exactly Florensky's understanding of creation that made him become radically opposed to any "sophianism." In this sense, it is very hard to understand Gavrilyuk's excitement about Florensky's influence on Florovsky's specific focus on the doctrine of creation. I would agree with Fr. Matthew Baker that the "one-sidedly Russian focus, combined with a psychologizing hermeneutic of suspicion Gavrilyuk objects to in Florovsky but then applies to him, adds to a portrait which exaggerates the polemical, and misconstrues some points of Florovsky's thinking."[53] One could also sense a tendency to "deconstruct" Florovsky by identifying the sources of all his theological opinions in a particular earlier scholar or Renaissance "father," such as, for example, Solovyov, Khomiakov or Florensky, as if he did not read for himself the primary patristic sources but needed someone else to help him in shaping his most valuable theological points. It should be pointed out that Gavrilyuk's statements above directly contradict what Florovsky said about himself in the theological testament that was mentioned earlier:

> I studied primary sources before I turned to the learned literature. It is probably for that reason that I appear to be so much "old-fashioned." I did not start with the "higher criticism," and for that reason was never confused or corrupted by it. But, for the same reason, I was immunized forever against the routine, against the "theology of repetition" which is addicted simply to archaic forms and phrases, but so often misses completely the quickening spirit. The Fathers have taught me Christian Freedom.[54]

52. Ibid.

53. Baker, Panel presentation on Paul Gavrilyuk's book *George Florovsky and the Russian Religious Renaissance*. I am grateful to Fr. Matthew Baker, of blessed memory, who shared with me the text of his panel presentation

54. Blane, *Georges Florovsky*, 153.

Interestingly, Gavrilyuk does not see Florovsky and St. Maximus on one side of the spectrum of the patristic tradition, and Bulgakov on the opposite, less patristic, side, because for him:

> What is at stake here is a general antinomy that the human mind comes to when pondering the boundary between the uncreated (God and everything "around" God) and the created world. For if the concept of such a boundary has any meaning at all, the boundary itself has to be both created and uncreated—the fundamental insight that Bulgakov was trying to convey by insisting on this dual nature of the Sophia.[55]

According to Gavrolyuk, Florovsky's objections to Bulgakov's panentheism were quite serious but his own position also raised a number of questions, which are related to the teaching on the Divine essence and energies:

> First, how does one differentiate between an act of divine essence resulting in the generation of the Son and an act of divine will resulting in the creation of the world? In other words, what distinguishes a divine action that results in that which is divine (e.g., the generation of the Son) and a divine action that results in something non-divine (e.g., the creation of the world)? More generally, how should one conceive of a boundary between the uncreated God and the created order: as something entirely uncreated, or entirely created, or both?[56]

Gavrilyuk suggests that for Florovsky the very concept of a "boundary" was a category mistake and a mere spatial analogy that was not applicable to God and the world, because they did not belong to the same order of being. However, for him such an answer, while consistent, would not help in resolving other open issues, such as the metaphysical status of God's thought, will, or plan about the world—whether or not the Divine plan is created or uncreated, contingent or eternal.[57] It appears that Gavrilyuk's analytical attitude tends to relativize the theological opposition between Bugakov and Florovsky by questioning Florovsky's grounding in patristics and aiming at presenting Bulgakov's sophiologcal and panentheistic ideas as a valuable alternative to the patristic doctrine of creation. Even though this is a very sympathetic attempt, it is not methodologically convincing since it mixes philosophical and theological arguments, and aligns patristic references with heretical opinions. In fact, Gavrilyuk does not seem to

---

55. Gavrilyuk, *Georges Florovsky's Reading of Maximus*, 415.

56. Gavrilyuk, *George Florovsky and the Russian Religious Renaissance*, 149.

57. Ibid.

seriously appreciate the value of patristic theological insights. His searches for answers that do not to go beyond the times of the Russian "Renaissance fathers" thus diminishing his theological analysis to a kind of social science research resulting in relativizing statements about who said what and how difficult it is to make a judgment about who is right or wrong, and on what grounds. In doing so Gavrilyuk seems to misunderstand the apophatic mindset of the Eastern Christian Church, which is manifested in a subtle understanding of theological antinomies. For him Bulgakov's panentheism and Florovsky's account of creation out of nothing tend to prioritize one side of theological antinomies at the expense of the other side:

> Bulgakov prioritized the union of Creator and creation at the expense of their ontological difference; the connection between the eternal nature of God and the divine self-manifestation at the expense of the uniqueness of the historical divine revelation; divine providence at the expense of human freedom; the fullness of divine life at the expense of human creativity, and so on. Florovsky, with his "intuition of creaturehood," on the contrary, prioritized the ontological difference between God and the world at the expense of the divine-human communion; the uniqueness of the historical divine revelation in Christ at the expense of the eternal divine counsel regarding human salvation; the indeterminate character of human freedom at the expense of divine providence; the genuine novelty of contingent historical events at the expense of the divine omniscience.[58]

Using the language of theological antinomies conveniently implies that the two opposing positions refer to some generic understanding of the reality of Divine-human communion. Although there is good rhetorical value in such comparison, it blurs out Bulgakov's problem with mixing up divine and creaturely Sophia. According to Fr. N. Loudovikos, such statements by Gavrilyuk do not clarify

> whether or not this "mixed nature" of Sophia is ultimately projected upon Christ as the Sophiologists usually do, . . . or this Sophia becomes reminiscent of the mode of unity of natures implied by moderate Monophysitism. . . . [A]ccording to St. Maximus' account of a "mixed nature," a salad of mixed divine and crated qualities is created, instead of two countable natures: non-real otherness results in non-real communion, or, better, no clear selfhood means no real other. . . . So the problem with Sophia, according to Maximus' criteria, is precisely that

---

58. Gavrilyuk, *George Florovsky and the Russian Religious Renaissance*, 150.

she cannot safeguard the real union of real and intact natures, because she confuses them, and thus she cannot be thought of as fitting to the patristic theology concerning Chalcedonian Christ, who forms the model of any Orthodox understanding of the ontological connection between created and uncreated.[59]

Fr. Nicholas Loudovikos provided the most recent and probably the most insightful analysis of sophiology within the context of the theological contributions of St. Maximus the Confessor and St. Gregory Palamas.[60] He has adopted a balanced approach that is critical but also fair in locating what would be found theologically valuable for Orthodox theology, especially in the context of his apophatic ecclesiology of consubstantiality. Fr. Loudovikos is very clear that Russian sophiology is Schellingian and neo-Platonic in its inspirations. At the same time, according to him, Bulgakov "tried to directly connect his understanding of Sophia not only with the Bible, but also with a series of patristic concepts, such as *paradeigmata*, *logoi*, *proorismoi* prototypes of the Areopagite, Maximus the Confessor, Gregory of Nyssa, and even with the doctrine of the uncreated energies as promulgated by St. Gregory Palamas. That means that the sophiologists' fundamental interest was to re-establish and re-assess the mystery of God-in-creation and creation-in-God: this is what is meant by Bulgakov's term *panentheism* (all things in God)."[61] Fr. N. Loudovikos points out that "all these ideas have also many positive aspects . . . only if they are corrected through some Maximian and Palamite clarifications." In this sense, for him the ultimate criterion for the orthodoxy of Bulgakov's sophiology is its proper alignment with the theological insights of St. Maximus and St. Gregory Palamas.

In his recent book *Church in the Making: An Apophatic Ecclesiology of Consubstantiality*, Fr. N. Loudovikos makes an honest effort to incorporate sophiological terminology and ideas into his own theological approach of dialogical reciprocity and consubstansiality. He points out that for the main line of patristic thought, including St. Maximus, the incarnate Wisdom of God is Christ and the sophianic work of Christ in the realm of creation is consubstantiality.

The work of the incarnate Wisdom of God is the raising of creation to the Sophia of consubstantiality, that is to say, to the "identity," "innateness," and "undivided harmony" of beings that have been separated on account of the Fall, with the One of the body in the incarnate Wisdom of God—i.e., of Christ—which

59. Loudovikos, *Church in the Making*, 221.

60. Ibid., 196–211.

61. Ibid., 205.

is the Church. The Church is thus shown, as the sophianicity of creation, to be the manifestation of consubstantiality as the mode of existence of the whole-in-its-diversity. . . . Each person in Christ becomes a differentiated and unrepeatable hypostatic bearer of the consubstantiality of creation; without being lost, individual otherness becomes open to catholicity. It is precisely this that is the Sophia that the Wisdom of God, the Logos-Christ, has inserted, as a potentiality fulfilled through the Church, into the nature of beings. . . . Wisdom/Sophia/Consubstantiality expresses the God's unity, and unifies things in God: this is what all above patristic concepts (the Areopagitic proorismoi, the Maximian logoi, and the Palamite energies) have in common with the Bulgakovian Sophia. They all emanate from the one and united nature of God, they are God Himself ad extra, and at the same time they cause a glorious divine unity in the world, precisely as Sophia does.[62]

The theological approach of Fr. N. Loudovikos resonates very well with Florovsky's dynamic theological vision of creation.

The Sophia of God in beings is ultimately the uncreated logoi of their being in the plenitudinous, sophianic, hierurgic movement, through humankind toward the Logos-Sophia. These uncreated logoi of beings lie at the core of created natures, without being confused with them, and exist in a state of stable referentiality to the Logos-Sophia, a referentiality that only personal human freedom can activate as a free dialogue (*dia-logos*) of love between humankind and the Logos.[63]

Fr. N. Ludovikos finds therefore the ideas of Russian sophiologists fruitful, even though they tend to "ontologically confuse created and uncreated Sophia, created and uncreated logoi and energies, the divine Sophia and the world soul," but emphasizes again that Russian sophiology "can be accepted (especially in its Bulgakovian form) only after its correction through the relevant patristic tradition."[64]

The relation of Bulgakov's philosophical theology to the theology of St. Gregory Palamas did not escape the attention of non-Orthodox scholars as well. One good representative example would be the philosophers and theologians associated with the so-called Radical Orthodoxy movement for which Russian religious philosophy, and Bulgakov's theology in particular,

62. Ibid., 208–9.

63. Ibid., 209.

64. Ibid., 210.

represents a valuable theological resource.[65] For example, Adrian Pabst and Christoph Schneider point out that "[t]he theologies of language developed by the Russian philosophers Pavel Florensky, Sergii Bulgakov, and Aleksei Losev . . . draw on specifically Eastern Orthodox doctrines such as the theology of icons or the essence-energy distinction."[66] In addition, John Milbank, one of the founders of the Radical Orthodoxy movement, has clearly indicated that his "growing interest in Eastern Orthodoxy has led him to develop his account of ontology in the direction of a metaphysical-theological *methexis* of donation which draws on the Eastern Orthodox thematic of energy (ἐνέργεια) and wisdom (σοφία)."[67] According to him:

> Above all, we cannot distinguish, in Gregory Palamas' fashion (and I think that Bulgakov in the end implies a rejection of this), between divine essence and the divine uncreated energies which enable the economy of human redemption. It is clearly not the case that Palamas distinguished them in any simple fashion that would entirely forego the divine simplicity. Nonetheless, the distinction which he did make appears to have something in common with the almost contemporary Western Scotist "formal distinction"—less than a real one, more than merely one made by our minds: rather a kind of latent division within a real unity permitting a real if partial separation on some arising occasion. In this respect the Palamite theology does appear slightly to ontologise the epistemological truth that God "in himself" remains beyond the grasp of even the beatific vision, as though this reserved aspect were a real ultimate "area." . . . Clearly, for Bulgakov, the Palamite energies played the same role as Sophia, and infused human actions with theurgic power; nevertheless, sophiology is superior to the Palamite theology precisely *because* it moves away from a literal between and allows the energies simultaneously to be identical with the divine essence itself and yet also to be created as well as uncreated.

65. Pabst and Schneider, "Transfiguring the World through the Word," 7. The authors appear to be more than just interested in the theology of Fr. S. Bulgakov: "Most of today's Orthodox theologians operate within a theological framework that is close to the 'Neo-patristic synthesis' advocated by Vladimir Lossky, Georges Florovsky and others. Very few theologians try to work along the lines of the circle around Sergii Bulgakov, which developed a more sophisticated understanding of a 'living tradition' and which was much better equipped for a constructive *and* critical engagement with other denominations and contemporary thought." They identify Bulgakov's theology as a challenge and even a stumbling block for Orthodox theology, and point out to their way of engagement with it as a lesson learned, especially for Orthodox theologians.

66. Ibid., 14.

67. Ibid., 20.

This actually brings Eastern theology more in line with best of Thomism for which has to be created as well as uncreated if it is ever to reach us—but occupies no phantom and limboesque border territory.[68]

Without going into a more detailed analysis of the above statement, it could be pointed out that the question about the difference between the distinctions made by St. Gregory Palamas and Duns Scot has already been addressed explicitly by some of the Orthodox theologians and philosophers.[69] For example, in a recent book including the contributions of several scholars discussing David Bradshaw's monograph *Aristotle East and West: Metaphysics and the Division of Christendom*,[70] Fr. N. Loudovikos points out that for Palamas

> God in his wholeness of divinity is present in each one of the energies and, consequently, anyone who participates in any of these energies participates truly in God as he is, since in each energy "there is God in his wholeness being present in his creatures, imparting himself to them and absolutely participated in, according to the image of the sunbeam, in a little part of which we can see the sun in its wholeness."[71]

"It is really difficult," continues Fr. Loudovikos,

> after all these texts, to speak of any "Scotist" formal distinction or separation, as some sort of *fundamentum in re*, in Palamas, as Milbank so persistently claims. . . . Concerning Palamas, I think that it is clear enough that he would not endorse either a real or a formal distinction between essence and energies, in the sense given to these terms by Milbank. This is why great Palamists of the next generation after Palamas, such as Markus Eugenicus, following an analogous Palamite expression in his fifth treatise *Against Gregoras*, without any hesitation and without encountering any objection, used the term *kat' epinoian* (i.e., made by mind) in order to describe this distinction-in-identity between essence and energies in the Palamite oeuvre.[72]

---

68. Milbank, "Sophiology and theurgy," 70–71.

69. Romanides, "Notes on the Palamite Controversy," 193–202; Kapriev, *Philosophie in Byzanz*, 344; Loudovikos, "Striving for Participation," 125–26.

70. Bradshaw, *Aristotle East and West*.

71. Loudovikos, "Striving for Participation," 126.

72. Ibid., referring to Boulovich, "The Mystery of Essence-Energies Distinction in the Holy Trinity," 153–59.

Interestingly, David Bradshaw is very cautious regarding the statement that the distinction between essence and energy is *kat' epinoian*. According to him, everything depends on how this phrase is understood, since one could interpret *epinoia* (following St. John of Damascus) in two different ways:

> The first type of *epinoia* is the act of discovering in the object of thought a reality or distinction that is truly there, although thought is needed to identify and clarify it—for example, the distinction of body and soul; the second is the act of inventing something that has no reality apart from its being thought. Palamas himself, no doubt aware of this ambiguity, seems to have deliberately avoided saying that the distinction of essence and energies is *kat' epinoian*. Nonetheless later Palamites . . . adopted such language freely. Precisely what each meant by this must be determined from his own writings, but in general the early Palamites, at least, seem to have adhered quite closely to Palamas' actual meaning, if not to his words. As regards the phrase *kat' epinoian*, this is shown particularly by their holding that the distinction between the Father and the Son is also *kat' epinoian*, a statement plainly not intended to undermine its reality or to suggest that it is merely imposed by human thought.[73]

In support of Bradshaw's point, one could refer to a recent paper by Georgi Kapriev, who has specifically discussed the similarity between the Scotist formal distinction and the distinction between essence and energies in the Palamite tradition by reexamining its articulation in the works of Georgios Scholarios (known also as Gennadius II, Patriarch of Constantinople, 1454–56).[74] The comparison between Palamas and Scholarios suggested by Georgi Kapriev is of significant interest and deserves a special attention. Since the second quarter of the twentieth century Scholarios has been considered as one of the greatest Byzantine Thomists, even though after 1444 he was the leader of the Palamite party in Constantinople.[75] It was Martin Jugie (again) who in the beginning of the 1930s promoted the opinion that, in his articulation of the distinction between Divine essence and energies, Scholarios adopted the distinctions used by John Duns Scotus with a preference for *distinctio formalis a parte rei*.[76] According to Kapriev, this is the dominant opinion among many scholars even today. What is

---

73. Ibid., 258–59.

74. Kapriev, "The Scotist Distinction between Essence and Energies," 232–66.

75. Podskalsky, *Theologie und Philosophie in Byzanz*, 179.

76. Jugie, "Introduction," XVIII.

more interesting however is that since the 1930s some of the scholars have been trying to contrast Scholarios's *distinctio formalis* to a *distinctio realis,* which has been automatically assigned to St. Gregory Palamas. For Kapriev the intention was to point out that there was a misalignment between the positions of the two Byzantine theologians and, more specifically, that the adoption of a Latin metaphysical logic (Thomist, but also Scotist) by Scholarios had actually offered a solution to the logical and philosophical inconsistencies of Palamas's thought. Kapriev offers a rather detailed and insightful comparison of the distinctions made by Scholarios and Palamas, showing that one should actually consider Scholarios as someone who had adopted an authentically Palamite position but expressed it in a way that was compatible with the positions of Bonaventure and Duns Scot.

Did really Bulgakov simply reject Palamism, as Milbank suggested? It was already shown that Bulgakov's sophiological approach to Palamism was rather more subtle than a mere rejection. Milbank's opinion only demonstrates the need for a more careful analysis of any possible relationship between Bulgakov's sophiology and the teaching of St. Gregory which, to a certain degree, the present chapter offers. What is more interesting however in Milbank's quotation above is the point about the potential relationship between sophiology and Thomism. A similar point was also made recently by Joost van Rossum in a paper about Vladimir Lossky's reading of St. Gregory Palamas.[77] Joost van Rossum discusses Bulgakov's essentialistic approach to sophiology by characterizing it as Thomistic as far as it does not clearly distinguish between Divine essence and existence and "internalizes" the energy of the Divine Wisdom (Sophia) by identifying it with the Divine essence. The link between Bulgakov's sophiology and the essentialistic aspects of Thomistic thought touches on an important issue since it provides another hermeneutical tool in the analysis of the sophiological controversy. It is definitely helpful in providing some insights about the philosophico-theological background on and against which the teaching on the Divine essence and energies reemerged in the twentieth century—a background that seems to be very similar to the one in the middle of the fourteenth century.[78] It may also help in identifying some of the reasons for the sophiological "excitement" of the Radical Orthodox movement. According to Milbank, the sophiological tradition of Pavel Florensky and Sergii Bulgakov is crucial in refining and extending the key concepts of Radical Orthodoxy in terms of participation, mediation, and deification since it conceives mediation

---

77. Van Rossum, "Vladimir Lossky et sa lecture de Grégoire Palamas," 42.

78. Hierotheos, *Saint Gregory as a Hagiorite,* 23.

between the persons of the Trinity in terms of substantive relations.[79] For Milbank relations at the level of the substance mean (in the same way as in Bulgakov) that there is no need of any third term in addition to essence and person, i.e., there can be no third term between the two natures of Christ, nor between both the natures and the divine hypostasis. There is no need of a third term because "there is nothing more general or fundamental than the three divine persons and the Trinitarian relations that pertain between them." At the same time (in the same way as in Bulgakov), there is a need of the term *Sophia*, which however is seen as not introducing any semantic inconsistency since "Σοφία names a relation or μεταξύ (a term central to Bulgakov's work) which is not situated between two poles but rather remains—simultaneously and paradoxically—at both poles at once."[80] Sophia is not a fourth divine person, "but is equally (though also differently) of the Father, the Son and the Holy Spirit, a kind of energy that both unifies and differentiates the One triune God and infuses his glorious creation with the wisdom of knowing him as the Creator."[81] One could provocatively summarize the logic of the Radical Orthodox position as follows: a) there is no need of a third term, however, b) there is a need of the term Sophia, which is c) used in the sense of energy, i.e., exactly the term that had been used by St. Gregory Palamas and many other Church Fathers.

The similarity between the Radical Orthodox and Bulgakov's positions is quite evident and appears to emerge from their common ontological presuppositions.[82] The reason for us to discuss it in more detail here was to point out that for Bulgakov the introduction of the term Sophia was not an attempt to elaborate a necessary third theological term in addition to οὐσία and ὑπόστασις, but rather an attempt to (unnecessarily) replace one that was already in patristic use—ἐνέργεια—by forcing into it a meaning that was alien to patristics. Using the similarity with the Radical Orthodox ontological presuppositions has shown a tendency in sophiology to collapse the Divine persons into substantive relations and, thus, into the substance or essence. Such collapse seems to exhausts the possibility for an epistemological opening between God and man. It defines a static *a priori* relation between God and man that does not leave space for a relationship based on love and personal freedom. Sophia *a priori* contains in itself the whole of creation. Containing all of creation and being also God's substance or

79. Pabst and Schneider, "Transfiguring the World through the Word," 20.

80. Ibid.

81. Ibid.

82. For a more detailed analysis of the Radical Orthodox position from an Orthodox perspective the reader could refer to: Loudovikos, "Ontology Celebrated," 141–55.

nature, Sophia implies no difference between the Creator and His creation and removes the freedom in the relationship between them, thus, infecting Bulgakov's sophiological system with the seeds of pantheism.[83] In response to such static relation one could use a statement by the late Fr. Dumitru Popescu according to whom

> the Holy Trinity cannot become a prisoner of unity, because it is moved by love, through the uncreated energies, imparted by the Holy Spirit. If the person and the relations were simultaneous, man would have to elevate himself to reach out to the Holy Trinity, because the Trinity would not descend to reach man. The uncreated energies, radiating from the internal constitution of the Holy Trinity, are the means through which the incarnate Logos descends into the world, so that the world may ascend to God. If the Trinity remained closed upon Itself, it would be hard to see that God loved the world so much, that He gave His only begotten Son as a redeeming price for it. In its turn, the world is not representing a monad closed upon itself, like a monolithic divine nature, but it has an internal ontological rationality, which stems from the Divine rationalities, which proceed from the Logos and have their center of gravity in the Logos. This rationality, which manifests itself in the created energies of the world, constitutes the means through which the Divine reasons (λόγοι) work within creation, with man's participation, to evolve to its final perfection, according to God's will.[84]

In his statement Fr. Poposecu refers to the *Orthodox Dogmatic Theology* of Fr. Dumitru Staniloae[85] which appears to be in full agreement with Fr. Florovsky's teaching on the distinction between Divine essence and energies,[86] and demonstrates the link between the sophiological theme, the teaching on the Divine energies and the doctrine of creation.

The Doctrine of Creation in Bulgakov's *The Bride of the Lamb*

It was already pointed out that the indirect theological debate between Fr. George Florovsky and Fr. Sergius Bulgakov focused on the Christian doctrine of creation. For both of them the doctrine of creation played a keystone

---

83. Sergeev, *Sophiology in Russian Orthodoxy*, 109.

84. Popescu, "Logos, Trinity, Creation," 63.

85. Staniloae, *The World: Creation and Deification*, 13.

86. Florovsky, "Creation and Creaturehood," 43–78.

role for a proper understanding of Christian theology. For Bulgakov the concept of Sophia naturally emerges as a theological prerequisite for the understanding of the relationship between God as Trinity and the world. The doctrine of creation, therefore, is crucial to understanding Bulgakov's sophiology, and he devotes almost the entire first half of *The Bride of the Lamb* to a detailed treatise on the nature of created beings and the relationship between Creator and creation, including some of the specific aspects of *creatio ex nihilo*. According to Bulgakov's translator Boris Jakim, *The Bride of the Lamb* is "the greatest sophiological work ever written," and "the most mature development of his sophiology."[87] The next sections will focus on a parallel exploration of some of the diverging points between Bulgakov and Florovsky aiming at showing that the teaching on the distinction between the Divine essence and energies emerges as a solution to Bulgakov's sophiological problematics.

In Bulgakov's terminology, the Divine nature can be analyzed in two aspects, namely, as οὐσία—the Divine nature in the aspect of God-for-Himself, and Σοφία—the Divine nature in the aspect of God-for-Others. Sophia can be understood only in relation to, but not as, οὐσία, because without God-in-Himself there is no God-for-Others. Οὐσία is necessarily more than Sophia, because God never completely reveals Himself. Nonetheless, they both represent the same nature of God in relation to the Creator Himself (οὐσία) or the creature (Σοφία). In this sense, Divine Wisdom or Sophia is understood as the nature of God revealed to creation and, respectively, in creation:

> One and the same Sophia is revealed in God and in creation. Therefore, if the negative definition, "God created the world out of nothing" eliminates the idea of any nondivine or extradivine principle in creation, its *positive* content can only be such that God created the world out of himself, out of His essence. And the idea that the content of world was invented ad hoc by God at the creation of the world must be fundamentally rejected. The *positive* content of the world's being is just as divine as its foundation in God, for there is no other principle for it. But that which exists pre-eternally in God, in His self-revelation, exists in the world only in becoming, as becoming divinity. And metaphysically the creation of the world consists in the fact that God established His proper divine world not as an eternally existing world but as a *becoming* world. In this sense, He mixed it with nothing, immersing it in becoming as *another form* of being of one and the same divine world. And this divine world is the

---

87. Bulgakov, *The Bride of the Lamb*, xiii.

foundation, content, entelechy, and meaning of the creaturely world. The Divine Sophia became also the creaturely Sophia. God repeated Himself in creation, so to speak; He reflected Himself in nonbeing.[88]

One of the main concerns of Bulgakov in *The Bride of the Lamb* is to re-establish the place of the world in its ontological relation to God and, in a sense, to reconcile the world to God. "If there is such a place, it must be established by God, for there is nothing that is outside of or apart from God and that in this sense is not-God."[89] It is here that the dogmatic formula on the creation *ex nihilo* comes into play. In looking at the problematic of creation *ex nihilo*, Bulgakov transfers the question, in his own words, from a static to a dynamic plane. To do that he starts with Plato and Aristotle in whom, he asserts, we find "Divinity without God."[90] In Plato, the createdness of the world finds no role in his ideas and the ideas are hovering above the world in the eternal Divine Sophia, and are "duplicated," as it were, in the empirical world. There is no answer that could overcome this "ontological hiatus," and Platonism remains "only an abstract sophiology," which slides into idealism or monism.

Aristotle, on the other hand, transposed these ideas from the domain of the Divine Sophia to the domain of the creaturely Sophia, in a system of "sophiological cosmology."[91] "God" (the Prime Mover) and the world merge to the point of indistinguishability,[92] where in the final analysis Aristotle equates God with the world. His cosmology "is nothing but a sophiology," but a sophiology that is impersonalistic and "deprived of its trinitarian-theological foundation."[93] Sophiology can be justified not in itself but "*only in connection with* theology," when the former occupies its proper place in the latter, "but does not supplant it."[94] At the same time, Bulgakov believes that ancient religion and philosophy attested so powerfully to the *sophianicity* of the world, that their contribution has yet to be illuminated in its full significance.

Moving to the discussion of patristics Bulgakov employs an approach that could be characterized as typical of him—he sees the Church Fathers through his sophiological prism and ends up identifying them as bad

88. Ibid., 126.
89. Ibid., 6.
90. Ibid., 8.
91. Ibid., 9.
92. Ibid., 10.
93. Ibid.
94. Ibid., 15.

"sophiologists." He finds the key flaw of patristic theology in "the confusion of sophiology with logology"[95] and openly argues against the patristic identification of the Logos, the second hypostasis in the Holy Trinity, with the Divine Sophia, calling this identification "the primordial defect of all patristic sophiology." His approach to patristics therefore is to take the core of patristic theology for a sophiology and then judge it on the basis of his own understanding of what sophiology is and what it should be. All of his theological reflections show a continuous unhappiness with the underdeveloped sophiology of the Church Fathers and a clear commitment to its theological correction or constructive renewal. This is a point that will become a key issue in the indirect theological debate between him and Florovsky for whom a proper understanding of the Church Fathers becomes the most authentic resource for a constructive contemporary theological reflection.

Bulgakov's Emphasis on the Doctrine of the Divine Prototypes or Ideas

Bulgakov finds a patristic sophiological opportunity in the fact that "logological sophiology does not exhaust the entire content the patristic doctrine of Sophia" leaving space for the emergence of what he calls an "*applied* sophiology." This applied sophiology is based on the doctrine of the prototypes, paradigms, or ideas of creaturely being in God in the way it was articulated by St. Gregory the Divine, St. John of Damascus, St. Maximus the Confessor, Pseudo-Dionysius, and St. Augustine. But, again, he ends up with the criticism that, while patristic and scholastic doctrines converge in appreciating the theological value of the Divine paradigms or ideas of creaturely being in God, they are incomplete because of a lack of sophiological substance. For him the lack of sophiology leads to the attribution of an "accidental" character to the Divine ideas whereas a full understanding of patristic sophiology requires considering both "logological sophiology, on the one hand, and the theory of ideas in their mutual interrelation and harmonization, on the other."[96] Bulgakov points out that in connection with this

> arises a fundamental question, which, however, was not understood as such in patristics itself, and therefore did not find an answer for itself there: the question of how one should properly understand the relation of these prototypes of the world to the Logos, and then to the Divine Sophia and the creaturely Sophia.

95. Ibid., 16.
96. Ibid., 17.

In particular, do these ideas have a divine and eternal character? Do they refer to Divine being? Or are they created ad hoc, so to speak, as the ideal foundation of the world, a "heaven" in relation to "earth"? In other words, is it a question here of the Divine Sophia or of the creaturely Sophia?[97]

These questions again demonstrate the peculiarity of Bulgakov's approach—he imposes his sophiological presuppositions on patristic theology and keeps asking questions that would have never emerged from its own premises. As a result, he finds solutions that are alien to it:

> In the first place, these divine ideas of the world can be equated with the Divine Sophia, since the Divine Sophia includes the ideal *all*, the ontic seeds of the Logos. By a creative act theses seeds are implanted in 'nothing' and form the foundation of the being of the creaturely world, that is, the creaturely Sophia, who also shines with the light of eternity in the heavens, in the Divine Sophia. In the Divine Sophia, these seeds belong to the self-revelation of divinity in the Holy Trinity or to the divine world, whereas in the creaturely world they are its divine goal-causes, or entelechies. . . . The main trait of these prototypes of creaturely being is that they are *not* created, but have a divine, eternal being proper to them. This is the uncreated heaven, the glory of God. But these prototypes, or ideas, can also be considered as *created* by God as the prototypes of the world *before* creation, as it were. They ontologically presuppose creation but are connected with it. . . . If one calls this too Sophia (of course, with violence done to terminology), one would have then to say that Sophia is created, and that in general only the creaturely Sophia exists, although she is not an independent part of this created world but only its plan. This is indeed the understanding of some of the theologians, though for us this idea of a solely creaturely, *ad hoc* created Sophia contains a number of irreconcilable contradictions and dogmatic absurdities. In particular, it introduces changeability into the very essence of God. God in creation is different from God before creation: He creates something new even for himself, namely, the creaturely Sophia.[98]

We can return now to the point about the similarity between Bulgakov's sophiology and the theology of Thomas Aquinas in their relation to the doctrine of creation (in the section of the *Bride of the Lamb* dedicated to the creation of the world out of nothing, the discussion of the teaching of

97. Ibid.
98. Ibid., 17.

Aquinas and Western theology is the largest in the volume).[99] In the quotation above one could identify an affinity to Aquinas' concept of creation in which the beginning of the world is decoupled from its creation in time and "being created" is not equivalent to "having began to exist" but just to "being depended on someone"—an approach that could be considered as an "audacious novelty" for Thomas' times.[100] It seems again that, although Bulgakov appears to be quite critical towards Aquinas, considering Bulgakov's sophiological ideas in parallel with Thomas' doctrine of creation would be quite worthwhile in providing another hermeneutical insight for a contemporary re-evaluation of his theology and a new fresh look at the sophiological controversy in general.

Divine Necessity vs. Freedom in *The Bride of the Lamb*

A key point in Bulgakov's sophiology is emphasizing the contrast of the difference between creation by Divine necessity and by Divine freedom. For him "patristics affirmed only the general notion of the creation of the world by God's free will, in contradistinction to the necessity that reigns in divinity's internal self-determinations."[101] He sees "an anthropomorphism in the acceptance of this dishonorable doctrine of (and even opposition) in God between necessity and freedom."[102] These latter are permissible, he writes, only for creaturely limitedness, and the "antinomic conjugacy of freedom and necessity" not only determine creaturely life, but "the very distinction and opposition between the two finds its origin here."[103] For God, "all is equally necessary and equally free," and "occasionalism . . . is not appropriate to God's magnificence and absoluteness."[104]

> If God created the world, this means that He *could not have refrained from creating it*, although the Creator's act belongs to the fullness of God's life and this act contains no external compulsion that would contradict divine freedom. And if one can speak of the *will* to creation in God, this will, as synonymous with freedom, is not an anthropomorphic will, which can desire or not desire, but the divine will, which invariably and

99. Ibid., 19

100. Putallas, "Audace et limites de la raison"; see also Heller, "Where Physics Meets Metaphysics," 238–77.

101. Bulgakov, *Bride of the Lamb*, 29.

102. Ibid.

103. Ibid.

104. Ibid., 32.

absolutely desires. In general, the distinction between God's being and his creation, defined according to the feature of freedom
and understood in the sense of different *possibilities*, must be
completely eliminated, for such a distinction does not exist.
Having in himself the power of creation, God cannot fail to be
the Creator. . . . The world's "creation" is not something *extra*,
not something *plus* to God's proper life. This creation enters into
the divine life with all the force of "necessity," or of the freedom
that, in God, is completely identical with "necessity."[105]

It appears then that for Bulgakov the world's creation is "God's own
life, inseparable from *personal* divinity, as his self-revelation." He emphasizes the importance of understanding the Divine Sophia as divinity in God
in her connection with the hypostases of the Trinity. As divinity, she does
not have her own hypostasis, but is eternally hypostatized in the Holy Trinity and cannot exist otherwise. She belongs to the tri-hypostases as their life
and self-revelation.[106] Thus,

the Divine Sophia is God's *exhaustive* self-revelation, the fullness of divinity, and therefore has absolute content. There can
be no positive principle of being that does not enter into this
fullness of sophianic life and revelation. . . . The Divine Sophia
(also known as the divine world) is therefore a *living* essence in
God. However, she is not a "hypostasis" but "hypostatizedness"
which belongs to the personal life of the hypostasis, and because
of this, she is a living essence.[107]

God as Try-hypostatic Person?

In discussing the meaning of Divine Sophia in relation to creation Bulgakov
provides another key passage:

Sophia must also be understood in the sense of *creative* self-
determination, the supra-eternal creative act of the Holy Trinity,
the self-creativity of the Holy Trinity, the *actus purus* of God.
. . . In our theology there exist certain ossified formulae that
fundamentally contradict this divine self-creative actuality. This
includes the usual dogmatic formula relating to the Holy Trinity: God "has" tree persons and one nature. The formulation that

105. Ibid. See also Лосский, "Спор о Софии."
106. Bulgakov, *Bride of the Lamb*, 38–39.
107. Ibid., 39.

God has three persons is imprecise if it is not also stated that
God himself is a tri-hypostatic person. But we can ignore this
imprecision; it will not necessarily lead to incorrect conclusions.
But the formula that the Holy Trinity *has* one *nature* is, in this
form, unsatisfactory in general. For what this "nature" and this
"has" signify? . . . "Nature," to be sure is divinity itself, God's own
life in its self-revelation. . . . This life is divinity's eternal *act*. . . .
God's nature is, in this sense, the creative self-positing of divinity, God's personal—trihypostatic—act. This act is the Divine
Sophia, the self-positing and self-revelation of the Holy Trinity.
. . . She is the creative act of the divine trihypostatic person. . . .
Only on the basis of such a conception of the divine nature, or
Sophia, as God's self-creative act can we wholly overcome the
rationalistically reified concept of God and think of him not
statically, but dynamically, as *actus purus*.[108]

There are two significant points to make in relation to this passage.
The first one is Bulgakov's comfort in using the concept of *actus purus*
which, for an Orthodox ear, clearly indicates a tendency to collapsing the
essence or nature of God and His activities and manifestations *ad extra*.
The second one is the discussion of Divine Sophia as the creative act of the
divine trihypostatic *person*, i.e., Bulgakov makes a distinction between the
three hypostases in God and His . . . person. According to A. Arjakovsky,
if one has to state in a few words the principal response of Bulgakov to the
enigma of Chalcedon, one would say "God does not have three persons,
God is Himself a tri-hypostatic Person."[109] According to Fr. N. Loudovikos,
the adoption of such terminology suggests an association with Sabellian-
ism.[110] Arjakovsky's point helps in opening the important question about
Bulgakov's understanding of the nature of the relation between the three
Divine hypostases and the Divine essence or nature. A careful look in his
earlier work *The Lamb of God* provides some additional insights about it:[111]

The Divine nature entirely and totally belongs to God; it is
personally realized in Him as "His eternal power and Godhead" (Rom. 1:20). But in virtue of this realized state, even if
the nature in God must be distinguished from His personality,
one must not oppose to it, as another principle, a "fourth" in

108. Ibid., 42.

109. Arjakovsky, "The Sophiology of Father Sergius Bulgakov," 219–35.

110. Loudovikos, *Church in the Making*, 198.

111. At the same time, any comparative analysis of Bulgakov's works should be
done very carefully. It could easily create a sense of conceptual confusion due to the fact
that his opinions have developed in time.

the Holy Trinity, a "Divinity" in God. . . . The Divine nature is totally transparent for the Divine hypostases, and to that extent it is identified with them, while preserving its proper being. The nature is eternally hypostasized in God as the adequate life of the hypostases, whereas the hypostases are eternally connected in their life with the nature, while remaining distinct from it.[112]

Bulgakov points out that there is a fundamental relation between personality and nature in Divinity. It is not entirely clear what the difference between the Divine personality, the tri-hypostatic Divine Person and each of the three hypostases is. However, it seems that by personality he refers to some kind of pre-hypostatic state of intentionality or an autonomous dynamic living principle in association with the Divine nature that makes it to be hypostasized. It should be therefore fully open or transparent for the three hypostases.

This transparence of the nature for the hypostases and its total adequacy are realized in the unity of the tri-hypostatic life in conformity with the try-hypostatizedness of the Divine Person. God has his nature by a *personal* self-positing, but one that is personally tri-hypostatic. . . . The principle (ἀρχή) of the nature of Divinity, as of the entire Holy Trinity, is God the Father. He has his own nature, and His possession of it is a hypostatic, co-hypostatic, and inter-hypostatic act. . . . The Father actualizes *His own*, His own hypostatically transparent nature, in the hypostasis of the Son, who is His Word, the "image of his person [ὑπόστασις]" (Heb. 1:3). . . . In the Divine Spirit the relation between person and nature is defined in another manner. In the Divine Spirit, there is nothing in a given or unrealized state. . . . Therefore, although nature is other than hypostasis in God as well, it is entirely hypostasized, rendered conscious in the personal life of the Divinity, manifested and actualized.[113]

Reading the above quotations makes it difficult to disagree with A. Arjakovsky about Bulgakov's theological innovativeness with respect to patristics. It is, however, equally difficult to agree with him that this theological innovativeness is a natural development of patristic theology. During Bulgakov's own times it was Vladimir Lossky who reacted vigorously to such statements because "it seemed to him a mixing of the nature and the person of God."[114] Today there is not much to add to such criticisms,

112. Bulgakov, *The Lamb of God*, 97.

113. Ibid.

114. Cited by A. Arjakovsky in: Антуан Аржаковски, Журнал Путь *(1925–1940)*,

especially when one could see the theological implications of the collapsing of the Divine essence into the Divine activities, and of Divine nature into the Divine "person":

> Only the divinity of the existent God *is*, and there is nothing apart from and outside divinity. . . . The existent God has being, that is, essence and existence. The tryhypostatic Person of God has His own nature or His own divine world, and all belongs to this life and world. Therefore, the assertion that there is nothing apart from God is only a negative expression of this positive conception. In fact, such an extra-divine nothing simply does not exist. . . . And if we believe that the world is created out of nothing, then, in the positive sense, this can mean only that God created the world out of Himself. . . . One must include the world's creation in God's own life, correlate God's world-creating act with the act of His self-determination. One must know how to simultaneously unite, identify, and distinguish creation and God's life, which in fact is possible in the doctrine of Divine Sophia, Divine and creaturely, identical and distinct.[115]

For Bulgakov there cannot be a basis for the separation in God of His being and creativity, contrary to His self-identity and simplicity.

> It is thought that God did not have to become the Creator, that He does not need the world, that He could remain in the absolute solitude and glory of His magnificence. Corresponding to this is the confused notion that God supposedly began to be the Creator in a time that proceeded the time of His being *before* creation. But all such attempts to measure God's being by time, namely before and after creation, or to define different modes of necessity and freedom in God, as well as their degree, are exposed as absurd, as contradicting God's eternity and unchangeability. . . . God's all simple essence is one and unchanging, and if God is the Creator, He is the Creator from all eternity.[116]

425; See also Лосский, "Спор о Софии." In a private communication Fr. Nicholas Lossky pointed out to me that his father V. Lossky did not want this last text to be openly published. For him it was part of a private report requested by the Metropolitan of Moscow and, if it was going be openly published, it should have been much more positive towards Fr. Sergius Bulgakov. According to Fr. N. Lossky, his father had a great respect towards Fr. Sergius as a theologian and believed that, with some small corrections, his theology could easily become fully Orthodox.

115. Bulgakov, *Bride of the Lamb*, 49.

116. Ibid., 45.

Thus, God is both God in Himself and the Creator, with a completely equal necessity and freedom of His being. In other words, God cannot fail to be the Creator, just as the Creator cannot fail to be God. The plan of the world's creation is as co-eternal to God as His own being in the Divine Sophia. In this sense (but only in this sense), God cannot do without the world, and the world is necessary for God's own being. . . . For this reason, we must consider inadmissible and contradictory the anthropomorphic principle that God 'freely' or accidentally, as it were, created the world, and the world therefore did not have to be created.[117]

Based on his analysis Bulgakov concludes that the Divine Sophia is not only God's project or His pre-eternal ideas of the creaturely world but also creation's eternal and uncreated foundation and essence. In this sense, the creaturely world does not contain any ontological novelty for God and is not subject to time. "Rather, it is eternal with all of God's eternity, as eternal as the Holy Trinity and its self-revelation in the Divine Sophia, as eternal as God's life."[118]

117. Ibid., 46.
118. Ibid.

Chapter 3

Energeia vs. *Sophia* in the Works of Fr. Georges Florovsky

Florovsky on Sophia

Interestingly enough, Florovsky rarely talks about Sophia. "It is particularly startling to discover that there seems to be absolutely nothing" in Florovsky's lifetime corpus of published writing that could qualify as an explicit attack on sophiology.[1] However, Florovsky's writings abound in what can be characterized as indirect criticism of sophiology. Most of them were scholarly studies which aimed "to expose weaknesses in the theoretical or historical underpinnings of the sophiological edifice, doing so, however, without referring to the sophiological teaching by name."[2] One of the few places where Florovsky discusses the concept of Sophia is in a letter written to Bulgakov on July 4 (July 22, New Style), 1926, where he argues that acquaintance with Palamas would have made his Sophia unnecessary:[3]

> As I have been saying for a long time, there are *two* teachings about Sophia and even *two* Sophias, or more accurately, *two images* of Sophia: the true and real, and the imaginary one. Holy churches were built in Byzantium and in Rus' in the name of the former. The latter inspired Soloviev and his Masonic and western teachers—and goes right back to the Gnostics and Philo. Soloviev did not at all know the *Church Sophia*: he knew Sophia from Boehme and the Boehmenists, from Valentinus and Kabbalah. And *this* Sophiology is heretical and renounced.

1. Klimoff, "Georges Florovsky and the Sophiological Controversy," 75.

2. Ibid., 76.

3. The letter has been published in Russian: Пентковски, "Письма Г. Флоровского С. Булгакову и С. Тышкевичу," 205, and translated in English: http://ishmaelite.blogspot.com/2009/05/palamas-florovsky-bulgakov-and.html.

56

That which you find in Athanasius relates to the other Sophia. And one may find even more about Her in Basil the Great and Gregory of Nyssa, from which there is a direct line to Palamas. The very terminology—*ousia* and *energeia* has its beginning in Basil the Great. I see no difficulty in this terminology. Aristotle has nothing to do with this. The basic thought of Cappadocian theology can be reduced to a precise distinction of the inner-divine Pleroma, of the Triune fullness of all-sufficient life, and it is this that is the *ousia, pelagas, tis ousias* in Damascene,—and: the "outward" [*vo vne*] direction of Mercy, Grace, Love, *Activity–Energeia.* The entire question (speculatively very difficult) is in this distinction. In the perceptible sense, this is the explanation of the very idea of *creation,* as a Divine *plan-will about the other, about not-God.* Ousia—according to Basil the Great and according to Palamas—is unreachable and unknowable, it is "in light unapproachable." But "*the very same God*" (Palamas' expression) *creates,* that is, offers *another,* and for that reason is revealed "outward" [*vo vne*]. It is this that is "Energy," "Glory," "Sophia"—a non-hypostatic revelation of "*the same*" God. Not "essence," not "personhood," not "hypostasis." If you like, yes,—Divine accidentia, but *accidentia* of "the very same" God or God "*Himself.*" And it is precisely to this that Palamas' thought leads—the accent is on the fullness and full meaning *tis Theotitos.* If you like, Sophia is Deus revelatus, that is, Grace. Grace—this is God to the world, *pros ton kosmon* (and not *pros ton Theon,* as in John 1:1 about the Logos). Sophia is eternal, inasmuch as it is thought—the will of the Eternal God, but it is willed—a thought about *Time.* There is much on this theme in Blessed Augustine. Sophia—is not only thought, "idea," *kosmos noitos,* but is will, power. . . . And in God there is not, God does not have non-eternal powers and wills, but there is will about time. Sophia never is world. The world is *other,* both in relation to grace and in relation to the "original image." Therefore "pre-eternity" and "pre-temporality" of will—thoughts about time does [sic] not convert time into eternity. "Ideal creation," "pre-eternal council," *toto genere* is different from real creative *fiat.* Sophia is not the "soul of the world." This negative statement distinguishes the Church teaching about Sophia from the Gnostic and Boehmenist teachings about her. Sophia *is not* a created subject, it is not a substance or substrata of created coming-into-being [*stanovleniia*]. This is *gratia* and not *natura.* And natura = creatura. Sophia—is not creatura. Along with this, it is *not hypostasis,* but *thrice-radiant glory.*

This letter is most representative for the identification of some of the key characteristics of Florovsky's theological approach: the overall rejection of Soloviev's legacy in Russian religious philosophy; the firm foundation of his theology in patristics, starting with the theological contribution of St. Athanasius the Great; the clear distinction between Divine nature and will as well as the location of the solution of the sophiogical problematics in the Palamite distinction between Divine essence and energies; last but not least, the relevance of the doctrine of creation for Christian theology in general. Florovsky developed further these ideas in a number of future works.[4]

Florovsky's Understandning of the Doctrine of Creation

Florovsky summarizes the Christian teaching on creation *ex nihilo* in his "Creation and Creaturehood" and "The Idea of Creation in Christian Philosophy." For him the doctrine of creation *ex nihilo* was a striking Christian innovation in philosophy and still a stumbling-block for philosophers who, up to the present day, are still thinking in Greek categories. At the same time for Florovsky, in the same way as for Bulgakov, an adequate idea of Creation is the distinctive test of the integrity of Christian mind and faith.

Some of the first messages that could be found in "Creation and Creaturehood" are that there is no necessity whatsoever in the creation of the world; creation became possible as a result of the Divine will; there is a fundamental difference between created and uncreated:

> The world exists. But it began to exist. And that means; the world could have not existed. There is no necessity whatsoever for the existence of the world. Creaturely existence is not self-sufficient and is not independent. In the created world itself there is no foundation, no basis for genesis and being. . . . By its very existence creation points beyond its own limits. The cause and foundation of the world is outside the world. The world's being is possible only through the supra-mundane will of the merciful and Almighty God, *"Who calls the things that be not, to be"*(Rom. 4:17). But, unexpectedly it is precisely in its creaturehood and createdness that the stability and substantiality of the world is rooted. Because the origin from out of nothing

---

4. Florovsky, "Creation and Creaturehood," 43–78; "The Concept of Creation in Saint Athanasius," 36–57; "St. Athanasius' Concept of Creation," 39–62; "The Idea of Creation in Christian Philosophy," 53–77; "St. Gregory Palamas and the tradition of the Fathers," 165–76.

determines the otherness, the "non-consubstantiality" of the
world and of God. It is insufficient and inexact to say that things
are created and placed *outside of God*. The *"outside"* itself is
posited only in creation, and creation "from out of nothing" [*ex
nihilo*] is precisely such a positing of the "outside," the positing
of an "other" side by side with God.[5]

The Difference between Divine Nature
and Human Nature

The striking difference between Florovsky's and Bulgakov's theological positions can be easily identified: for Florovsky the world could not have existed
and there is no necessity whatsoever in God for the existence of the world
since the world's being became possible through the Divine will. In addition, there is an infinite distance between God and creation which is due to
the differences in nature, i.e., there is no relationship whatsoever between
the Divine nature and created nature, except the creative act of the Holy
Trinity which is related not to the Divine nature but to the Divine will:

> In creation something *absolutely new*, an extra-divine *reality* is
> posited and built up. It is precisely in this that the supremely
> great and incomprehensible miracle of creation consists—that
> an "other" springs up, that heterogeneous drops of creation exist
> side by side with "the illimitable and infinite Ocean of being," as
> St. Gregory of Nazianzus says of God. There is an infinite dis-
> tance between God and creation, and this is a *distance of natures*.
> All is distant from God, and is *remote* from Him not by place but
> *by nature*—οὐ τόπῳ ἀλλὰ φύσει—as St. John Damascene ex-
> plains. And this distance is never removed, but is only, as it were,
> overlapped by immeasurable Divine love. As St. Augustine said,
> in creation "there is nothing related to the Trinity, except the
> fact that the Trinity has created it"—*nihilique in ea esse quod ad
> Trinitatem pertineat, nisi quod Trinitas condidit ...*.[6]

> Will and volition precede creating. Creating is *an act of will*
> [*ek vulimatos, εκ βουληματος*], and therefore is sharply distin-
> guished from the Divine generation, which is an *act of nature*
> [γεννᾷ κατὰ φύσιν]. A similar interpretation was given by St.
> Cyril of Alexandria. The generation is out of the substance, κατὰ

5. Florovsky, "Creation and Creaturehood," 45.
6. Ibid., 46.

φύσιν. Creating is an act, and is not done out of the creator's own substance; and therefore a creation is heterogeneous to its creator.[7]

A key of difference with respect to Bulgakov can be found in the statement that "in creation something *absolutely new*" and "an extra-divine *reality* is posited and built up."

> Any transubstantiation of creaturely nature into the Divine is as impossible as the changing of God into creation, and any "coalescence" and "fusion" of natures is excluded. In the one and only hypostasis and person of Christ—the God-Man—in spite of the completeness of the mutual interpenetration of the two natures, the two natures remain with their unchanged, immutable difference; "without the distinction of natures being taken away by such union, but rather the specific property of each nature being preserved." . . . The vague "out of two natures" the Fathers of Chalcedon replaced by the strong and clear "*in* two natures," and by the confession of the double and bilateral consubstantiality of the God-Man they established an unshakeable and indisputable criterion and rule of faith. The real existence of a created human nature, that is, of an other and second nature outside of God and side by side with Him, is an indispensable prerequisite for the accomplishment of the Incarnation without any change in or transmutation of the Divine nature.[8]

In all quotations above there are no references to Bulgakov or to sophiology. However, they appear to be almost antithetically developed and articulated against specific Bulgakovian positions. For example, the claim that the independent and autonomous existence of the created human nature is an "indispensable prerequisite for the accomplishment of the Incarnation" would not fit Bulgakov's overall theological vision. The reference to the Incarnation indicates Florovsky's ultimate soteriological concerns as well as the Christological grounds of the Divine-human communion and human Salvation in general. If it was not God Himself, the second person of the Trinity, who became incarnate for us by uniting our human nature to His Divine nature, the Salvation of man would have been impossible. This is why the fundamental difference between the Divine and human natures is critically important in Christian theology and it is exactly this difference that makes the Divine plan of creation and salvation so great and beautiful. By preserving his Divine nature intact and unmixed with the creaturely one,

7. Ibid., 48.
8. Ibid., 47.

God opens and secures the way to Himself by providing the meaning, the direction, and the ultimate goal of human existence and perfection. Man, however, is not programmed *a priori*, by force, to reach Divine communion and needs to embrace on his own the road to perfection by following Christ and His commandments in freedom and love.

Florovsky's focus on Christology shows a key difference in the two points of departure. For Bulgakov, as it was already shown, all theological articulation of the relationship between God and man, including creation, starts from within a Trinitarian perspective and this perspective for Bulgakov is necessarily sophiological, i.e., it is positioned within the one essence of the Trinity itself in its two aspects as Divine and creaturely Sophia. For Florovsky the only proper approach to Trinitarian theology is Christological, since it is only in Christ that the Trinitarian worship is revealed[9] and it is only from history and from historical experience that we could understand the creaturehood of creation and the eternity of the Divine thought-will about it. For him Bulgakov's sophiological approach leads to a kind of automatically arranged deification of man and makes his communion with God too naturalistic and human-centered by cutting it away from the reach and the operation of the Divine Grace.[10]

Divine Ideas or Prototypes

In a way similar to Bulgakov, Florovsky offers a detailed discussion of the Divine prototypes or ideas focusing on the writings of St. John Damascene, Pseudo-Dionysius, and St. Maximus the Confessor—the same Church Fathers that were discussed by Bulgakov. According to St. John of Damascus, God contemplated everything in His mind before the beginning and each thing receives its being at a determinate time according to His timeless and decisive thought, image, and pattern. This "counsel" of God is eternal and unchanging, pre-temporal, and without beginning, since everything Divine is immutable. It is the *image of God* turned towards the creation. According to St. Maximus the Confessor the eternal counsel is God's design and decision concerning the world and must be rigorously distinguished from the world itself.

> The Divine idea of creation is not creation itself; it is not the substance of creation; it is not the bearer of the cosmic-process; and the "transition" from "design" [$\dot{\epsilon}\nu\nu\acute{o}\eta\mu\alpha$] to "deed" [$\ddot{\epsilon}\rho\gamma o\nu$] is

---

9. Пентковски, "Письма Г. Флоровского С. Булгакову и С. Тышкевичу," 205.
10. Ibid.

not a process within the Divine idea, but the appearance, formation, and the realization of another substratum, of a multiplicity of created subjects. The Divine idea remains unchangeable
and unchanged, it is not involved in the process of formation. It
remains always outside the created world, transcending it. The
world is created *according to the idea*, in accordance with the
pattern—it is the realization of the pattern—but this pattern is
not the subject of becoming.[11]

Here Florovsky turns to St. Augustine for whom "Things before their
becoming are as though non-existent, they both were and were not before
they originated; they were in God's knowledge: but were not in their own
nature."[12] In creation there is a new reality which is projected from out of
nothing to become the bearer of the Divine idea and realize it in its own
becoming.

In this context the pantheistic tendency of Platonic ideology
and of the Stoic theory of "seminal reasons" [σπερματικοὶ λόγοι]
is altogether overcome and avoided. For Platonism the identification of the "essence" of each thing with its Divine idea is
characteristic, the endowment of substances with absolute and
eternal (beginningless) properties and predicates, as well as the
introduction of the "idea" into real things. On the contrary, the
created nucleus of things must be rigorously distinguished from
the *Divine idea* about things.[13]

The last paragraphs use the full power of the patristic theological arse-
nal to directly reject Bulgakov's positioning of the co-eternity of the created
world in the Divine ideas and prototypes. The Divine pattern of a thing
before its creation is not its substance or hypostasis, but, rather, its truth,
and the truth of a thing and its substance are not identical. It is therefore
out of question to talk about any possible aspects of co-eternity between the
Divine ideas about things before creation and the created things themselves
after creation:

The idea of the world, God's design and will concerning the
world, is obviously *eternal*, but in some sense *not co-eternal*, and
not conjointly everlasting with Him, because "distinct and separated," as it were, from His "essence" by His *volition*. One should
say rather that the Divine idea of the world is eternal by *another
kind* of eternity than the Divine essence. Although paradoxical,

11. Ibid., 61
12. Ibid.
13. Ibid., 62

this distinction of types and kinds of eternity is necessary for the expression of the incontestable distinction between the *essence* (*nature*) of God and the *will* of God. This distinction would not introduce any kind of separation or split into the Divine Being, but by analogy expresses the distinction between *will* and *nature*, the fundamental distinction made so strikingly explicit by the Fathers of the fourth century. The idea of the world has its basis *not in the essence, but in the will of God*. God does not so much have as "think up" the idea of creation. And He "thinks it up" in perfect freedom; and it is only by virtue of this wholly free "thinking up" and good pleasure of His that He as it were "becomes" Creator, even though from everlasting. But nevertheless He could also not have created.[14]

Divine and Human Freedom vs. Necessity

In contrast to Bulgakov, who emphasized the relationship between necessity and freedom in God's creative act, Florovsky focused on creaturely freedom as a key for understanding the idea of creation:

> The reality and substantiality of created nature is manifested first of all in *creaturely freedom*. Freedom is not exhausted by the possibility of choice, but presupposes it and starts with it. And creaturely freedom is disclosed first of all in the equal possibility of two ways: to God and away from God. . . . As St. Gregory the Theologian says, "God legislates human self-determination." "He honored man with freedom that good might belong no less to him who chose it than to Him Who planted its seed." Creation must ascend to and unite with God by its own efforts and achievements.[15]

For Florovsky it is critically important to emphasize the mutual freedom in the relationship between God and man.

> The reality and substantiality of created nature is manifested first of all in *creaturely freedom*. Freedom is not exhausted by the possibility of choice, but presupposes it and starts with it. And creaturely freedom is disclosed first of all in the equal possibility of two ways: to God and away from God. This duality of ways is not a mere formal or logical possibility, but a

14. Ibid., 56.
15. Ibid., 49.

real possibility, dependent on the effectual presence of powers and capacities not only for a choice between, but also for the following of, the two ways. Freedom consists not only in the possibility, but also in the *necessity* of autonomous choice, the resolution and resoluteness of choice. Without this autonomy, nothing happens in creation.[16]

By stepping into being creation is given the freedom of will to the extent of being able to reject the Creator Himself. And the beauty of creation consists in the fact that human freedom cannot be left unused. The creaturehood of humanity makes it impossible for man to avoid or abandon that choice:

> In her primordial and ultimate vocation, creation is destined for union with God, for communion and participation in His life. But this is not a binding necessity of creaturely nature. Of course, outside of God there is no life for creation. But as Augustine happily phrased it, *being and life do not coincide* in creation. And therefore *existence in death* is possible. . . . The possibility of metaphysical suicide is open. . . . But the power of self-annihilation is not given. Creation is indestructible—and not only that creation which is rooted in God as in the source of true being and eternal life, but also that creation which has set herself against God.[17]

All this is because the world was created so that "it might have being." In creation God and man fell into a personal relationship and the personal freedom of both, God and man, is a key for the proper understanding this relationship. It could be interpreted as a kind of realistic Christian "anthropological maximalism"—the road to salvation and deification is fully open to everyone, but it has to be willed and followed through spiritual struggle cooperation with God.

Florovsky addresses directly the question about the existence of any necessity in God's act of creation of the world and somewhat rhetorically points out that it is not so easy to demonstrate the absence of any internal necessity in this revelation of God *ad extra*: "Is the attribute of Creator and Sustainer to be considered as belonging to the essential and formative properties of the Divine Being?" He seems to be rhetorically introducing the reader into the problematic of the theories on the Divine necessity of creation in order to sharply and unconditionally express his own firm opinion which is based again on the distinction between Divine nature and will:

16. Ibid.
17. Ibid.

"And it must be said at once that any such admission means introducing the world into the ultra-Trinitarian life of the Godhead as a co-determinant principle. And we must firmly and uncompromisingly reject any such notion."[18] This firm rejection is very representative in demonstrating the differences between Bulgakov's and Florovsky's approaches. By focusing on the distinction between Divine nature and will Florovsky augments his argumentation by introducing the discussion of the distinction between the essence and energies:

> One has to admit distinctions within the very co-eternity and immutability of the Divine Being. In the wholly simple Divine life there is an absolute rational or logical order [τάξις] of Hypostases, which is irreversible and inexchangeable for the simple reason that there is a "first principle" or "source" of Godhead, and that there is the enumeration of *First, Second,* and *Third* Persons. And likewise it is possible to say that the Trinitarian structure is antecedent to the will and thought of God, because the Divine will is the common and undivided will of the All-Holy Trinity, as it is also antecedent to all the Divine acts and "energies."[19]

Divine Essence vs. Energies

Florovsky opens the discussion of the distinction between Divine essence and energies by pointing out that the absolute creatureliness and non-self-sufficiency of the world leads to the distinguishing of two kinds of predicates and acts in God. In this he follows again the legacy of the Church Fathers, where a primary distinction between "theology" and "economy" has already been made. "The Fathers and Doctors of the Church endeavored to distinguish clearly and sharply those definitions and names which referred to God on the 'theological' plane and those used on the 'economical.' Behind this stands the distinction between 'nature' and 'will.' And bound up with it is the distinction in God between 'essence' and 'that which surrounds the essence,' 'that which is related to the nature.'"[20] According to St. John of Damascus, the Divine essence is unattainable and only the powers and operations of God are accessible to knowledge. This distinction is connected to God's relation to the world. For Florovsky the theological response

18. Ibid., 56.

19. Ibid., 58.

20. Ibid., 63.

to sophiology is rooted in Trinitarian theology, since it is the Trinitarian theology of the Fathers of the fourth century that has already provided a basis for an adequate formulation of God's relation to the world: the whole entire and undivided operation (ἐνέργειαι) of the consubstantial Trinity is revealed in God's acts and deeds. But the essence (οὐσία) of the undivided Trinity remains beyond the reach of knowledge and understanding. St. Basil the Great affirms that "we know our God by His energies, but we do not presume that it is possible to approach the essence itself. Because although His energies descend to us, His essence remains inaccessible."[21] The Divine energies are real, essential, life-giving manifestations of the Divine life. They are real images of God's relation to creation, connected with the image of creation in God's eternal knowledge and counsel. They are that aspect of God which is turned towards creation.

Florovsky points out that the doctrine of the energies of God received its final formulation in the Byzantine theology of the fourteenth century, and above all in St. Gregory Palamas, for whom there is a real distinction, but no separation, between the *essence* or *entity* of God and His *energies*. The creatures have access to and communicate with the Divine energies only, but this participation is critical for them to enter into a genuine and perfect communion and union with God—the ultimate goal of their creation and existence, their deification. Any refusal to make a real distinction between the Divine essence and energy removes the boundary between generation and creation and they both appear then to be acts of essence.

> And as St. Mark of Ephesus explained, "Being and energy, completely and wholly coincide in equivalent necessity. Distinction between essence and will [θέλησις] is abolished; then God only begets and does not create, and does not exercise His will. Then the difference between foreknowledge and actual making becomes indefinite, and creation seems to be coeternally created." None of these energies is hypostatic, nor hypostasis in itself, and their incalculable multiplicity introduces no composition into the Divine Being. The totality of the Divine "energies" constitutes His pre-temporal will, His design—His good pleasure—concerning the "other," His eternal counsel. This is God Himself, not His essence, but *His will*. The distinction between "essence" and "energies"—or, it could be said, between "nature" and "grace" [φύσις and χάρις]—corresponds to the mysterious distinction in God between "necessity" and "freedom," understood in a proper sense.[22]

21. Ibid., 64.
22. Ibid., 68.

The distinction between Divine essence and energies is directly related to the distinction between Divine nature and will and appears as critically important for the articulation of the Orthodox teaching on creation. In his final discussion Fr. George unfolds the implications of the distinction between essence and energies within a context that addresses many of the issues raised by Bulgakov. The distinction enables the use of a "necessity language" with respect to the Divine essence and "with permissible boldness" one may say that God cannot but be the Trinity of persons. However, the Triad of Hypostases is above the Divine will and its necessity is a law of Divine nature which is expressed in the consubstantiality, the indivisibility and the mutual co-inherence of the three Persons. Florovsky refers to St. Maximus the Confessor in pointing out that it would be inappropriate to introduce the notion of will into the internal life of the Godhead for the sake of defining the relations between the Hypostases, because the Persons of the All-Holy Trinity exist together above any kind of relation, will, or action, and the ground of Trinitarian being is not in the economy or revelation of God *ad extra*.

At the same time creation and the act of creation presuppose the Trinity and creation cannot be considered apart from the Trinity. The natural fullness of the Divine essence is contained within the Trinity including the free actualization of the Divine plan for creation as a result of a creative act through the operation of the common to the Trinity Divine will. "The distinction between the names of 'God in Himself,' in His eternal being, and those names which describe God in revelation, 'economy,' action, is not only a subjective distinction of our analytical thinking; it has an objective and ontological meaning, and expresses the absolute freedom of Divine creativity and operation."[23]

The Divine freedom includes the economy of salvation in which from everlasting times the Son of God is destined to the Incarnation and the Cross. However, the predicates referring to the economy of salvation do not coincide with the predicates referring to the Hypostatic Being of the Second Person of the Trinity since revelation is an act of love and freedom and does not affect the Divine nature. It is through a similar creative act that the world was created out of nothing in freedom and love. It should, however, advance in accordance with its own creaturely freedom, the standard of the Divine economy and the standard of its pre-temporal image in God. God sees and wills each and every being in the completeness of its destiny including both its future and sin beholding all and manifesting himself to each one of them in a different way by means of an inseparable distribution of His grace or

---

23. Ibid., 71.

energy. His grace and energy is beneficently imparted to thousands upon myriads of thousands of hypostases and

> each hypostasis, in its own being and existence, is sealed by a particular ray of the good pleasure of God's love and will. And in this sense, all things are in God in "image" [ἐν ἰδέᾳ καὶ παραδείγματι] *but not by nature*, the created "all" being infinitely remote from Uncreated Nature. This remoteness is bridged by Divine love, its impenetrability done away by the Incarnation of the Divine Word. Yet this remoteness remains. *The image of creation* in God transcends created nature and does not coincide with "the image of God" in creation.[24]

In creation the free participation in and union with God is set as an invitation and challenging goal. This is a challenge that transcends created nature, but it is only by responding to it that created nature reaches its completeness in a process of created becoming which is real in its freedom, and free in its reality. It is by this becoming that what is out of nothing reaches its authentic fulfillment—deification:

> With the Incarnation of the Word the first fruit of human nature is unalterably grafted into the Divine Life, and hence to all creatures the way to communion with this Life is open, the way of *adoption* by God. In the phrase of St. Athanasius, the Word "became man in order to *deify* [θεοποιήσῃ] us in Himself," in order that "the sons of men might become the sons of God." But this "divinization" is acquired because Christ, the Incarnate Word, has made us "receptive to the Spirit," that He has prepared for us both the ascension and the resurrection as well as the indwelling and appropriation of the Holy Spirit. Through the "flesh-bearing God" we have become "Spirit-bearing men"; we have become sons "by grace," "sons of God in the likeness of the Son of God." And thus is recovered what had been lost since the original sin, when "the transgression of the commandment turned man into what he was by nature," over which he had been elevated in his very first adoption or birth from God, coinciding with his initial creation.[25]

We can see here that Florovsky's Trinitarian approach to the distinction between Divine essence and energies is ultimately rooted in Christology and Pneumatology.

---

24. Ibid., 73.
25. Ibid., 75.

The main goal of the initial chapters was to show that the teaching on the distinction between the Divine essence energies in the twentieth century emerged in the context of the Name-worshiper controversy associated with theological articulation of the spiritual on Mount Athos as well as a natural patristic response to sophiology. The key difference in the theological approaches of Fr. George Florovsky and Fr. Sergius Bulgakov could be found to be in the different perception or attitude to the legacy of patristic theology. For Florovsly, the legacy of the Church Fathers was the main source of theological reflection. For Bulgakov there was a need for a sophiological renewal of patristic theology and he tried to do that by imposing on it his philosophical presuppositions. The difference between the two theologians can be also expressed in terms of two different understandings of a Christian anthropological maximalism. Bulgakov could be characterized by a radical maximalist with regard to the scope of human deification, which seems to abolish the ontological difference between God and deified man. By insisting on the divine-like character of human nature he goes as far as to say that "if man were capable of freeing himself from his natural essence by the power of spiritual life, he would simply be God, and his life would be *fused* with Divine life."[26] According to Nicholas Sakharov "this is indeed a break with the Eastern patristic tradition."[27] In the case of Florovsky, one could talk about an anthropological maximalism rooted in the dynamic realism of Divine-human communion which is based on his commitment to remain faithful to the patristic tradition and its foundation in ascetic experience[28] with an explicit focus on safeguarding the ontological difference and the mutual freedom in the relationship between God and man. For him the fundamental difference between created and uncreated natures does not abolish the possibility for human deification, which is based on the cooperation of the Divine and human energies.[29] The sources of such anthropological maximalism could be found in the theology of St. Gregory Palamas: "man by grace possesses the infinite attributes of God— man becomes uncreated, omnipotent."[30] Ultimately, the difference between

26. Sakharov, *I Love Therefore I Am*, 155, referring to: Bulgakov, *The Lamb of God*, 94.

27. Ibid.

28. The comparison of the Christian anthropological maximalisms of Fr. G. Florovsky and Fr. S. Bulgakov follows the logic of a similar comparison between Fr. S. Bulgakov and Archimandrite Sophrony Sakharov that was done by Nicolas Sakharov in the reference above.

29. Dragas, "Divine and Human Synergy," 35–53

30. Meyendorff, *A Study of Gregory Palamas*, 176–77, referenced by Sakharov, *I Love Therefore I am*, 157.

the two theologians can be also expressed in terms of their different ways of interpreting the theology of St. Gregory Palamas. It is in fact the chasm between these two different interpretations that could explain the theological struggle associated with the sophiological controversy and that should be taken into account in its contemporary re-evaluations.

The present study partially addresses the need for a contemporary re-evaluation of the theology of Fr. S. Bulgakov. The theology of Fr. Bulgakov is becoming increasingly popular amongst both Orthodox and non-Orthodox theologians and a fresh evaluation of his works seems to be very much needed. In addition, there seems to be a tendency in recent Orthodox scholarly works to revive—sometimes against the achievements of Florovsky's neo-patristic theology—the thought of Soloviev and Bulgakov "as paradigms for Orthodox theology and a model of theological engagement with secular culture."[31] According to Fr. Matthew Baker, these tendencies raise important questions, and may offer potential new insights.

> Yet they also carry potential hazards, not only for the integrity of Orthodox theology itself, but ecumenically—not least because they tend to represent more the liberal cultural values of the Western-trained academics to whose interest they are generally confined than the faith and piety of the Orthodox churches as a whole. Neither the political orientations of contemporary contextual theologies nor the idealist speculations of sophiology could be said to underscore clearly the ancient, perennial fundaments of the apostolic faith which are able to unite Christians across diverse cultures and epochs.[32]

Fr. Matthew referred to the veteran ecumenist and Orthodox Bishop Emilianos Timiadis who indicated the presence of aberrant gnostic tendencies in Russian sophiology by pointing out that the "Orthodox teaching would have been misjudged by Western churches if such uncontrolled views had prevailed"[33] The key point here is that the theological contributions of Fr. S. Bulgakov should not be considered apart from the specific context of his proper theological motivations—the integration of his sophiology with the theology of St. Gregory Palamas. Bulgakov has never rejected the teaching on the distinction between the Divine essence and energies. He rather used

---

31. Baker, "Neopatristic Synthesis and Ecumenism," 235–60. Fr. Matthew refers to Valliere, *Modern Russian Theology*. According to him, although not Orthodox himself, P. Valliere has recently exercised a strong influence on Orthodox academics in the English speaking world with his championing of what he calls "liberal Orthodoxy."

32. Ibid.

33. Timiadis, "Georges Florovsky 1893–1979," 94–95.

it as a heological starting point for his philosophically inspired theological elaborations. A proof of this can be found in the multiple references to St. Gregory Palamas made by Bulgakov in his great trilogy on Divine-humanity which includes the three major works of Fr. Sergius Bulgakov that were recently published in English in the translation of Boris Jakim: *The Bride of the Lamb* (2002), *The Comforter* (2004), and *The Lamb of God* (2008). At the same time, although very important, the link between Bulgakov's sophiology and the teaching of St. Gregory Palamas should not be oversimplified. It would be completely wrong for example trying to see Fr. Sergius as a Palamist, or St. Gregory Palamas as a sophiologist (as Bulgakov himself was trying to do). The teaching of St. Gregory provides a very clear answer to sophiology: "the distinction between the divine essence and energies implies that the world, which has been created by God's energies, can never become identical with God's essence."[34] The appreciation of this link however provides a hermeneutical key to understanding Bulgakov's philosophico-theological system by showing that, instead of imposing his sophiological prism as a key to understanding the entire body of Orthodox theology, everyone (Orthodox or non-Orthodox alike) interested in Bulgakov's later thought should rather have a more integrative look at his works in parallel with a more comprehensive engagement with the theology of St. Gregory Palamas. What one would certainly find out is that some of his key theological inspirations emerged somehow independently of his sophiological constructions. According to Joost van Rossum, this was, "in fact, the tragedy of Fr. Sergius—who himself was aware of the 'tragedy of philosophy' (the title of one of his earliest books)—that he was more a philosopher than a theologian, and that his 'sophiology' as a system contradicts his theological intuitions."[35] It could turn out then, as Fr. George Florovsky and Vladimir Lossky were trying to demonstrate, that Bulgakov's sophiology appears as no more than an unnecessary attempt for a conceptual upgrade of the theological integrity of Byzantine theology. This unsuccessful attempt however should not diminish the appreciation of Bulgakov's dialogical role in formulating some of the key questions and generate the initial momentum for the authentic articulation of their answers in twentieth century Orthodox theology—a role that should be continuously highlighted as a tribute to his life and works. In addition, the proper appreciation of Bulgakov's life and works offers the opportunity to emphasize the role of Fr. G. Florovsky for contributing to the proper rediscovery of the theology of St. Gregory Palamas in the twentieth century.

---

34. Van Rossum, "Deification in Palamas and Aquinas," 375.
35. Van Rossum, "Паламизм и софиология," 66.

Chapter 4

Fr. John Meyendorff on Divine *Sophia* and *Energeia* in Fourteenth- and Twentieth-century Orthodox Theology

Fr. John Meyendorff is one of the Orthodox theologians who have significantly contributed to the articulation of the theology of the Divine energies in the twentieth century. However, his theological legacy includes several other contributions, one of which consists in the insightful interpretation of the sophiological controversy.[1] His ability to discern the key theological issues emerging within the context of specific historical situations allowed him to see the sophiological controversy as one of the two occasions in the history of Orthodox theology when the doctrine of creation was vigorously debated[2]—the first one was in connection with Origen; the second one was in connection with Russian sophiology where, as in the case of Origen's thought, the doctrine of creation stood at the center of both, its main theological concerns and the criticisms against it. It should be pointed out that these two contributions should not be considered independently of each other and some scholars have rightly considered Fr. John's work on St. Gregory Palamas as a direct continuation of the work of his two closest teachers—Fr. G. Florovsky and V. Lossky—in refuting the sophiological inspirations of Fr. S. Bulgakov.[3]

It is quite significant that in his last lectures in Minsk Fr. John specifically pointed out that he should be considered "absolutely and almost

1. Meyendorff, "Wisdom—Sophia," 391–401; *Byzantine Theology*, 21; "Creation in the History of Orthodox Theology," 27–37; "L'iconographie de la Sagesse Divine dans la tradition Byzantine," 259–77; Мейендорф, "Тема 'Премудрости'," 244–52.

2. Meyendorff, "Creation in the history of Orthodox theology," 27.

3. See the Afterward of: Мейендорф, *Жизнь и труды святителя Григория Паламы*, 327–72.

unconditionally" a disciple of Fr. G. Florovsky.[4] One of the ways to understand this statement is by referring to the announcement of a recent Colloquium dedicated to the life and works of Fr. John Meyendorff, which points
out that "[t]he theological works of Fr. John Meyendorff are essentially
shaped by an historical approach that left its profound mark on Orthodox
theology in the twentieth century. In this regard, he demonstrated himself
to be a student *par excellence* of Fr. Florovsky."[5] It appears however that
there is another way to interpret the above statement by referring to the
contribution of Fr. John Meyendorff to the rediscovery of the teaching of
St. Gregory Palamas in the second half of the twentieth century. Fr. John
Meyendorff translated the some of the key works and promoted the theology of St. Gregory Palamas and, in this regard, became a true disciple
of Fr. G. Florovsky. Indeed, it was Florovsky who was the first to engage
into a more systematic theological response to sophiology by referring to
the theology of St. Gregory Palamas.[6] A brief passage from a letter from
Fr. S. Bulgakov to Florovsky is particularly interesting since it shows that
the theology of St. Gregory Palamas was part of the discussions between
Bulgakov and Florovsky as early as 1926: "And I am very glad," says Fr.
Sergius, "that the direction of your thought leads you to that central point
which I, although in a preliminary way, was referring to—the problematic
of the energies and, in particular, St. Gregory Palamas."[7] The line of thought
linking the rediscovery of the Palamite teaching on the Divine essence and
energies in the twentieth century with the sophiological circle including Fr.

4. Мейендорф, "Православное свидетельство в современном мире," 53: "Я
являюсь абсолютно и почти безоговорочно учеником отца Георгия Флоровского
и, очень уважая его, считаю, что он был прав. Это не значит, что он был прав
в деталях, но его основная цель и точка зрения, по-моему, правильная, и его
критика всех софиологов и Бердяева совершенно справедлива."

5. The text is from the conference web page of the Colloque international sur
"L'héritage du Père Jean Meyendorff, érudit et homme d'Eglise (1926–1992) à l'Institut
Saint-Serge à Paris, 9–11 février 2012.

6. Флоровский, "Тварь и тварьность," 176–212; Florovsky, "Creation and Creaturehood," 43–78; Florovsky, Letter to Bulgakov on July 4 (July 22, New Style), 1926 in:
Пентковский, "Письма Г. Флоровского С. Булгакову и С. Тышкевичу," 205, English
translation: http://ishmaelite.blogspot.com/2009/05/palamas-florovsky-bulgakov-and.
html.

7. Letter from Bulgakov to Florovsky on 27 April 1926 (10 May 1926), Princeton
University Library, Rare books and special collections: Georges Florovsky Papers, p.
1: "И меня радует, что направление Вашей мысли ведет Вас именно к той самой
центральной точке, которую я Вам сразу, хотя тогда еще преждевременно,
указывал, к проблематике 'энергий', и в частности, у св. Григория Паламы." Fr. S.
Bulgakov has a section on St. Gregory Palamas in: *Булгаков*, Свет невечерний.

Pavel Florensky and Fr. S. Bulgakov is of particular relevance.[8] It leads to the realization that the rediscovery was driven by the theological controversies in Russia (1912–13) associated with the interpretation of the spiritual practices of the Name-worshipers (Imiaslavtzi) on Mount Athos who were claiming that they were followers of St. Gregory Palamas. Both Florensky and Bulgakov engaged into a philosophical and theological defence of the Name-worshipers by suggesting a sophiological interpretation of the theology of St. Gregory Palamas.[9] As it was already pointed out, the link to the theology of St. Gregory Palamas appears to have been initiated and inspired by Florensky, but it was Bulgakov who provided the most systematic defense of the Name-worshipers by linking the Palamite teaching on the distinction between Divine essence and energies to Soloviev's metaphysics of All-Unity.[10] In fact, it was exactly Bulgakov's specific (non-patristic) interpretation that appears to have forced Fr. George Florovsky to engage in reaffirming the place of St. Gregory Palamas "within mainline patristic tradition, in this sense refuting Bulgakov's claim that St. Gregory can be seen as one of the originators of Sophiology."[11] Fr. S. Bulgakov interpreted the adoption of Palamism during the Council of 1351 as Church's first serious commitment to a sophiological agenda but also found it in need of further sophiologocial development. Fr. G. Florovsky offered an alternative interpretation by referring to some of the key resources of patristic theology. Florovsky's programmatic paper "Creature and Creaturehood,"[12] which he himself considered as one of his finest theological works,[13] makes a direct reference to the theol-

8. Evtuhov, *The Cross and the Sickle*; Horujy, "The idea of energy in the Moscow school of Christian neo-Platonism," 1; Van Rossum, "Паламизм и софиология," 66.

9. For more details on Name-worshiper controversy see Evtuhov, *The Cross and the Sickle*; van Rossum, "Паламизм и софиология"; Horuzhy, *"Neo-Patristic Synthesis and Russian Philosophy"*; Horujy, "The Idea of Energy in the Moscow School of Christian Neo-Platonism"; Sergeev, *Sophiology in Russian Orthodoxy*; Alfeev, *Le Mystère sacré de l'Église*.

10. Evtuhov, *The Cross and the Sickle*, 210.

11. Klimoff, "Georges Florovsky and the Sophiological Controversy," 96.

12. Софроний (Сахаров), Переписка с протоиереем Георгием Флоровским, Письмо № 10.

13. Horuzhy, *"Neo-Patristic Synthesis and Russian Philosophy,"* 17. In his article Horuzhy refers to a statement by Florovsky in a talk he gave, or intended to give as a kind of theological will, in response to a honor that was being bestowed upon him: "It should be more than just a collection of Patristic sayings or statements. It must be a synthesis, a creative reassessment of those insights which were granted to the Holy Men of old. It must be Patristic, faithful to the spirit and vision of the Fathers, ad mentem Patrum. Yet, it must be also Neo-Patristic, since it is to be addressed to the new age, with its own problems and queries. It was in that mood that I have written, already thirty years ago, my two theological essays, on the Doctrine of Creation and on the Doctrine

ogy of St. Gregory Palamas and was first published as early as 1927.[14] In this paper the discussion of the teaching about the distinction between Divine essence and energies within the context of the doctrine of creation provides a first substantial elaboration on the theology of St. Gregory Palamas, an elaboration that will later become a reference point for Vladimir Lossky and Fr. John Meyendorff. The importance of Florovsky's paper "Creature and Creaturehood" could be illustrated by a reference to a letter that was sent to him by Archimandrite *Sophrony* (Saharov), written on Pascha, 1958. In this letter the Elder Sophrony points out that it was amazing for him to realize to what extent the majority of the positions expressed in Lossky's book *The Mystical Theology of the Eastern Church*[15] were articulated some fifteen years earlier by Florovsky in his paper "Creature and Creaturehood": "Of course nobody works alone and independently of the others: in terms of language, references etc., . . . but despite all of that the entire book of Lossky was so much prepared by you, that I found it really striking."[16]

The publication of *"Creature and Creaturehood"* was rightly perceived by some of his Russian compatriots in Paris as a direct opposition to Bulgakov's sophiology.[17] A careful reading of the paper together with the first section of *The Bride of the Lamb*[18] (The Creator and Creation) of Fr. S. Bulgakov reveals the antithetical nature of their key theological points. As Fr. John Meyendorff has pointed out, the confrontation between these two approaches materialized in different understandings of the doctrine of creation *ex nihilo* and "was probably the most interesting episode in the history of Orthodox theology in the twentieth century."[19]

---

of Redemption, which I am still regarding as my best achievements, and probably my only ones. Unfortunately, soon after that I was discarded. . . . I have written less than I ought to have written, or probably than I could have written." The entire statement can be found in: Blane, *Georges Florovsky*, 154.

14. Флоровский, "Тварь и тварность," 176–212; Florovsky, "Creation and Creaturehood," 43–78.

15. Lossky, *Essai sur la théologie mystique.*

16. Софроний (Сахаров), Переписка с протоиереем Георгием Флоровским, Письмо № 10.

17. See Florovsky's letter to N. A. Struve (Feb. 18, 1971): "А у меня статья о Софии (Флоренского) вызвала серьезные философские недоумения, как и последующая работа о платонизме (в юбилейном сборнике МДА). Но именно Флоренский направил мою мысль к проблеме Творения, и я пришел этим путем к радикальному противлению всякому 'софианству'. См. мою позднейшую статью 'Тварь и тварность' в 1-м выпуске 'Православной мысли'. В свое время, кажется, только о. Сергий и отчасти о. Василий Зеньковский сообразили, что это была противософианская статья, иные, напротив, нашли, что я сам 'софианец.'"

18. Bulgakov, *The Bride of the Lamb.*

19. Meyendorff, "Creation in the History of Orthodox Theology," 27–37.

It is not by accident that in his *Introduction à l'Etude de Grégoire Palamas* Fr. John Meyendorff discusses St. Gregory's understanding of Sophia—the Wisdom of God and points out the differences with its modern sophiological interpretations:

> In his polemics with Akindynos St. Gregory was forced to consider the Wisdom of God not only from the traditional Christological point of view which identifies the Divine Wisdom with the Logos, but also as an essential Divine attribute since it is all three hypostases who participate in the Divine creative act. However, he is very careful in not identifying the Divine Wisdom with the Divine essence as the Russian "sophiologists" did and, actually, accuses his opponents in this very mistake which leads to pantheism.[20]

Fr. John also points out that the problematic associated with the Divine Wisdom was of great interest to the Byzantines in the fourteenth century and that this interest found an expression in iconography. This is not the only place where Fr. John made an insightful relationship between the theological issues that emerged in the fourteenth and in the twentieth centuries by focusing on the relationship between the teaching on Divine essence and energies, and the understanding of Sophia, the Wisdom of God.[21] For example, in other works he pointed out that the meaning of Sophia, the Wisdom of God, has naturally emerged as an issue in the debate between St. Gregory Palamas and the philosopher Nicephorus Gregoras.[22] In this debate the followers of the Philosopher (Gregoras) have directly asked the Thessalonian (Palamas): "Tell us, is the Divine Wisdom different form His essence?"[23] In his reply St. Gregory refers to St. Maximus according to whom "God, that is the Father, the Son and the Holy Spirit, knows Himself from within His essence; but we know from the works—not the Divine essence but His creative power and Wisdom which is common to the Father, the Son and the Holy Spirit, through which, and in which, He created everything."[24] Fr. John has also referred to one of the most important works of the Patriarch Philotheos Kokkinos[25] where the same issue is addressed from a Palamite

20. Мейендорф, *Жизнь и труды Святителя Григория Паламы*, 301.

21. Meyendorff, "L'iconographie de la Sagesse Divine dans la tradition Byzantine," 259–77; Meyendorff, "Wisdom–Sophia: Contrasting Approaches to a Complex Theme," 391–401; Мейендорф, "Тема 'Премудрости,'" 244–52.

22. Ibid., See also: Фраксис, *Диспут свт. Григория Паламы с Григорой философом.*

23. Фраксис, *Диспут свт. Григория Паламы с Григорой философом*, 55.

24. Ibid., 57.

25. Philotheos, Patriarch of Constantinople, *On the Text of Proverbs*, 132.

theological point of view. In this work the Divine Wisdom is considered not only as a Divine Person but also as a divine manifestation or energy. The Patriarch speaks, on the one hand, of Wisdom as "a common, natural wisdom and energy of the One and consubstantial Trinity," but he also says that "The wise theologians also affirmed that the role and the image of Divine Wisdom belonged in particular to the Son who, in the last days, in His love for man assumed a flesh similar to ours; thus (the theologians) attributed the particular meaning of the term 'Wisdom' to His unique composite hypostasis."[26] The fourteenth-century controversy provided Patriarch Philotheos with an opportunity to make a fine distinction between the two ways of understanding Divine Wisdom—as an attribute or energy of the Trinity and as Divine Logos to the extent to which He was incarnated.[27] And it is exactly through the Incarnated Wisdom that the Wisdom-Energy acts within the community of the Church members. The fact that the Wisdom-Energy is common to the entire Trinity does not go against the belief that the Son alone is the Wisdom incarnated.[28]

One could complement the theological insights of Fr. John by a reference to the works of David Dissipat,[29] one of the closer followers of St. Gregory Palamas who was involved in the debates from the very beginning and whose works represent a significant interest for contemporary scholarship on the theological debates in the fourteenth century. In his treatise *David Disypatou Logos kata Barlaam kai Akindynou pros Nikolaon Kabasilan Dissipat* provides one of the most refined elaborations on how the Son of God could be called the Wisdom of God and how such name refers to the energies belonging to Him by nature.[30] The recent Russian

26. Meyendorff, "Wisdom—Sophia," 392.

27. Meyendorff, "L'iconographie de la Sagesse Divine dans la tradition Byzantine," 262.

28. Ibid.

29. Дисипат, Монах Давид. "Слово господина Давида Дисипата о богохульствах Варлаама и Акиндина," 220–35.

30. Ibid., Ch. 50, 223: "Каково же слово истины? Каким образом Сын называется силой, премудростью Отца и другими наименованиями энергий, и как этими словами [не отрицается, а], скорее, подтверждается [бытие] природных и общих энергий Троицы? . . . Сын называется такими именами не потому, что общая премудрость и сила у Троицы природно не созерцается, а потому что и [Сын] природно имеет всю [премудрость и силу], равно как и Отец, от Которого у Него, по причине равночестности природы, и бытие, и обладание всеми свойствами Божества."; Ch. 55, 231: "Единородный же, будучи Сыном от Отца, ипостасью от ипостаси, Богом совершенным от совершенного, воспринимает по природе все Отчее, [то есть] жизнь, силу, благость, премудрость – все то, что дает знание о совершенном Боге, [но вместе с тем, Он же,] как ты уже слышал, согласно принятому в Писании образному выражению, именуется Словом, Силой и

translation and detailed commentary of Dissipat's work provides a great opportunity for further more comprehensive research focusing on the reception of the Palamite theology in the fourteenth century. An additional source pointing to the existence of the Wisdom-Energy trend in Byzantine theology is the *Treatise about the light of Tabor* of Theophanus of Nicaea.[31] In his treatise, Theophanus also understands the Divine Wisdom as being common to all three Persons of the Trinity and as one of the names of the energies of the Holy Trinity.[32]

The theological insights of Fr. John Meyendorff provide an opportunity to identify a special kind of contextual antinomy between the theological debates in the fourteenth and in the twentieth century: i) in the fourteenths century it was the theological controversy on the distinction between essence and energies that led to the need of discussing the meaning of *Sophia*, the Wisdom of God; ii) in the twentieth century it was the theological controversy on the meaning of *Sophia*, the Wisdom of God, that led to the need of discussing of the Orthodox teaching on the distinction between Divine essence and energies.[33] The identification of this antinomy is quite relevant. It demonstrates the theological affinity between the concepts of *Sophia* and *Energeia* and shows, again and again, that there were deeper theological and historical reasons behind the rediscovery of the teaching of the Divine energies in the twentieth century.[34] Why is this point relevant within the context of contemporary Orthodox theology?

First, there seems to be an ongoing tendency to relativize the emergence of the teaching on the Divine energies by arguing that it was the result of: i) the need for self-identification of the Russian immigrant theologians in the first quarter of the twentieth century in Paris who needed to talk about themselves to the Western people, whom they studied with, worked with and lived with; ii) a reaction to an article written in 1931 by the Roman Catholic theologian Martin Jugie, who said that Orthodox theologians have abandoned Palamas for the last seven hundred years.[35]

Премудростью, по причине, как говорит [Григорий] бесстрастности рождения и сопряженности с Отцом."; See also the insightful analysis provided by: Бирюков, "Давид Дисипат, его учение и место в паламитских спорах," 7–61.

31. For more information on Theophanus of Nicea see Polemis, *Theophanes of Nicaea*; Беневич и Бирюков, *Антология восточно-христианской богословской мысли*, 572.

32. See commentary by D. Makarov and statements by Theophanus on p. 108 of: Фраксис, *Диспут свт. Григория Паламы с Григорой Философом*.

33. This second point was elaborated by Tanev, "ΕΝΕΡΓΕΙΑ vs. ΣΟΦΙΑ"

34. Ibid.

35. See the interview of Peter Korolev with Fr. John Behr, Dean of St. Vladimir's

One of the main points of the present chapter is to firmly reject such misinterpretation. A careful reading of the works of Fr. John Meyendorff would clearly support such a rejection. Fortunately, there is a growing body of research dedicated to Name-worshiper controversy that continues to provide valuable insights concerning the theological and the historical context of the rediscovery of the theology of Divine energies in the twentieth century. One should also point out the inconsistency of the so-called "self-identification theory" which is being currently promoted by some of the representatives of the newer generation of Orthodox theologians as an interpretation focusing on the contingent character of some of the key Orthodox theological insights in the twentieth century by considering them as emerging in a mere opposition to a forcefully created and illusionary non-Orthodox "West."[36] Interestingly enough, it seems that such theory could be used in a much better way to explain the theological attitude of its own creators than the attitude of Russian immigrant theologians in the first half of the twentieth century Paris.

Second, there seems to be an ongoing crisis in the interpretations of the teaching on the Divine essence and energies that could be roughly expressed as a kind of polarization in the arguments for or against its relevance

---

Seminary, NY, USA, April 7, 2007. Fr. John points out that: "In the twentieth century, Russian theologians, diasporas, emigrants coming to the West had to talk about themselves to the Western people, whom they studied with, worked with, and lived with. That meant being more conscious of oneself. . . . [I]t's only because of that circle of Russian emigrate theologians that Orthodoxy came to rediscover Saint Gregory Palamas. In nineteenth-century Russia, Saint Gregory Palamas was not taught. He was not part of the catechism, his works were not published, and there was no Greek printed edition of the text. In some ways, that rediscovery of Saint Gregory of Palamas was a response to an article written by Roman Catholic theologian Jugie, who said that Orthodox theologians have abandoned Palamas for the last seven hundred years: they haven't taught him, he wasn't part of the catechism, and he hasn't been part of theology. You keep his name for the second Sunday of the Lent, but nowhere do you find him in the teachings of the Church. In response to that, theologians in the West began to reexplore Palamas, and that brought about the rediscovery of Palamism. And I don't think that anybody would regard that negatively." See also a more recent comment in Russell, *Fellow Workers with God*, 14, who points out that the rediscovery of St. Gregory Palamas "was occasioned by the publication in 1931 of an article on St. Gregory by Martin Jugie in the authoritative *Dictionnaire de théologie catholoque*. Jugie, a member of an Augustinian religious congregation and a great expert on Byzantine theology, declared Palamas' distinction between the essence and the energies of God to be fundamentally wrong and his notion of deifying uncreated grace to be 'near to heresy.' This provoked a vigorous response from the Russian community that had established itself in Paris after the Bolshevik revolution of 1917 and Lenin's expulsion of prominent intellectuals in 1922. Their defense of Palamas soon led to exposition of theosis, which was perceived to rest primarily on the essence-energies distinction."

36. Gallaher, "Waiting for the Barbarians," 659–91.

for Orthodox theology in general.[37] The works of Fr. John Meyendorff offer some of the best historical and theological resources in addressing such polarization. In addition, most recent Orthodox scholarship has also greatly contributed to affirming the fundamental place of the teaching within Orthodox theology in general.[38]

Third, there seems to be a renewed interest, from both Orthodox and non-Orthodox, in the theology of Fr. S. Bulgakov requiring a sober reevaluation of his theological contributions. It is quite important that such re-evaluation should be done within the specific context of his proper theological motivations—the sophianic development of the theology of St. Gregory Palamas. Bulgakov has never explicitly adopted or rejected the teaching on the distinction between the Divine essence and energies.[39] It could be even suggested that some of the sophianic insights of Fr. Sergius Bulgakov have been driven by his philosophical appropriation and specific interpretation of the theology of St. Gregory Palamas. The works of Fr. John Meyendorff offer an example of a critical interpretative approach to sophiology that

37. See Russell, "Theosis and Gregory Palamas," 357–79: "The opponents of Palamism were not heretics. But, like many of the Fathers of the fourth century who had reservations about the word *homoousios*, they rejected novel terminology and insisted on what they took to be 'the ancestral doctrines'—*tapatria dogmata*. Palamas's torrent of treatises convinced some of them but his final victory was chiefly brought about by his supporters' capture of the patriarchal office. His version of theosis was enshrined in Orthodox teaching as a result of his canonization by the synod of 1368, but among the intellectuals for whom it was intended it remained—and still remains—controversial." See also the opinion of David Bentley Hart in: Pabst and Schneider, *Encounter between Eastern Orthodoxy*, xiii: "Some Eastern theologians might be emboldened partly to abandon the Neo-Palamite theology that has become so dominant in their Church since the middle of the last century, and frankly acknowledge its incoherence, and come to recognize that in many ways Augustine or Thomas was closer to the Greek Fathers in his understanding of divine transcendence than was Palamas (at least, Palamas as he has come to be understood); these theologians might even feel freer to avail themselves of many of the riches of their own tradition that have been forgotten as a result of the triumph of the Neo-Palamite synthesis." See also: Zizioulas, *Communion and Otherness*, 26, for whom the teaching of St. Gregory Palamas on the Divine essence and energies deserves to be mentioned only for historical reasons. According to Torrance ("Personhood and Patristics," 704) the concern of Metropolitan Zizioulas "is above all to affirm a eucharistic and ecclesial ethos, and thus he distances himself from any language which might evoke an individualistic, non-ecclesial piety. This ecclesial-centred theology also accounts, it seems, for his general distaste for any overemphasis on the theology of the divine energies (or rather, the potential abuse of this theology), an otherwise prominent feature of contemporary Orthodox theology." For a recent critic of Metropolitan Zizioulas's interpretation of the teaching on the Divine energies see Larchet, *Personne et nature*, 307–12.

38. See Христов, *Византийското богословие през XIV век*; Larchet, *La théologie des energies divines*; Kapriev, *Philosophie in Byzanz*; Bradshaw, *Aristotle East and West*.

39. Tanev, "ΕΝΕΡΓΕΙΑ vs. ΣΟΦΙΑ."

could be used for a meaningful contemporary appropriation of the best of the theological legacy of Fr. Sergius in the specific context of the history of Orthodox theology in the twentieth century.

Fourth, there seems to be an ongoing tendency to undervalue the role of Fr. G. Florovsky for the development of twentieth-century Orthodox theology by promoting the need for a new meta-patristic, post-neo-patristic or post-Florovsky approach as a way for the revival of Orthodox theology in the twenty-first century. One of the aspects of this tendency is exactly associated with the teaching on the Divine essence and energies, namely, the tendency to ignore his bold reminder that: "This basic distinction (i.e., between divine essence and energies) has been formally accepted and elaborated at the Great Councils of Constantinople in 1341 and 1351. Those who would deny this distinction were anathematized and excommunicated. The anathematisms of the council of 1351 were included in the rite for the Sunday Orthodoxy, in the Triodion. Orthodox theologians are bound by this decision."[40]

40. Florovsky, "St. Gregory Palamas and the Tradition of the Fathers," 105–20.

Part II

The Encounter between Theology and Physics

Chapter 5

The Possible Grounds for a Parallel Study of Energy in Orthodox Theology and Physics

The relevance of the concept of energy in Orthodox theology and in physics naturally poses the question about the possibility for a parallel study of its meaning in both contexts as well as about the potential value of such study. This question has at least two aspects. The first aspect has a scholarly grounding since it would be highly valuable to constructively correlate our understandings of a single term in two obviously different yet important fields of human engagement with reality. This exploration can be placed within the context of the ongoing conflict/dialogue between science and theology. The value of the approach used here could be found in the breaking of and moving away from the conflict/dialogue paradigm. Without any doubt, the universal nature of the energy concept in such an approach is particularly fruitful as a starting point. I truly believe that some of the epistemological insights of Orthodox theology will be found very illuminating by physicists providing the possibility for a reversal of the predominantly existing pattern of science-theology interactions—a pattern that could be characterized by the unidirectional (and unsuccessful) scientific attempts to provide an explanation of the mysteries of faith.

The second aspect of the question is theological and evangelical in nature. It is associated with the answer to a simple question: "In the end, who cares about any existing parallels between the meanings of energy in physics and theology?" I am certain that many believers will find such study irrelevant and useless—a life in Christ based on a personal relationship with the living God does not need additional reasons. Others among them, however, may enjoy it since it was God Himself who created the world and man in it, opening the possibility for us to know Him in everything He did, still does, and will do, i.e., knowing more about some of the common heuristic

structures underlying our knowledge of God and the world would only en-
rich the experience of the Divine presence in us and in everything around
us. Most non-believers, both scientists and non-scientists, will find the topic
meaningless. Others among them, however, with or without a scientific
background, may find in it an opportunity for an opening to the realm of
faith, since, ultimately, it points to the inherent empirical and existential
nature of both faith and science. In the beginning of the twenty-first century it is precisely scientific progress that has come to enlighten the mystery
of the world by answering questions that have remained unanswered for
centuries,[1] but also to reveal the epistemological subtleties of our scientific
approach to the mysteries of nature and open new horizons for a fuller appreciation of our human presence and destiny in it.

What are then the possible grounds on which a parallel exploration
of the concept of energy in Orthodox theology and in physics could be un-
dertaken? The articulation of these grounds is not foreign to contemporary
theological discourse, where there always remains the question about the
existence of "any real possibility of language—and the human thought forms
which are intrinsically bound up with language—and therefore of God-talk
of any kind if we do not hold to some kind of continuity of meaning"[2] across
the supposed gulf between God and the created world. The clarification of
these grounds is of critical importance for the articulation of our theological
terms and statements which, as Orthodox theology believes, do not exactly
describe but incorporate the imprints of and point to the experience and
knowledge of God.[3]

Anthropological and Cosmological Implications of the Event of the Incarnation

The first ground is rooted in the anthropological and cosmological implications of the event of the Incarnation. It was articulated for the first time in
the fourth century by St. Athanasius of Alexandria and, more recently, in
the scientific theology of Thomas F. Torrance[4] and by his former student
Fr. George Dragas in his lecture on the anthropic principle delivered at
Aristotle University of Thessaloniki in 2005. Thomas Torrance points out

1. Yannaras, *Elements of Faith*, 38.
2. Torrance, *Persons in Communion*, 126.
3. Ware, "The Debate about Palamism," 46.
4. Thomas F. Torrance (1913–2007) is one of the most important Reformed theologians of his era who has been influential by his works on patristics, theological method,
and the relationship between theology and science.

that theology should operate within the context of "a triadic relation between God, man and world, or God, world and man: for it is this world unfolding its mysteries to our scientific questioning which is the medium of God's revelation and of man's responsible knowledge of him." This implies a connection between theological concepts and physical concepts, spiritual and natural concepts, between theological science and natural science.[5] Scientific concepts are related to natural order of the universe. Theological concepts look through the rational structures of the universe to the Creator, i.e., they indicate but do not exhaust or describe the reality to which they refer. However, since they refer from our world to God, their worldly starting point is essential to them.[6]

In a very similar vein, Fr. George Dragas emphasizes the patristic understanding of the relationship between God, man, and the world:

> The Incarnation and Inhomination of God the Creator, which constitutes the basic chapter of Theology, makes the cosmos the context of the revelation of God and of God's renewing action upon it whereby it is brought back to its natural evolution towards its final fulfillment. . . . The basis of the universe is the uncreated energy of God and the will of God which transcends nothingness—the empty space that lacks existence and on which the limited existence of the created universe is established and floats. This is confirmed by the stunning event of the Incarnation of the Creator Word, whereby not only God communicates with man, but also this communication enters into the creaturely space of human existence and is expressed mystically with human terms, human thought, language, and symbolism.[7]

Another contemporary Orthodox theologian, Archbishop Lazar Puhalo, articulated the fundamental difference in the levels of knowledge that are found in modern physics and theology.[8] Science is a values-neutral endeavor seeking to discover the nature of created things. It "studies the nature of the 'creature,' but does not pertain to worship."[9] Theology, on the other hand, is an ascent in the realm of grace, toward a knowledge that is a gift from God. "God is so far removed from the creature that we dare not even represent Him except as He appeared in the flesh in the person of our Lord Jesus Christ." By becoming one of us in the person of Jesus Christ,

5. Torrance, *Reality and Scientific Theology*, 68.
6. Ibid., 69.
7. Dragas, "The Anthropic Principle: Christ's Humanity."
8. Puhalo, *The Evidence of Things Not Seen*, 27.
9. Ibid.

God provided the key to the understanding of the universe and of Himself. The Holy Scripture clearly tells us that we can know the Creator from the things that were created by Him and it is the same God Who has created the universe and Who is the author of our theology. This unity of Divine authorship makes modern physics something that is not to be feared by theologians; rather it makes it an intriguing and fascinating contribution to the integrity of our knowledge which could only substantiate our basic theological concepts.[10]

The Universal Nature of the Distinction between Essence and Energy

The second ground is based on the belief in the universality of the distinction between essence and energy that can be found in the works of the Byzantine Church Fathers. I will use a few citations from patristic literature to illustrate my point. The first one is from the trial of St. Maximus the Confessor, which took place in Constantinople in June 654. On the question "Is it altogether necessary to speak of wills and energies on the subject of Christ?" he answered:

> Altogether necessary if we want to worship in truth, for no being exists without natural activity. Indeed, the holy Fathers say plainly that it is impossible for any nature at all to be or to be known apart from its essential activity. And if there is no such thing as a nature to be or to be known without its characteristic activity, how is it possible for Christ to be or to be known as truly God and man by nature without the Divine and human activities?[11]

The second citation is from St. John of Damascus and defines energy as "the natural force and activity of each essence" or the activity innate in every essence: "For no essence can be devoid of natural energy. Natural energy again is the force in each essence by which its nature is made manifest."[12] The next two citations are from the *Triads* of St. Gregory Palamas, written during the time of his debates with Barlaam the Calabrian.[13]

---

10. Ibid.

11. Maximus the Confessor, *Selected Writings*, 23.

12. John of Damascus, *Writings, Orthodox Faith*, Book II, Ch. 23.

13. Meyendorff, *A Study of Gregory Palamas*; *Byzantine Hesychasm*.

As Basil the Great says, 'The guarantee of the existence of every essence is its natural energy which leads the mind to the nature.' And according to St. Gregory of Nyssa and all the other Fathers, the natural energy is the power which manifests every essence, and only nonbeing is deprived of this power; for the being which participates in an essence will also surely participate in the power which naturally manifests that essence.[14]

The reason for me to provide these citations was to point out that for the Byzantine Fathers (in our case St. Basil the Great, St. Gregory of Nyssa, St. Maximus the Confessor, St. John of Damascus and St. Gregory Palamas) the distinction between essence and energy applies to both God and created beings. The universality of the essence-energy distinction provides a basis for the development of the methodological background for the parallel exploration of the concept of energy in Orthodox theology and physics.

Methodological Remarks[15]

The methodological framework adopted here is based on the so-called conceptual or analogical isomorphism method that was previously used, for example, by the Canadian theologian Bernard Lonergan[16] within the context of a parallel analysis of Thomist and scientific thought. Analogical isomorphism presupposes two sets of terms from two different systems of thought. It neither affirms nor denies similarity between the terms of one set and those of other set, but it does assert that the network of relations in one set of terms is similar to the networks of relations in the other set. If the first set involves the terms A and B, and the second set—P and Q, the set (A, B) is said to be isomorphic to the set (P, Q) if the relation of A to B is similar to the relation of P to Q. Both sets are to be considered at once aiming at bringing to light an isomorphism or analogy of proportion that concentrates on the structural similarity of the two sets of terms moving away from the specific meanings of the terms within each of the sets. Finally, as Lonergan suggests, if this analogy is grasped, it may appear that the conceptual differences between the terms are less significant than what they seem to be when considered alone and the structure of the two sets is ignored.

14. Gregory Palamas, *The Triads*, II, 2.7, 95.

15. I am grateful to Prof. Dr. Andreas Speer, Director of the Thomas Institute in Cologne, Germany, for pointing out to me the importance of clarifying the methodological justification of the comparative analysis provided here.

16. Lonergan, "Isomorphism of Thomist and Scientific Thought," 133.

Lonergan's approach could be used as a methodological background for our study if we identify the (A, B) set of terms with the concepts of essence and energy in Orthodox theology and the (P, Q) set of terms with the concept of essence and energy in physics. It is, however, necessary to address a key issue raised by the problem of analogy that concerns not only the manner in which the terms are used but the nature of the underlying ontology controlling their use. It is the ontological foundation of the terms that governs whether they are being used in their legitimately proper functions and warrants.[17] The issue seems to be automatically taken care of since the term essence, which is the initial term of both sets (A, B) and (P, Q), is inherently ontological in nature. The methodological fit of Lonergan's approach here is further justified by the fact that the term energy, i.e., the second term in both sets (A, B) and (P, Q), plays a clearly epistemological role, thus providing the proper setting for the development of the relationship between any ontological and epistemological considerations.

The main purpose of employing the method of analogical isomorphism is to build on existing works and established knowledge in examining the occasions upon which the concept of energy is used, together with the characteristic ways the concept behaves on those occasions.[18] The expected outcome of such approach is the identification of specific common themes, issues, or patterns of use emerging from the examination of relationships between essence and energy in Orthodox theology and physics. This approach could be compared to the grounded theory approach in social sciences research—a general method of comparative analysis allowing for the emergence of categories, concepts, and relationships between them, from data (most often found in a textual representation of multiple-case narratives) by literally ignoring all existing conceptual and theoretical pre-assumptions in order to assure that the emergence of the concepts and relationships will not be contaminated by these pre-assumptions.[19] The grounded theory approach is mostly appropriate in situations where there is insufficient knowledge about the subject under study, which, as I believe, is our present situation.[20]

---

17. Torrance, *Persons in Communion*, 129.

18. Theobald, *The Concept of Energy*, xiii.

19. Glaser and Strauss, *The Discovery of Grounded Theory*; Dey, *Grounding Grounded Theory*.

20. I should point out that there have been previous works that addressed this topic although in different and less systematic ways, for example: Murphy, "Energy and the Creation of the World"; Rogich, "Divine Energy: Quantum Mechanics, Psychotherapy and World Religions," Ch. 5 in Rogich, *Becoming Uncreated*.

Chapter 6 _____

The Concept of Energy in Physics

The Concept of Energy in Classical Physics

Preliminary remarks

The discussion of the concept of energy usually starts with an emphasis on mechanics, but it is all-embracing. According to Eugene Hecht, "it influences our thinking about every branch of physics, indeed, about every aspect of our existence. Yet, there is no completely satisfactory definition of energy. Even so," he continues, "we will quantify its various manifestations as we struggle to define it."[1] In its most popular meaning, the concept was used at least since the late 1500s and was associated with the capacity of physical objects and systems to do work. In 1638 Galileo employed the term *energia*, though he never defined it. It was only in the 1850s that the idea had taken on a scientific meaning—a meaning that is not altogether satisfactory defined. "In very general terms, energy describes the state of a system in relation to the action of four forces"[2]—gravitational, electromagnetic, strong,[3] and weak.[4] It is therefore a relational concept, a concept which is inherently associated with the description of motion, change, and the interaction between physical objects and systems in general.

1. Hecht, *Physics*, Vol. 1, 222.

2. Ibid., 223.

3. The strong nuclear force is the force responsible for the structural integrity of atomic nuclei.

4. The weak nuclear force is responsible for the decay of particles that are part of the atomic nucleus. Its most familiar effect is the beta decay of neutrons in atomic nuclei, which is associated with the phenomenon of radioactivity. The word "weak" derives from the fact that the field strength is some 1,013 times less than that of the strong force.

Energy and change

Energy is a property of all matter and is observed indirectly through changes in physical objects' speed, mass, position, and so forth. The change in the energy of a system, which is all we can ever measure in an experiment, is a measure of the physical change in that system. Force is the agent of change, whereas energy is the measure of change. Because a system can change through the action of different forces in different ways, there are several distinct manifestations of energy.

> By observing the changing behavior of matter, we "infer" the presence of one form or another of energy. Still, energy is not an entity in and of itself—there is no such thing as pure energy. Energy is always the energy of something. The concept of energy provides a means of quantitatively accounting for physical change. When a material system manifests an observable change due to some interaction, we associate an amount of energy with the extent of that change. Interaction is crucial; if matter did not interact, the concept of energy would be superfluous.[5]

Mario Bunge points out that, since it is ubiquitous, the concept of energy must be philosophical and, in particular, metaphysical, belonging in the same league as the concepts of thing and property, event and process, space and time, causation and chance. He identifies energy with changeability.[6]

Kinetic and potential energy

It is interesting to point out that the concept of energy is associated with the concept of work. This association makes a lot of sense given the semantic meaning of the word *energeia* in Greek, which comes from *energos*: *en* (at) + *ergon* (work). In mechanics work is defined by the product of force and distance, and happens to be equal to the change of energy resulting from the application of that force to a body as that body moves through a distance in space. This type of energy is naturally associated with motion and is called *kinetic energy*, a term introduced by Lord Kelvin (William Thomson) in 1849. It was defined as the square of the velocity v of an object multiplied by its mass m divided by two: $mv2/2$. If, however, the force acting upon the body is naturally present after its displacement and the body is kept motionless but potentially susceptible to the force action, the potential for

5. Hecht, *Physics*, Vol. 1, 223.
6. Bunge, "Energy: From Physics to Metaphysics," 458.

generating the kinetic energy is still there because of the presence of the force. This type of energy is known as *potential energy* and exists by virtue of the position of the body in relation to a naturally present force. Such is the situation when the gravitational force causes the free fall of objects which are left on their own without any support at some height above the surface of the earth. In summary, kinetic energy is associated with the capacity to do work by virtue of motion; potential energy is associated with the capacity to do work by virtue of position.

Energy conservation law and symmetry

R. B. Lindsay defines the concept of energy through the concept of change, pointing out, however, that the basis of its usage today is the idea of *invariance,* which means constancy in the midst of change.[7] Lindsay's shift of focus from change to invariance alludes to the energy conservation law—the empirical fact that, whenever an amount of energy is transferred from one entity to another, the total amount of energy always remains unchanged. This shows that "the importance of energy springs not just from its variety of form, but form its conservation: the total amount of energy in the cosmos remains always the same, since the loss of one kind of energy is always being compensated by the gain of another kind of energy."[8] It is important to note that the conservation of energy applies to systems and not to individual bodies. The total energy of a system of bodies includes contributions from both kinetic energy of motion and potential energy that reflects the interaction between the bodies. The potential energy contributions depend on the distances between the bodies, their electrical charges, and possibly other things. It is only the *total* energy that is conserved.

Conservation laws are commonly considered as the deepest and most significant types of scientific laws because they give insights into the symmetry of the physical systems, but, more importantly, into the symmetries of space and time (space-time). More involved mathematical manipulations of classical physics' laws of motion reveal that energy conservation stems from the "smooth" nature of time, i.e., from the fact that "it spreads smoothly from the past into the future with no squashed bits or stretched bits."[9] What this really means is that the energy conservation law could be mathematically derived from the invariance of the physical laws to forward and back-

7. Lindsay, "The Concept of Energy and its Early Historical Development," 384; "The Scientific and Theological Revolutions," 219.

8. Word, *The Quantum World*, 18.

9. Atkins, *Galileo's Finger*, 98.

ward time changes. So deep is the relationship between conservation laws and the symmetry of space-time that the conservation laws survive even when classical physics laws of motion fail and there is a need to move into the realm of relativity and quantum mechanics. This relationship shows that the stability and the sustainability of the physical world are deeply rooted into the symmetry principles of its most fundamental inner structure.[10]

From visible to invisible

Historically the concept of kinetic energy was introduced first. The introduction of potential energy provided continuity to the idea of energy in general, since its change was associated with the work done on a body against a naturally present external force. Its relevance to the development of physics was found to be critically important:

> The concept of kinetic energy, as it stands, is a derivative concept since it is directly definable in terms of observables, namely mass and velocity. To this extent its usefulness is limited, and it affords no deeper understanding of the nature of mechanical systems; its logical distance from observation is too slight. But the value and significance of the concept are immeasurably increased, both for mechanics and as it turns out for physical science as a whole, by the introduction of the additional concept of potential energy. This move at one stroke places energy among the most important of physical concepts. The new notion of energy thus created, represents a considerable conceptual sophistication of the old one; its logical distance from observation is now very much greater, and the concept casts its net more widely.[11]

It is, therefore, the logical distance from observation that provided the concept of energy its metaphysical relevance. It is the shift from the description of the visible properties of physical objects and systems to the manifestation of their invisible ones that makes it universally meaningful.

Energy and fields

The relevance of the concept of potential energy is inherently associated with the emergence of the field concept. To clarify what a field is, we could

10. Ibid.
11. Theobald, *The Concept of Energy*, 39.

use an example from electrostatics—the part of physics dealing with electrical charges, fields, and their interactions. The concept of electrical charge is fundamental and cannot be described in simpler, more basic concepts. In the words of Eugene Hecht: "We know it by what it does and not by what it is—if you like, it is what it does, and that's that."[12] A charged particle, such as the electron, interacts with other charged particles by creating a web of interaction around itself that extends out into space. We say that one charge creates an electric field in space and when another charge is immersed in that field, it interacts directly with it. The field that surrounds an electrical charge is part of it and becomes the media or mediator of the interaction with the other charge.

The picture is quite straightforward, but it raises many questions. The main question is why do we need the field concept on the first place? The answer is: to deal with the explanation of "action at a distance," and the principle of "locality"—the expectation that effects must be co-located with their causes, both in space and in time. One electron causes another, second, electron, located at some distance away from the first electron, to experience a certain force. This force seems to have no cause located any nearer to the second electron than the distance to the first one. It seems, therefore, that there is no visible local cause for the force experienced by the second electron. The introduction of the field concept by Michael Faraday enabled electric interactions to satisfy spatio-temporal locality and explain the action at a distance, i.e., that the electric force acting on a charged body at a given moment in time is caused by the electrical field at its location. The field is invisible, but it becomes visible by its effects. Its energy is manifested by the work done by the electrical field force for moving the charge away at a given distance. Even this simple exposition of the field theory clearly shows in what sense the concepts of energy and field are interrelated. Energy "becomes the basic 'substance' of field physics, as matter was the basic 'substance' of Newtonian physics. Energy is not a way of characterizing particles, but a way of characterizing processes in the field."[13] "It is so because the field is characterized by the presence of energy. . . . A field is nothing more than a spatial distribution of energy which varies with time. Energy has thus been freed from its dependence upon physical vehicles such as particles; it has achieved the status of independent scientific existence."[14]

12. Hecht, *Physics*, Vol. 2, 610.
13. Theobald, *The Concept of Energy*, 50.
14. Ibid., 98.

Are fields and their energies real?

The inherent relationship between the energy and field concepts makes the questions about their existence somehow interchangeable. It is interesting to discover that in physics the existence of the physical reality behind the concept of energy might be questioned:

> The reality of the field is self-consciously inculcated in our elementary teaching, often with considerable difficulty for the student. This view is usually credited to Faraday and is considered the most fundamental concept of all modern electrical theory. Yet in spite of this I believe that a critical examination will show that the ascription of physical reality to the electric field is entirely without justification. I cannot find a single physical phenomenon or a single physical operation by which evidence of the existence of the field may be obtained independent of the operations which entered into the definition. The only physical evidence we ever have of the existence of a field is obtained by going there with an electric charge and observing the action on the charge . . . , which is precisely the operation of the definition. . . . The electromagnetic field itself is an invention and is never subject to direct observation. What we observe are material bodies with or without charges (including eventually in this category electrons), their positions, motions, and the forces to which they are subject.[15]

This statement may seem strange, but there is one aspect in which it is not so trivial. In the case of the system of two electrons considered above, does the field of the first electron exist when the second one is not present, i.e., independently of it, or its presence is *enabled* by the proximity of the second electron? The question here may be considered as being not about the reality of the field in general but about its reality independently of the second electron. Such question, however, does not seem to fall within the scope of interest of the majority of physicists, whose reasoning functions under the premises of operationism—the view that the meaning of every scientific term must be specifiable by identifying a definite testing operation that provides a criterion for its application. This means that for most physicists "the whole of physics is about operations, chiefly measurements and computations, rather than about nature."[16] This approach is clearly visible in a longer quote by Richard Feynman: "It is important to realize that

---

15. Bridgman, *The Nature of Thermodynamics*, 57–58, 136. This work was referenced by: Lange, *An Introduction to the Philosophy of Physics*, 41.

16. Bunge, *Philosophy of Physics*, 1–4.

in physics today, we have no knowledge of what energy 'is.' We do not have a picture that energy comes in little blobs of a definite amount. It is not that way. However, there are formulas for calculating some numerical quantity and when we add it all together it always gives . . . the same number. It is an abstract thing in that it does not tell us the mechanism or the reason for the various formulas. . . . Conservation of energy can be understood only if we know the formula for all of its forms."[17] For Feynman every specific meaning of the energy concept should be based on a specific formula, on a carefully defined measurement and on some calculation procedures. Such an approach to the definition of a concept is called *operational*. The operationist attitude to scientific concepts has a long history and, as we see, tends to put aside questions of whether the object of the definition really exists or not.[18]

Electrodynamics and the objective reality of electromagnetic fields

The ambiguity of the question about the real existence of the electric field seems to appear due to the fact that we were silently focusing on static fields, i.e., the electric fields of electrical charges that do not move in time and space. Electrodynamics deals with dynamic, i.e., changing in time, electric and magnetic fields. When an electrical charge undergoes some acceleration, a portion of its field "detaches" itself and travels off at the speed of light, carrying with it energy. This is what we call electromagnetic wave radiation. It is impossible to question the reality of electromagnetic waves. "It existence invites (if not *compels*) us to regard the fields as independent dynamical entities in their own right, every bit as 'real' as atoms or baseballs. . . . But it takes a charge to *produce* an electromagnetic field and a charge to *detect* one . . . ."[19] Thus, the dynamic nature of the electromagnetic fields helps in resolving the ontological ambiguities associated with the reality of their existence.

A classical epistemology

Before moving to quantum physics we should stop for a moment and see how to characterize the epistemology of classical physics at the end of the nineteenth and the beginning of the twentieth century. But why are we

17. Feynman et al., *The Feynman Lectures on Physics*, Vol. I, 4-2.
18. Harrison, *The Concept of Energy*.
19. Griffiths, *Introduction to Electrodynamics*, xiv.

talking about epistemology here? One of my underlying assumptions is that, in order to escape the trap of operationism, a discussion of the concept of energy in theology and physics should be developed within an epistemological context. A second underlying assumption is that the epistemic power of a science is dependent on its ontological presuppositions, i.e., on the foundational insights about the nature of the realities it is dealing with. This second assumption is found to be methodologically important since it reflects the proper positioning of the two terms—essence and energy—as the two poles of the analogical isomorphic analytical approach.[20]

There is no doubt that one of the main features of classical physics was the development of a refined mathematical language.

> Visualizable aspects of physical reality were translated into the map space of newly invented mathematical and geometrical relationships—the calculus and analytical geometry. And the remarkable result was that the correspondence between points in the new map space of physical theory and the actual behavior of matter in physical reality seemed to confirm a one-to-one correspondence between every element in the physical theory and the physical reality.[21]

> The enormous success of classical physics soon convinced more secular Enlightenment thinkers, however, that metaphysics had nothing to do with the conduct of physics, and that any appeal to God in efforts to understand the essences of physical reality in physical theory was ad hoc and unnecessary. The divorce between subjective constructions of reality in ordinary language and constructions of physical reality in mathematical theory was allegedly made final by the positivists in the nineteenth century. This small group of physicists and mathematicians decreed that the full and certain truth about physical reality resides only in the mathematical description, that concepts exist in this description only as quantities, and that any concerns about the nature or source of physical phenomena in ordinary language do not lie within the domain of science.[22]

20. Lonergan, "Isomorphism of Thomist and Scientific Thought."

21. Here and in the following discussions of classical and quantum epistemology I will be closely following the logic of the insights provided by: Nadeau and Kafatos, *The Non-Local Universe*. I am grateful to Archbishop Lazar Puhalo for pointing out to me some of the previous works of Robert Nadeau and Menas Kafatos.

22. Ibid.

The result was the emergence of the belief that the real is, in its essence, geometrical, rigorously describable, exactly measurable, and, therefore, predictable and manageable. The truths of classical physics were considered as literally "revealed" truths, fully given for exploration and able to be visually studied in completeness, independently of the specific inner nature of their corresponding realities. This metaphysical presupposition became in the history of science what we could call today the "hidden ontology of classical epistemology"—a kind of universal ontology leading to the universality of the scientific method and to the "epistemological arrogance" of the rationalism of the eighteenth and nineteenth centuries, which, surprisingly, may be still commonly found today.

Final reflections on the concept of energy in classical physics

By focusing so far on classical physics we have seen that the concept of energy is always associated with a physical reality behind it—energy is always the energy *of something*. Its universal nature lies in its distance from the observable, i.e., in its ability to articulate the dynamic properties and manifestations of invisible realities. What physics is actually dealing with are the (energetic) manifestations of these realities, which are invoked or actualized by making acts of observation or measurement performed in a way suitable to the dynamics of their inner nature. In this sense, we could say that the energy concept is used in an inherently epistemological manner. It seems, however, that the physics community has traditionally neglected the epistemological aspects of its use by operating within the framework of a predominantly operationist approach. The predominance of operationism, which is mainly driven by the challenges of dealing with the invisible and dynamic nature of physical realities, gives raise to another challenge associated with the interpretation of the reality of their existence.

Energy in Quantum Physics

In this section I will intentionally stay away from the discussion of the concept of energy in Einstein's special and general theory of relativity and focus on quantum physics. There are two reasons to do that. First, any discussion of relativistic concepts will be unavoidably based on heavy mathematics and will put me in danger of loosing the connection with the reader. In the words of Roland Omnès, an expert in quantum physics and philosopher of science, "It is so easy to dream with the help of some heavy mathematics in the wonderland of general relativity."[23] Second, recent progress in quantum physics sheds new light on important epistemological issues that are found to be more relevant for the present study. I will, therefore, follow Omnès' example by focusing first on what is generally admitted by highlighting the outstanding features of Niles Bohr's epistemological insights.[24] In the next section I will briefly discuss the concept of energy in Special and General theory of relativity and cosmology by focusing on the contributions of Albert Einstein.

Max Plank and the quantum of energy and action

The idea of the quantum of energy was introduced as a kind of energetic atomism, in which energy could not be divided into arbitrarily small amounts but existed as discrete, tiny packets.[25] In its origins, the introduction of the concept of energy quantization was driven by deeply practical reasons. In 1900 it allowed the German physicist Max Planck to create an adequate mathematical model of a troubling problem—so called black-body radiation, i.e., the radiation that is emitted by a specific type of heated bodies. Planck worked with careful experimental measurements of the actual energy distribution trying to develop a correct theoretical model to describe it. Eventually, he found out that he could do that only if he assumed that the emitted energy could change only in jumps, from one energy level to the next. This assumption in Planck's model violated the usual way of thinking about energy—as a quantity that could vary smoothly, increasing or decreasing gradually, rather than being confined to stepwise change. Some people consider Planck's assumption as a "desperate" move, but the only one possible, enabling him to fit the empirical data on black-body radiation. Planck called these discrete energy changes "quanta" of energy. He assumed that their necessity in the theory would soon be explained, and that the explanation would not require energy itself to exist only in bundles of specific sizes. He, however, was not able to come up with such an explanation himself.

23. Omnès, *Quantum Philosophy*, 147.

24. Ibid.

25. For an insightful description of the early stages of the emergence of quantum physics see Dear, *The Intelligibility of Nature*, 142.

The universal meaning of the energy quantum concept

Very soon other physicists began to see the more universal meaning in Planck's idea. In a paper from 1905 dedicated to the photoelectric effect, Albert Einstein argued that light itself should not be understood simply as wave motion but should also be understood in terms of light quanta—mass-less packets of energy that were later to be called "photons." The energy of a single photon E was found to be proportional to the light's frequency v by means of a universal constant h: $E = hv$. The constant h was first derived by Planck and, therefore, known as Planck's constant or the "quantum of action." Soon after the emergence of the photon, the idea of the quantum nature of energy was extensively infiltrated into microphysics.

In 1913 the Danish physicist Niels Bohr opened up a critically im-portant new arena for the use of the concept—atomic spectra. It was the exploration of this arena that led to the emergence of quantum physics. Bohr adopted Planck's quantum to study the internal structure of atoms in a way that was "in obvious contrast to the ordinary ideas of electrodynamics but appears to be necessary in order to account for experimental facts."[26] He started with the commonly accepted "solar system" model of the atom, wherein negatively charged electrons orbit around the central positively charged nucleus like planets.

> The size of an electron's orbit corresponded to the orbit's en-ergy, and Bohr postulated that the only orbits permitted to such electrons were those whose energy corresponded to discrete, quantized levels—not just any amount of energy, or orbit, was allowed by his model. There were levels, or steps, of orbital ener-gy that the electrons could occupy; Bohr called them "stationary states." The only changes in orbital levels that an electron could undergo were ones in which it shifted, in a discrete jump, from one stationary state to another.[27]

Assuming the discrete nature of these changes allowed Bohr to in-terpret some experimental results that had been known for nearly thirty years. These results concerned the radiation emitted by hydrogen atoms when excited by heat. When the radiation was separated out according to frequency by a spectroscope, the spectrum showed a series of discrete bright lines that was uniquely related to the specific internal structure of the atom. Even though quantum theory was still at its initial stages, there was a major epistemological breakthrough that was associated with Niels Bohr's

26. Ibid., 144.
27. Ibid.

achievement—the demonstration that the behavior of light quanta and their energetic manifestations could be identified with the composition of atoms and the structure of matter in general. The dynamic structure of matter is manifested or known by the particular mode by which the smallest quantities of energy are presented to the observer. Or, in the poetical theological language of Christos Yannaras, "That means that the hypostasis of matter itself is energy, that matter contains the constituents of light, that light is the ideal matter."[28]

The classical epistemology of Albert Einstein

The mathematical description of physical reality that Planck, Einstein, Bohr, and others developed over the first thirty years of the twentieth century undermined or displaced virtually every major assumption about the nature of physical reality in classical physics. And the vision of reality in what came to be called the new physics immediately challenged the predominant epistemology without providing a clearly articulated new alternative.[29]

Albert Einstein has contributed enormously to the opening of the new era in physics, starting with his special theory of relativity. However, his underlying epistemology itself ended up being classical. The motivation behind his special theory of relativity was in fact a larger unification of physical theory that would serve to eliminate mathematical inconsistencies in some of its currently existing fundamentals. The fact that frames of reference in physical experiments are relative was known since Galileo's times. What Einstein did was to extend the so-called Galilean relativity principle from mechanics to electromagnetic theory by abandoning the Newtonian idea for the existence of an absolute reference frame. It was this abandonment that led to the radical shift in physics from the realm of the visualizable into the realm of the mathematically describable but unvisualizable. It is when we try to image the four-dimensional reality of space-time in relativity theory that we have our first encounter with modern physics.[30] It is not difficult to imagine the dramatic nature of this encounter. However, all subsequent attempts to forcefully visualize the unvisualizable have led to reductionism, to an idolization of the mathematical formalisms, and to an objectification of the physical models rather than of physical reality itself.[31]

28. Yannaras, *Elements of Faith*, 39.

29. In this section I am following again the logic of the insights provided by Nadeau and Kafatos, *The Non-Local Universe*.

30. Ibid., 23.

31. On the problem of visualization in modern physics within the context of

In 1915 and 1916 Einstein extended the principle of relativity to account for the more general case of accelerated frames of reference and developed his general theory of relativity. Here, again, visualization may only help in understanding what is implied by this theory, but it does not disclose what is really meant by it. A visual analogy is useful only to the extent that it helps in accepting that the reality of space-time and the fundamental physical phenomena in it are unvisualizable. Yet here, as in the special theory of relativity, there is no ambiguity in its mathematical description. Most physicists have made a firm commitment to Einstein's classical epistemology. Its fundamental precept is based on the assumption of one-to-one correspondence between every element in the theory and every aspect of the physical reality described by that theory.

A quantum or non-classical epistemology

Quantum physics began challenging this epistemology in the beginning of the 1920s in a twenty-three-year debate between Albert Einstein and Niels Bohr. It was just in the last few years of the twentieth century that modern physics experiments demonstrated that the fundamental issues in the famous Einstein-Bohr debate seem to have been resolved in Bohr's favor. The outcome of this debate was the disclosure of a profound new relationship between parts and whole that is completely non-classical. This new relationship suggests that the classical conception of the ability of a physical theory to disclose the whole as a sum of its parts, or to "see" reality-in-itself, is no longer acceptable. Modern physics experiments have made it perfectly clear that these classical assumptions are no longer valid.[32]

The principle of uncertainty & the shift from visible to invisible

It took more than two decades before it became possible to formulate a theory that was in a sense similar in its functioning to Newtonian mechanics. Quantum mechanics was introduced in 1925 and 1926 by Heisenberg and Schrödinger in two mathematically equivalent but epistemologically different versions. Heisenberg's version was presented in virtually non-classical terms and led to the formulation of the so-called *uncertainty principle*. When applied to a particle, Heisenberg's famous uncertainty

---

Orthodox theology see Puhalo, *The Evidence of Things not Seen*, 34.

32. Ibid.

relations mean that having more precision in the particle's position leads to less precision in its velocity, and vice versa. There are no states in which a particle has both a definite position and a definite velocity and the amount of uncertainty can never be reduced below the limit set by the principle. The radical nature of this principle is based on the fact that it makes a quantum physicist blind and wordless by somehow hiding or blurring the visual attributes of the particle.

The first insight that would open the door to an improved understanding of this situation came from Max Born in 1926, and it was not well received by the majority of physicists at the time. Born realized that it is not the exact position and velocity of a particle but the "probability" of finding the particle within a particular region and with a possible range of velocities that allows us to precisely predict where that particle will be found. What greatly disturbed physicists was that Born's definition of the term probability did not refer to the behavior of a system in a way that could be described in classical terms. He was referring to an inherent aspect of measurement of all quantum mechanical events, which does not allow predicting where a particle will be observed no matter what improvements are made in both theory and experiments. While there is a mathematically simple quantum recipe to describe this situation, the reality it describes is totally unvisualizable.

The principle of complementarity and the breakdown of classical logic

We have already seen that the particle-like understanding of light emerged after Planck's discovery of the quanta, primarily due to Einstein. It was around 1920 when light acquired an explicitly dual, i.e., wave and particle, character unexplainable by classical physics. Almost at the same time the pervasive nature of this duality at the quantum level became apparent as well. Both light and particles may manifest their existence in wavelike or particle-like phenomena under different circumstances.

It is quite significant that the point at which mathematical theory meets the realm of the unvisualizable is exactly the point at which classical logic breaks down as well. This required a new logical framework that was originally developed by Niels Bohr in an effort to explain wave-particle dualism in quantum physics.[33] Since physical reality in quantum physics is described on the most fundamental level in terms of exchange of quanta, Bohr realized that the fact that a quantum existed either as a wave or as a particle was

33. Ibid.

enormously significant. This mutual exclusivity was the basis for him to define the principle of complementarity—a single quantum mechanical entity can either behave as a particle or as wave, but never simultaneously as both.

One of the basic laws of Aristotelian logic is the law of the excluded middle stating that x is *either* y *or* not-y, or that an attribute either belongs or does not belong to an object and there is no middle ground on which two essentially opposite attributes could belong to the same object. We realize that normative logic, which is premised on this law, is based on our dealings with macro-level phenomena and does not hold in the quantum domain where the quantum nature of physical reality requires a new "quantum" logic and epistemology. Therefore, the principle of complementarity in quantum mechanics does not conform to classical logic.[34] The "total reality" of a quantum system is antinomic in nature and Bohr was among the first to realize that a proper understanding of the relationship between these two aspects of a single reality requires the use of a new logical framework.

What makes this logical framework new is that, in addition to representing profound oppositions that preclude one another in a given situation, both aspects are necessary to achieve a complete understanding of the entire situation. It not only applies to the measurability or knowability of some property of a physical entity but, more importantly, it applies to the limitations of the manifestation of this property in the physical world.[35] Thus, physical reality is determined and defined by the energetic manifestations of its properties which are limited by the trade-offs between the two aspects of its antinomic wave-particle nature. The emergence of complementarity in a quantum system occurs when one considers the specific circumstances under which one attempts to measure its properties. As Bohr noted, the principle of complementarity "implies the impossibility of any sharp separation between the behaviour of atomic objects and the interaction with the measuring instruments which serve to define the conditions under which the phenomena appear."[36]

The debate between Albert Einstein and Niels Bohr

The famous debate between Bohr and Einstein began at the fifth Solvay Congress in 1927 and continued intermittently until Einstein's death in 1955. The argument took the form of thought experiments in which Einstein

---

34. Birkhoff and von Neumann, "The Logics of Quantum Mechanics," 823–43.

35. http://en.wikipedia.org/wiki/Complementarity_%28physics%29

36. Bohr, "Discussion with Einstein," 210.

would try to demonstrate that it was theoretically possible to measure, or at least determine precise values for, two complementary constructs in quantum physics, like position and velocity, simultaneously. Bohr would then respond with a careful analysis of the conditions and results in Einstein's thought experiments and demonstrate that there were fundamental ambiguities he had failed to resolve.[37]

Einstein eventually accepted the idea that the uncertainty or indeterminacy principle is a fact of nature and the essential point of subsequent disagreement in the debate became whether quantum theory was a complete theory. Einstein's position can be expressed by one of his most famous quotes today "Quantum mechanics is certainly imposing. But an inner voice tells me that it is not yet the real thing. The theory says a lot, but does not really bring us any closer to the secret of the 'Old one.' I, at any rate, am convinced that He does not throw dice."[38] According to him, if our current understanding about the nature of quantum objects is probabilistic, this only shows that we are missing something and there should be some "hidden variables" that escape our knowledge but will be certainly discovered as our theories improve with time. In other words, our ignorance about these hidden variables makes quantum reality appear probabilistic, unpredictable, and unknowable in classical terms. Therefore, the knowledge of these hidden variables would supposedly make the description of quantum systems completely deterministic, i.e., although quantum indeterminacy may be a property of a quantum system in practice, it need not be so in principle. In this sense the physical attributes of quantum systems can be viewed as objective or real even in the absence of measurement and we could assume, as Einstein did, a one-to-one correspondence between every element of the physical theory and the physical reality. This is how the dialogue eventually revolved around the issues of non-locality and realism.

Bohr agreed that our existing theories may and will improve with time but believed that this improvement will not remove the principles of uncertainty and complementarity because they are inherent characteristics of the nature of quantum objects. He looked at quantum objects in terms of their energetic manifestations in the effects of their interaction with measuring instruments rather than in terms of their properties. In Bohr's ultimate

37. An insightful discussion of the nature of the debate between Einstein and Bohr can be found in Nadeau and Kafatos, *The Non-local Universe*, 162.

38. Letter to Max Born (December 4, 1926). In Born and Eisntein, *The Born-Einstein Letters*. Einstein used slightly different versions of this quote at other times. For example, in a 1943 conversation with William Hermanns recorded in Hermann, *Einstein and the Poet*, 58, where Einstein was quoted to have said: "As I have said so many times, God doesn't play dice with the world."

view all available quantum phenomena are defined strictly in terms of the manifestations of particular aspects of their inner nature in recorded effects, such as the click of a photo-detector, rather than in terms of properties of the quantum objects themselves. The assignment of such properties is unacceptable in view of the impossibility of any sharp separation between the behavior of atomic objects and the interaction with the measuring instruments which serve to define the conditions under which the observable phenomena appear. In this sense, quantum discreteness, discontinuity, individuality, and indivisibility are transferred to the level of the phenomena and their effects. This transfer requires a terminological adjustment. All terms now apply to certain physically complex and non-localized entities, each involving the whole experimental arrangement, rather than to single and localized in space physical entities, i.e., there is no God-like perspective from which we can know physical reality absolutely in itself. We are forced to recognize that our knowledge of the physical system is *in principle* local and, therefore, incomplete.

> If non-locality is a property of the entire universe, then we must also conclude that an undivided wholeness exists on the most primary and basic level in all aspects of physical reality. What we are actually dealing with in science per se, however, are manifestations of this reality, which are invoked or "actualized" in making acts of observation or measurement. Since the reality that exists between space-like separated regions is a whole whose existence can only be inferred in experiments, as opposed to proven, the correlations between the particles, or the sum of their parts, do not constitute the "invisible whole." Physical theory allows us to understand why correlations occur. But it cannot in principle disclose or describe the actual character of the invisible whole.[39]

Modern physics experiments have clearly confirmed this view.[40]

---

39. Nadeau and Kafatos, *The Non-local Universe*, 4.

40. See Freedman and Clauser, "Experimental Test of Local Hidden-Variable Theories"; Aspect, Grangier, and Roger, "Experimental Tests of Realistic Local Theories"; Aspect, Grangier, and Roger, "Experimental Realization of Einstein-Podolsky-Rosen-Bohm Gedankenexperiment"; Aspect, Dalibard, and Roger, "Experimental Test of Bell's Inequalities"; Tittel, Brendel, Zbinden, and Gisin, "Violations of Bell Inequalities more than 10km apart."

Quantum vs. classical language

Bohr grounded the language of quantum theory in the wave-particle model of matter. Wave-language is process-like, particle-language is object-and-event-like.[41] Two particles cannot be in the same place at the same time, whereas two waves can. Physical description can use one or other language, but clearly not both at once. There seems to be no logical continuity between the languages of macrophysics and microphysics, and it cannot be simply assumed that the categories of classical discourses will be the same as those of quantum discourse.[42] In Bohr's interpretation, the apparatus of quantum mechanics is viewed as a mathematical device for the description of a reality that cannot be directly measured or observed. It expresses the relationship between the quantum system, which is inaccessible to the observer, and the measuring device, which conforms to classical physics. The challenge is in viewing quantum reality with one set of assumptions, those of quantum physics, and the results of experiments with another set of assumptions, those of classical physics. This implies a categorical distinction between the micro and macro worlds.

Are quantum objects real?

Bohr confronts and resolves the epistemological implications of the quantum observation problem in entirely realistic terms. Some scientists have assumed that since Bohr's analysis of the conditions for observation precludes exact correspondence between every element of the physical theory and the physical reality, he is implying that this reality does not objectively exist or that we are not anymore objective observers of this reality. These conclusions are possible only if we equate physical reality with our ability to know it in an absolute sense. According to Bohr, we just reach a limit to our ability to know. Knowledge here can never be complete in the classical sense because we are unable to simultaneously apply the mutually exclusive constructs that constitute the complete description. This, however, does not make the quantum objects less real. In this sense the limits of knowledge and the unknowable itself have become an inherent part of our knowing process:

> This thinking and these theories radically redefine the nature
> of knowledge by making the unknowable an irreducible part of

41. Theobald, *The Concept of Energy*, 98.
42. Ibid.

knowledge, insofar as the ultimate objects under investigation by non-classical theories are seen as being beyond any knowledge or even conception, while, at the same time, affecting what is knowable. Thus, according to Niels Bohr's non-classical understanding of quantum mechanics . . . "we are not dealing with an arbitrary renunciation of a more detailed analysis of atomic phenomena, but with a recognition that such an analysis is in principle excluded" (Bohr's emphasis). It is this impossibility, in principle, of any analysis of the phenomena considered by non-classical theories beyond certain limits (which non-classical theories establish as well) that defines these theories.[43]

Reflections on the distinction between the quantum and the classical concepts of energy

One of the most obvious and important differences between classical and quantum physics is that the exchange and transformation of energy is not regarded as a continuous process. In classical physics the use of the energy concept is process-driven and descriptive in nature. It presupposed continuity and had to be abandoned when moving into the realm of quantum physics.[44] But concepts such as conservation of energy which do not require following the actual process of change are naturally still valid in quantum theory. In other words, the radical newness of quantum theory is associated with the way it describes the states of systems and has nothing to say of the processes by which states of affairs are realized. This does not mean that nothing ever happens; it simply means that continuous processes escape the conceptual apparatus of quantum theory. In quantum physics the concept of energy is associated with a deeper split between visible manifestations and the invisible realities. This is due to two reasons. First, in addition to the invisible nature of the quantum objects, there is also another radically different scale of dimensions—the sub-atomic. Second, quantum objects are not only invisible but also unimaginable—the fundamental concepts of quantum physics are not accessible to human imagination. This second reason leads to the need of interpretation. This "new" physics deals again with the energetic manifestations of physical realities, which are invoked or actualized in acts of observation performed in a way suitable to the dynamics of their inner nature, i.e., to observe the activity of a quantum object,

43. Plotnitsky, *The Knowable and the Unknowable*, xiii.
44. Theobald, *The Concept of Energy*, 117.

you must disturb it.[45] Although impersonal (i.e., there is no such thing as quantum object will), its energy is hypostatic in the sense of the Byzantine Church Fathers because it is always the energy of a (some)thing representing a particular instance of all things having the same essence and nature. The unimaginability, however, of this thing makes the need of the interpretation of its energetic manifestations unavoidable. Such an interpretation could happen only within the framework of activities of a given scientific community driven by its historically developed ontological and epistemological presuppositions. In contrast to classical physics, physical description at the quantum level operates by means of two languages—the classical or the macro-language and the quantum or the micro-one. One must use one or other language, but clearly not both at once. This implies a categorical distinction between the micro- and macro-descriptions, which is based on the necessity of using classical terminology and concepts, but also requiring an appropriate discontinuous quantum mechanical "correction" and conceptual "upgrade." Such logical discontinuity leads to the necessity of a new logical framework in accordance with the particular antinomic nature of quantum objects. Last, but not least, quantum physics operates with a completely new understanding of the relationship between whole and parts, which is due to the non-local nature of quantum objects. All these quantum "features" lead to the need of a more subtle understanding of the relationship between the quantum nature or essence of microphysical entities and their energy or energetic manifestations.

Energy in Relativity and Cosmology

This section will briefly discuss the concept of energy in the special theory of relativity, general theory of relativity, and cosmology, using the contribution of Albert Einstein as a case in study. The reason for this approach is twofold. First, it will point out Einstein's role in extending our understanding of energy by providing three major insights showing that: i) mass is a form of energy, ii) there is a close relationship between mass and energy, on the one hand and, the geometry of space-time and gravitation, on the other, iii) energy can exist in what can be called "vacuum"—the state of space with no matter present.[46] Second, it will somehow balance the discussion of the debate between Einstein and Bohr provided earlier, by pointing out Einstein's role in areas where Bohr did not contribute much. In fact, in a

45. Wilczek, *The Lightness of Being*, 74.
46. Randall, "Energy in Einstein's Universe," 299.

peculiar way, Einstein's opposition to quantum mechanics made him ignore part of the developments in fundamental physics after the late 1920s by focusing his efforts exclusively on general relativity, on the quest for a unified theory embracing gravity and electromagnetism, and on cosmology.[47]

Special theory of relativity and $E = mc^2$

The special relativity of Einstein came out of the study of electricity and magnetism. It arose from a description of the world based on the concept of field. As we have seen, fields are physical realities filling all space and mediating the interaction between physical particles, such as electrons, protons, and neutrons. This was a world different from Newton's world that was based on particles exerting forces on one another through empty space. The insights of special relativity, however, go far beyond electromagnetism since its essence is rooted in a symmetry principle—that the laws of physics should take the same form after an increase of the velocity of all objects by the same constant value. What Einstein really did was to change Newton's laws of classical physics of motion so that they obey the symmetry principle found it electromagnetism.[48]

The first of Einstein insights about the concept of energy was the association of mass with energy: "One more consequence of the electrodynamical paper has also occurred to me. The principle of relativity, together with Maxwell's equations, requires that mass be a direct measure of energy contained in a body; light transfers mass. . . . The argument is amusing and attractive; but I can't tell whether the Lord isn't laughing about it and playing a trick on me."[49] Einstein obviously talks about his famous equation $E = mc^2$ which holds for isolated bodies at rest. For moving bodies, the correct mass-energy equation becomes $E = \gamma mc^2$ and includes an additional factor $\gamma = 1/$

47. Gross, "Einstein and the Quest for a Unified Theory," 289.

48. Ibid., David Gross points out that this change of the laws of classical physics revolutionized the way we view symmetry and credits Einstein as the driver of this revolution. This point goes back to the fact that symmetries imply conservation laws such as the energy conservation law that was discussed earlier. Although conservation laws "were regarded to be of fundamental importance, they were regarded as consequences of the dynamic laws of nature rather than as consequences of symmetries that underlay these laws. . . . Einstein's great advance in 1905 was to put symmetry first, to regard the symmetry principle as the primary feature of nature that constrains the allowable dynamic laws." The symmetry implicit in the equations describing the electric and magnetic fields was elevated to symmetry of space-time itself. According to Gross, "this was the first instance of the *geometrization* of symmetry."

49. From a letter to Conrad Habicht in 1905, quoted by: Randall, "Energy in Einstein's Universe," 299 n. 97.

$(1-v^2/c^2)^{1/2}$ which depends on the velocity of the body v. Einstein's result implied that the mass of any body was equivalent to its energy at rest and did not assume a special role of the equation in electromagnetism.

The energy of being

The message coming from the equation $E = mc^2$ was rather radical—the concept energy associated with physical particles is not necessarily related to motion (kinetic energy) and positioning (potential energy): ". . . there is also an energy that a particle has from its mere existence, an energy that depends directly on the mass."[50] Therefore, in the world of isolated elementary particles "there are two significant forms of energy: the mass energy and the kinetic energy of motion. The mass energy of a particle is its energy of being."[51] Energy of being is proportional to mass. "Twice as much mass means twice as much energy, and no mass means no energy. . . . So mass represents a highly concentrated form of energy."[52]

It took many years before Einstein could assume in 1932 that his equation was experimentally confirmed[53] and it is now well known that $E = mc^2$ is correct. It is also known that the equation has significant consequences that could be seen in: i) the nuclear processes that sustain the burning of the sun, ii) the radioactivity, the reversed process of chemical element creation (it happened during the early stages of the evolution of the universe when particles and antiparticles were constantly created and destroyed as mass and energy were inter-converted—a process that happens today at particle accelerators),[54] iii) nuclear power and (hopefully not) in nuclear bombs, iv) the explanation of the origin of most (more than 95 percent) of the mass of known matter, which is due to the mass of protons and neutrons.

50. Feynman, *The Character of Physical Law*, 65.

51. Word, *The Quantum World*, 18.

52. Ibid., 19.

53. In 1932 Ernest Walton and John Cockcroft performed an experiment to split the Lithium atom nucleus by using accelerated protons and demonstrated that the kinetic energy gained by the two newly created Helium atom nuclei was equal to the mass that was lost during the experiment.

54. Randall, "Energy in Einstein's Universe," 303.

Energy, gravitation, and the geometry of space-time

The second of Einstein's insights about energy is related to his theory of gravitation. After the development of the special theory of relativity Einstein started looking for a way to include gravity into the new framework and, in the end, produced a field-based theory of gravity—general relativity. The fact that general relativity is a field theory should be of no surprise. One of the main insights from the special theory of relativity was the postulate that the velocity of light, c, is constant, but, even more importantly, limited. Therefore, the influence of one particle to another cannot be transmitted faster than that. Newton's law of the gravitational force did not obey that rule and was not consistent with special relativity theory. General relativity arose as an update of Newton's gravitation theory by fixing this inconsistency with the help of a field-based approach. Using the relativistic principles Einstein showed how energy creates a gravitational field playing the role that was previously occupied by mass alone. In his gravitation theory he related the metric or the curvature of the geometry of space-time to the gravitational field arising from any energy present, showing that gravity could be deeply encoded in the geometry of space-time. Mass and energy distort space-time, and the distorted space-time in turn accounts for gravitational effects on matter and energy (for example light) moving through it.[55]

Matter, dark matter, and dark energy

The third of Einstein's insights about energy is related to cosmology. In 1917, based on his two initial insights, Einstein derived the set of equations describing the metric of the space-time of the universe as a whole. He thought that the universe had a constant density in time and space, but eventually found out that there is no solution with those properties. To get the constant density solution Einstein added to the equations for gravity a new term called the "cosmological term" or the "cosmological constant."[56] The solution he found corresponded to a closed static universe—a big sphere with finite radius that stayed constant over time. This solution happened to be unstable. In addition, in 1929 Edwin Hubble provided convincing evidence that the universe is in fact expanding, leading Einstein to admit that the introduction of the cosmological term was his "greatest mistake" or "blunder."[57] Nevertheless, the possibility he identified, of adding a new term

55. Ibid.
56. Ibid., 304.
57. Penrose, "Causality, Quantum Theory and Cosmology," 149.

to the equations of general relativity to describe the universe, did not go away and became a matter of serious study in the following seventy years. Cosmological observations remained consistent with a cosmological constant equal to zero until about 1998, when convincing measurements began to indicate that there is indeed an accelerating cosmic expansion that could be explained by the presence of a cosmological term with a cc having a very small positive value.[58] Subsequent observations provided additional support for this and Einstein's introduction of the term in 1917, although introduced for the wrong reasons, was found to be prophetic.

The cc or the cosmic density was recently estimated by measuring its effects on the curvature of space through the distortion such curvature causes in images of distant galaxies.[59] It is a powerful new technique measuring some of the properties of the cosmic microwave background radiation (CMB).[60] Using this technique, by 2001 several groups made several important conclusions. First, the universe is made up of 30 percent matter. Second, only 5 percent of these 30 percent is the matter as we know it—the kind of matter we study in biology, chemistry, engineering, and geology and the kind of matter we are made from. The remaining 25 percent is a special type of (dark) matter—it is not uniformly distributed in space and its density is not constant in time. Observations suggest that it is based on a special (probably new) particle, but it is not clear what this particle is. The new Large Hadron Collider (LHC) in Geneva is expected to help in identifying the source of dark matter. Third, there is a 70 percent missing component which is not matter and which is considered as being contributed by the so-called dark energy. It appears to be very uniformly distributed in space and time and has been observed only through its gravitational influence on the motion of normal matter. This makes it look like a property of empty space. It has not been observed to absorb light, i.e., it is not dark in the usual sense, but transparent. The dark energy concept is directly associated with Einstein's cosmological term—although there are slight differences in the interpretation, they may refer to the same physical phenomenon.[61] "The theory of dark energy is in bad shape. It's a problem for the future."[62] The current guesses are that it is some sort of force field which permeates the vacuum, but there is no currently known theory of physics that could explain it.[63] On

58. Ibid.
59. Wilczek, *The Lightness of Being*, 108.
60. http://en.wikipedia.org/wiki/CMB
61. Wilczek, *The Lightness of Being*, 105.
62. Ibid., 195.
63. Wheeler, *Cosmic Catastrophes*, 282.

the other hand, "the dark-matter problem . . . is ripe for solution" and there are promising ideas that could explain what dark matter is.[64]

Final reflections on Einstein's contributions to the concept of energy

Some physicists believe that, with the addition of his cosmological term, Einstein in fact had identified a new form of energy that is associated with space-time itself—it is not carried by matter and not the result of the known forces, i.e., a kind of vacuum energy. This is the first time in physics when a new form of energy is identified together with a claim that there is maybe nothing carrying it. There are two other logical possibilities. Either we are now seeing the effects of some new substance that was not previously seen before, or there is something wrong with our theoretical worldview.[65] Nobody knows. What we clearly know, however, is that Einstein's work on energy was extraordinarily influential in providing the fundamental insights for our current understanding of this concept.

64. Ibid., 196.
65. Taylor, "The Dark Universe," 41.

Chapter 7

The Theology of St. Gregory Palamas in the Context of the Encounter between Theology and Physics

St. Gregory Palamas and the Distinction between Essence and Energy

The distinction between essence and energy is a key for the understanding of the theology of St. Gregory Palamas—it is the essence that is manifested through the energies and not vice versa. This is the fundamental epistemological premise of his theology—a premise that he applied also to all beings.

> With respect to the fact of its existence but not as to what it is, the substance is known from the energy, not the energy from the substance. And so, according to the theologians, God is known with respect to the fact of his existence not from his substance but from his providence. In this the energy is distinct from the substance, because the energy is what reveals, whereas the substance is that which is thereby revealed with respect to the fact of existence.[1]

Gregory Palamas did not define in great details the character of the distinction between essence and energy. For him the distinction is not just conceptual, but it is not real, either, in the sense of the scholastic terminology, where *distinctio realis* means a difference in substance. Energy is not an independent substance. The word reality (originating from the Latin word

1. Gregory Palamas, *One Hundred and Fifty Chapters*, Ch. 141, 247.

res) presupposes a difference in substance and it is difficult to express it in Greek. The Greek *pragma* means "something existing," but not necessarily an independent substance or essence. It belongs to the same group as the concept *praksis* and also means "something actual." In this sense St. Gregory Palamas usually calls the energies "things." He talks about an "actual distinction" (*pragmatike diakrisis*), opposing it, on the one hand, to the "actual division" that would remove the Divine unity and simplicity and, on the other hand, to a simple mental distinction (*diakrisis kat' epinoian*).[2]

The distinction between essence and energy in St. Gregory Palamas is directly associated with his theological point of departure—the real possibility for the knowledge of God and the deification of man.[3] This real distinction is unavoidable in connection with the doctrine of deification and Divine knowledge, since deification and Divine knowledge imply participation of man in the uncreated life of God[4] and God's essence remains transcendent and totally unparticipable.[5] For Palamas the energy *differs* from the essence, but is *not separated* from it. The essence refers to the immanent, self-identical being of God, while the energy means that God does something and He does it willingly. The energy does not denote something other in God than His essence, but is the *same* Divine being *as active ad extra*.[6] This activity ad extra includes God's works such as creating, sustaining, providing, deifying, etc. "When the activity is spoken 'objectively' as a divine work (*ergon*) or being, . . . we are not to imagine a something existing between the divine essence and creatures. The terms work and being denote . . . the reality of God's activity as a powerful presence."[7] God's works represent his activity or energies in relation to His creatures and God, as He is in Himself, should be distinguished from God as He related to something other than Himself. The Divine energies, however, are proper to God's essence even before God relates Himself to anything other through them. But it is only at the moment decided by the Divine will when the energies, which are eternally but potentially present in God, are actualized and actively manifested ad extra in relation to something other.[8] The articulation of this actualization of the Divine energies echoes St. Maximus the Confessor:

2. Krivoshein, "The Ascetic and Theological Doctrine of St. Gregory Palamas," 132.

3. Tollefsen, *The Christocentric Cosmology of St. Maximus the Confessor*, 140.

4. See the Gospel of John 17:3: "And this is eternal life, that they may know You, the only true God, and Jesus Christ whom you have sent."

5. Meyendorff, *Byzantine Theology*, 186.

6. Tollefsen, *The Christocentric Cosmology of St. Maximus the Confessor*, 141.

7. Ibid.

8. Ibid., 144–45.

"For I do not say that in these things providence is one thing and judgment another. But I know them as potentially one and the same, but having a differing and many-formed activity in relation to us."[9]

One of the main arguments of St. Gregory Palamas for the distinction between essence and energy is the plurality of the energies:

> As it has been made clear above by Basil the Great, the theologians treat the uncreated energy of God as multiple in that it is indivisibly divided. Since therefore the divine and divinizing illumination and grace is not the substance but the energy of God, for this reason it is treated not only in the singular but also in the plural. It is bestowed proportionately upon those who participate and, according to the capacity of those who receive it, it instills the divinizing radiance to a greater or lesser degree.[10]

The Divine energies are bestowed proportionally upon the participants according to the capacity of the recipients under the coordination of the Divine will and their plurality is due to the multiplicity of the hypostases of the participants. The Divine energy becomes multiple by being en-hypostasized by multiple participants but "God is indivisibly divided and united divisibly and experiences neither multiplicity nor composition."[11]

Ontology vs. epistemology

The Divine energy is what manifests *that* God is, while the essence is *what* He is. If there was no distinction between Divine essence and Divine energy, the fact that "God is" would have remained unknown. The focus here is on the knowledge of God, i.e., the distinction between essence and energy and the meaning of energy itself are articulated within an entirely epistemological context. Metropolitan Hierotheos Vlachos has clearly underlined the role of St. Gregory Palamas for Orthodox epistemology:

> We can see quite clearly the great significance of his teaching for Orthodoxy on the important issue of epistemology. When we say epistemology we mean the knowledge of God and, to be precise, we mean the way which we pursue in order to attain knowledge of God.[12]

9. Louth, *Maximus the Confessor* (Difficulty 10, 1136A), 113.

10. Gregory Palamas, *One Hundred and Fifty Chapters*, Ch. 69, 163.

11. Ibid., Ch. 81, 177.

12. Hierotheos, *Saint Gregory Palamas as a Hagiorite*, 23.

The ontology underlying St. Gregory's theological epistemology is the ontology of Divine-human communion, which is centered on the realism and experiential nature of the knowledge of the personal God. This ontology finds its source in the Incarnation and leads to an understanding of theology which is "antinomic" and rooted in the very being of God, which itself is being-in-antinomy insofar as He is simultaneously transcendent and immanent, revealed and hidden, visible and invisible, knowable and unknowable.[13] The antinomic theological terminology requires further clarifications that could be pointed out by a reference to Bishop Kallistos Ware, according to whom by "antinomy" in theology we mean:

> the affirmation of two contrasting or opposed truths, which cannot be reconciled on the level of discursive reason although a reconciliation is possible on the higher level of contemplative experience. Because God lies "beyond" the world in a unique sense, He cannot be precisely conceived by the human reason or exactly described by human language. But if there are no exact descriptions of God, there are many "pointers." In order to reach out towards that which is inconceivable, the Christian tradition speaks in "antinomic" fashion—as Newman put it, "saying and unsaying to a positive effect." If we rest satisfied with a strictly "logical" and "rational" theology—meaning by this the logic and reason of fallen man—then we risk making idols out of finite, human concepts. Antinomy helps us to shatter these idols and to point, beyond logic and discursive reason, to the living reality of the infinite and uncreated God.[14]

Although St. Gregory acknowledges the necessity of an antinomic terminology in the articulation of Divine realities, he keeps firm to the unity and coherence of the dogmatic teachings. According to him, the use of antinomies should not and must not lead to theological contradictions and inconsistencies which are a sign of theological and spiritual immaturity.[15] In fact, the value of true theology is exactly in moving beyond antinomies such as expressed in human discourse and in facing the Divine realities in Spirit and Truth. This, however, requires a ruthless application of logic and masterful avoiding of homonyms focusing on a clear discernment of the meaning of the terms and the things they signify.[16]

---

13. Papanikolaou, *Being with God*, 9.

14. Ware, "The Debate about Palamism," 46.

15. Kapriev, *Byzantica Minora*, 178.

16. Ibid.

The relationship between ontology and epistemology found in the theology of St. Gregory Palamas is different from the one that could be found in modern theological discourse where epistemology seems to be preceding ontology and is usually seeking to determine whether or not the so-called ontological questions are relevant.[17] St. Gregory's ontological presuppositions are also different from the ones found in the "classical physics epistemology" where all realities are considered as literally "revealed," fully given for exploration and able to be studied in completeness, independently of their inner nature. His epistemology, however, shows some trends that are very similar to the ones in non-classical or "quantum" epistemology, which is antinomic insofar as it could be described by the complementarity between waves and particles, between whole and its parts, between invisible properties and their visible energetic manifestations. The antinomic nature of the Divine realities is directly expressed in St. Gregory's comments on the Divine energies:

> God also possesses that which is not substance. Yet it is not the case that because it is not a substance it is an accident. For that which not only does not pass away but also admits or effects no increase or diminution whatever could not possibly be numbered among accidents. But it is not true that because this is neither an accident nor substance it belongs among totally non-existent things; rather, it exists and exists truly. It is not an accident since it is absolutely immutable, but it is not a substance for it is not one of those things that can subsist on its own. And so it is called a quasi-accident by some theologians who wish to indicate only that it is not a substance. What then? Since each of the hypostatic properties and each hypostasis is neither a substance nor an accident in God, are they each on this account ranked among non-existent things? Certainly not! Thus, in the same way, the Divine energy of God is neither a substance nor an accident nor is it classed among non-existent things.[18]

Relationship between parts and whole

The Divine epistemology of St. Gregory presupposes a special relationship between parts and whole. He, however, is not an innovator and follows the Byzantine tradition before him (especially St. Dionysius the Areopagite):

17. Papanikolaou, *Being with God*, 9.
18. Gregory Palamas, *One Hundred and Fifty Chapters*, Ch. 135, 241.

"God is spirit and those who worship him must worship in spirit and truth,"[19] that is, by conceiving the incorporeal incorporeally. For thus will they truly see him everywhere in his spirit and truth. Since God is spirit, he is incorporeal, but the incorporeal is not situated in place, nor circumscribed by spatial boundaries. Therefore, if someone says that God must be worshipped in some definite place among those in all earth and heaven, he does not speak truly nor does he worship truly. As incorporeal, God is nowhere; as God, he is everywhere. For if there is a mountain, place, or creature where God is not, he will be found circumscribed in something. He is everywhere then, for he is boundless. How then can he be everywhere? Because he is encompassed not by a part, but by the whole? Certainly not, for once again in that case he will be a body! Therefore, because he sustains and encompasses the universe, he is in himself both everywhere and also beyond the universe, worshipped by true worshippers in his spirit and truth.[20]

The debate between Barlaam the Calabrian and St. Gregory Palamas

The question about the use of normative or Aristotelian logic in the realm of the Divine realities was the major issue at the initial stage of the controversy between St. Gregory Palamas and Barlaam the Calabrian. Barlaam was the Byzantine representative in the discussions between Constantinople and Rome on the issue of the *Filioque*. The anti-Latin Treatises which Barlaam wrote in 1335 to explain the Orthodox point of view have as their object the refutation of the use of Aristotelian logistic proofs by scholastics in defending the *Filioque*. Barlaam's objective was to refute them by their own methods, by showing that their syllogisms prove to be fallacious. His point was that the truth-value of the *Filioque* cannot be demonstrated with syllogistic arguments such as expressed in Aristotle's *Posterior Analytics*. The fundamental movement of Barlaam's commentary in his preliminary debate with Gregory Palamas was an exposition of the epistemological ground of logical science, aimed at demonstrating the inappropriateness of its use in theology.[21]

19. John 4:24.

20. John 4:23.

21. Sinkewicz, "The Doctrine of Knowledge of God," 189.

The interest for us here lays in the fact that in this debate St. Gregory introduces the main concepts constituting his theology—being, existence, nature, essence, and energies—and uses them both theologically and in a broader philosophical context. In fact, it is during this initial stage of the controversy with Barlaam that the Athonite monk and future Metropolitan of Thessaloniki will articulate for the first time the core of his teaching on the essence and energies of God. It must be also noted that the articulation of the meaning of the above concepts and the doctrine itself emerged within an entirely epistemological context driven by the specifics of a discussion about the nature of human knowledge of God.[22] The particular use of the concepts provides us with the unique opportunity to explore the type of transformations they needed to undergo in order for them to function within the realm of the ontological intuitions of Byzantine theology.[23]

Points of clarification concerning the debate

Before moving forward, I need to point out that the initial stage of the controversy between Gregory Palamas and Baralaam seems to be quite understudied. Until recently, the major sources of information and interpretation of this debate available in English and French were Fr. John Meyendorff's original study on St. Gregory Palamas[24] and the works of Robert Sinkewicz.[25] Sinkewicz's opinion is that "the real winner of the first round of the debate was Barlaam"[26] and there are "serious doubts about whether Palamas has really understood Barlaam or even Aristotle, for the Athonite monk took certain liberties in his use of Aristotelian terminology which did not necessarily support his cause or further his true intentions."[27] More recently, Hakan Gunnarsson provided an additional analysis of some of the issues in this debate.[28] Gunnarsson also suggests that the discussion was fuelled by misunderstandings and that "Palamas never fully realized that the formal aspects of demonstration were at the heart of Barlaam's criticism of the Latins."[29] According to Gunnarsson "Palamas' argumentation sometimes

---

22. Ibid., 221.

23. Христов, "Битие и съществуване"; Христов, Византийското богословие през *XIV* век.

24. Meyendorff, *A Study of Gregory Palamas*; *Byzantine Hesychasm.*

25. Sinkewicz, "The Doctrine of Knowledge of God," 181–242.

26. Ibid., 188.

27. Ibid., 202.

28. Gunnarsson, *Mystical Realism in the Early Theology of Gregory Palamas.*

29. Ibid., 254.

does not meet the requirements of consistency, which could be explained by the fact that here and there he feels obliged to argue for ideas that he sees as fundamental principles, such as there *is* experience of the Divine, and hence is in danger of being trapped in circular reasoning."[30] St. Gregory was also found having "a tendency to escape into talking about paradoxes when he cannot sort things out."[31] Sinkewicz's and Gunnarsson's opinions have been recently echoed by other scholars.[32]

Both Sinkewicz and Gunnarsson clearly express their doubts about St. Gregory's correct understanding of Barlaam's precise use of Aristotelian terminology. At the same time, there is a clear awareness of the dangers of Barlaam's dominating Aristotelian perspective and ultimate unorthodoxy:

> Barlaam looked at knowledge through the eyes of a Platoniz-ing Aristotle and saw it as the way of human science whereby man understands the created world around him. The God who is infinitely transcendent to such a world cannot be subjected to the same type of knowledge. Palamas, on the contrary, ap-proached the problem from a patristic point of view and refused to acknowledge (or perhaps never understood) the validity and the importance of his opponent's treatment of the matter. Here once again Palamas failed to recognize the Calabrian's precise use of terminology and thus the distinction between Aristote-lian *episteme* (which was Barlaam's sole concern at the time) and *gnosis* in a different, a more general or theological sense (which for Barlaam was not the subject of discussion).[33]

> The discussion of demonstration in theology constitutes the first phase in the progressive, although not necessarily consistent, development of Barlaam's thought. This can be considered as his orthodox period, *pace* Palamas who never really understood what Barlaam was talking about.[34]

> The second letter to Palamas and the theories expressed there on illumination represent the second phase in the progression of Barlaam's thought which now begins to move away from the sure ground of orthodoxy.[35]

30. Ibid., 255.

31. Ibid.

32. Angold, "Byzantium and the West 1204–1453"; Krausmuller, "The Rise of He-sychasm"; Ierodiaknou, "The Anti-Logical Movement in the Fourteenth Century."

33. Sinkewicz, "The Doctrine of Knowledge of God," 219.

34. Ibid., 240.

35. Ibid., 241.

The opinions given above show some ambivalence—in an attempt to do justice to all possible details in the argumentation of the two opponents, they do not clearly point out to any logical pattern emerging from their positions. The major arguments used in support of the above opinions are based on two facts. *First*, at the Council of 1341 Barlaam was censured not about his views on the impossibility of using logical demonstration in theology but about "his opinions on the Light of Tabor and for having called the prayer of the Hesychasts Messalian or Bogomil," i.e., "Barlaam was never condemned for his criticism of the Latin's use of demonstration in theology."[36] *Second*, Neilos Kabasilas, the successor of Gregory Palamas as Metropolitan of Thessalonica, "in a treatise entitled 'That it is not possible for the Latins to demonstrate that the Holy Spirit proceeds from the Son' attacked the Latin, Thomistic theology, just as Barlaam had done, by criticizing the use of Aristotelian logic in theological arguments. . . . Neilos even went so far as to incorporate those passages that Barlaam had directed specifically against Palamas."[37]

The first point that needs to be underlined here is that the arguments of Gregory Palamas and Neilos Kabasilas were put forward against different opponents. Palamas' opponent was not a Latin theologian but Barlaam, i.e., supposedly one of his own Byzantines. Kabasilas' opponents were the Latins and he was trying, in the same way as Barlaam did, to refute them by their own methods, i.e., by showing them that their syllogisms proved to be fallacious. The important point here is that the early debate between Barlaam and St. Gregory was not about the fallaciousness of the Latin way of using syllogisms about Divine truths. St. Gregory admitted that Barlaam was justified in condemning the Latin way of using syllogisms. What he did not agree on were the reasons why they were fallacious. Barlaam was trying to refute the logical inconsistency of the Latin syllogisms based on the correct application of the rules of Aristotelian logic assuming as a premise the unknowability of God and His essence. St. Gregory's emphasis was on the reality of the knowledge of God, not in essence, but through His Divine energies, and he would not use this argument against the Latins since they would never accept it as a premise:

> If mathematicians do not have to answer a person who is totally
> ignorant of geometry and another ignorant of harmony partici-
> pating in a discourse dealing with statements about geometry
> or music, while he clearly does not adhere to the principles of
> geometry or music—although they both seek the principles

36. Ibid., 240.
37. Ibid.

themselves, we are much more entitled not to answer or discuss with anyone or reasoning syllogistically about the properties of God who is not employing the premises from theology.[38]

This quotation could provide a better glimpse on the reasons for Kabasilas' way of criticizing the Latins—he was trying to find the most efficient way for the refutation of his particular opponents' views. In other words, the difference in the opponents was driving a difference in the argumentation techniques.

The second point that needs to be underlined is that St. Gregory himself did not seem to look so dramatically at his early discussions with Barlaam. In his first direct letter to Barlaam, Palamas pointed out that he had merely been setting forth an alternative opinion and that Barlaam's view was equally legitimate, i.e., "it was unimportant if one spoke proof in a general sense or more specifically of apodictic demonstration, so long as the truth is preserved in all its clarity."[39] In the same time, he attacked the Calabrian both for his overly enthusiastic Hellenism and for his acceptance of the Divine illumination of the pagan philosophers. "On the surface, there is nothing particularly shocking in this, at least not to the modern reader. Palamas, however, perceived that there was something suspicious behind these statements and attacked Barlaam regarding them."[40] The suspicions of St. Gregory Palamas were proven correct since, as we know now, Barlaam was censured later on for his unorthodox views about the Hesychast way of prayer.

A third point that might be helpful in the interpretation of the facts is the existing contrast and confrontation between the lovers of secular "Hellenic" learning and the more spiritually driven monastic circles that had already distinctly emerged in fourteenth century Byzantium.[41] The domination of a "monastic" trend in the Byzantine Church was completed in 1347 with the victory of the civil war by John Cantacuzenos, but the process had begun much earlier. It was associated with a theological revival which was not directly connected with the negotiations for Church union or with anti-Latin polemics, but emerged within the Byzantine Church itself, reflecting its intellectual, spiritual, and social concerns. This spiritual orientation of the monastic theologians contrasted with the preoccupations of the Byzantine humanists and intellectuals, for whom the preservation of Greek heri-

---

38. Referenced by Gunnarsson, *Mystical Realism in the Early Theology of Gregory Palamas*, 107.

39. As referenced by Sinkewicz, "The Doctrine of Knowledge of God," 208.

40. Ibid., 241.

41. Meyendorff, *Byzantium and the Rise of Russia*, 100.

tage and Hellenic culture was of major importance. "There is no doubt that the leadership of Byzantine monasticism in the fourteenth century shared the traditional monastic distrust for 'secular studies' and Palamas attacked Barlaam precisely on the grounds that he forgot the only possible Christian meaning of the word *Hellēn*—that of 'pagan'—and accepted the ancient philosophers as guides in defining the criteria of Christian theology."[42]

This predominant trend in Byzantine intellectual life could explain the way Palamas used his knowledge of Aristotle in the temporal development of the controversy. In a sense, it was a provocative demonstration of a masterful handling of Aristotelian logic in the theological domain aiming at a meaningful reply to Barlaam's intellectualistic challenge expressed in his first letter to Gregory Palamas where "Not without a touch of mockery, Barlaam opened his letter to the Athonite by saying that, if Palamas had gone off to seek the heights of contemplation and forgotten the skills of expression, he should be more careful in his criticisms, because he has in fact failed to understand the problems at question."[43]

Another approach to the interpretation of the early stage of the debate

In this book I have adopted an interpretative perspective suggested by Ivan Christov[44] in a 1996 paper focusing on the distinction between being and existence in the theology of St. Gregory Palamas. It is based on the assumption that St. Gregory was very well versed in Aristotelian logic[45] and knew exactly what is going on. In fact St. Gregory, in his own turn, was trying to refute Barlaam in a way very similar to the one Barlaam himself used to refute the Latins—by arguing against what Barlaam believed to be his strength and accusing him of ignorance of Aristotelian logic. According to Christov, what St. Gregory really did was to go beyond the substantialist understanding of the logical forms by means of a specific existential interpretation, i.e., by reconsidering the ontological foundations of Aristotelian logic and enabling a radical transformation of the nature of the syllogistic

---

42. Ibid.

43. Sinkewicz, "The Doctrine of Knowledge of God," 223.

44. Христов, "Битие и съществуване," 36–48; Христов, *Византийското богословие през XIV век*, I.4; Христов, "Естествения разум и свръхестественото озарение," 125–34.

45. Comments on the validity of this assumption can be found in Gunnarsson, *Mystical Realism in the Early Theology of Gregory Palamas*, 24; 95.

proof within an entirely theological perspective. In a recent article[46] Julia Konstantinovsky provided a very similar interpretation, i.e., that "Palamas was as interested in and knowledgeable of Aristotelian logic as Barlaam or as any Western scholastic. Being a man of his age, Palamas used Aristotle as an intellectual framework for his own philosophical theology. Crucially, Palamas' syllogizing is at the service of Christian dogmatic theology and epistemology, and as such pursues theological purposes of its own. Palamas, therefore uses Aristotle creatively and transforms him."[47] In his approach St. Gregory was following the Church Fathers:

> With the folly of the Gospel the Fathers are secure masters in the school of theology, for the Spirit of true wisdom inhabits their spirits and renders taught by God those who turn to them as teachers. And if an element of profane learning is not discordant, they incorporate it and harmonize it with the melody of the Spirit.[48]

The Fathers did not hesitate to alter the speculations of Greek philosophers in order to harmonize them with the theology of the Church without being constrained by the restrictions imposed upon their usage by secular philosophy.[49] It is worth noting that Sinkewicz and Gunnarsson also indicated the fact that St. Gregory has put forward a new understanding of the logical demonstration.

> There emerges from this letter a notion of demonstration quite distinct from that advocated by Barlaam and ultimately by Aristotle. It is a notion that seeks its justification not in the Greek philosophers but in the tradition of the Fathers. . . . Ultimately, his overriding concern was to affirm that man possesses a true and clear knowledge of God which is free from the uncertainties of human science since it is granted by God himself.[50]

> Along with the statements of the Fathers, Palamas refers to some arguments which make it clear that his notion of demonstration does comprise much more than the Aristotelian scientific demonstration. Gregory Palamas expresses the idea that any knowledge requires demonstration; therefore, from Palamas'

---

46. Konstantinovsky, "Dionysius the Areopagite versus Aristotle?," 313–20.

47. Ibid., 318.

48. First letter of Gregory Palamas to Barlaam, as referenced by Sinkewicz, "The Doctrine of Knowledge of God," 210.

49. Romanides, *Patristic Theology*, 85.

50. Sinkewicz, "The Doctrine of Knowledge of God," 202.

epistemology the very denial of demonstration of Divine truths leads to the denial of *any* sure knowledge of God.[51]

Christov's starting point is historically well grounded[52] and helps in seeing the nature of the debate within a perspective that could very well be interpreted in the context of the analogical isomorphic approach suggested in the beginning of this essay. The situation looks very much like the situation in quantum physics where a new "quantum" logical framework was suggested by Bohr as a way to address the inconsistencies of the ontological presuppositions that emerged right in the heart of the new physics.

In the realm of the Divine, Aristotelian logic breaks down

Barlaam's approach is based on his own (inaccurate) understanding of the apophatic nature of Byzantine theology. He excludes the possibility that any reasoning about God could have a syllogistic character, i.e., the character of a proof. His argumentation is based on the direct application of Aristotelian logic to the Divine realities without any theological correction due to their uncreated and antinomic nature. According to him, there is a basic difference between Divine realities and realities that are subject to demonstration by human science. Created realities can never be more not-x than x, i.e., they must be or x or not-x and, since Dionysius the Areopagite indicates that such restriction does not apply to God, Barlaam concluded that God transcends the boundaries of Aristotelian logic.[53]

Barlaam's approach to the discussions with the Latins aimed at proving that their syllogisms are neither apodictic nor dialectic and, therefore, fallacious. In order to show the impropriety of the demonstrative syllogisms in the discussions over the *Filioque*, Barlaam took the basic requirements for such syllogisms which Aristotle laid down in the first section of his *Posterior Analytics*. According to him an apodictic proof should have the following characteristics: i) have the form of a syllogism which is general, affirmative and in the first figure;[54] ii) its middle term must exceed the minor term and be lesser in extent than the major term; iii) its premises must be true, primary, immediate, better known than and prior to the conclusion by nature; iv) the premises should reveal the essence of the object and must be the

---

51. Gunnarsson, *Mystical Realism in the Early Theology of Gregory Palamas*, 108.

52. Ibid., 24; 95.

53. Sinkewicz, "The Doctrine of Knowledge of God," 213.

54. The discussion here follows the logic of Христов, "Битие и съществуване," 41; Христов, *Византийското богословие през XIV век*, I.4.

cause of the conclusion, and v) the premises must refer to the same genus as the proposition to be proved. Using these characteristics Barlaam showed that they could not be applied to truths concerning God. His arguments could be grouped along two dimensions according to i) the nature of the terms, and ii) the nature of the premises.[55]

Barlaam's arguments according to the nature of the terms

In an apodictic syllogism which is affirmative and in the first figure the middle term must exceed the minor term and be lesser in extent than the major term. But in a theological proposition the minor term is God Who is One. Therefore, the minor term is singular. However, there is no proof for singulars.[56] According to Aristotle's logic the main advantage of using syllogisms in the first figure over those in the third figure is rooted in the fact that they are general and this is exactly what makes them better as logical proofs. In addition, the middle and the major terms must exceed the minor term, but nothing could exceed God Who is considered here as the minor term. [57]

Barlaam's arguments according to the nature of the premises

In an apodictic syllogism the premises should reveal the essence of the object and be the cause of the conclusion. In theological syllogisms, however, the premises cannot express the essence of God, which is unknowable. The premises must also refer to the same genus as the proposition to be proved, but no being is in the same genus as the Divine realities. In addition, the premises must be the causes of the conclusion, but no humanly conceived definition could be the cause of any reality in the realm of the Divine.[58]

Barlaam's approach to the refutation of the dialectic argumentation of the Latins was based on a similar procedure—he summarized Aristotle's basic principles on the subject and indicated how the Latin arguments did not meet these requirements. He insisted that in dialectic syllogisms it is necessary to formulate one's arguments on the basis of opinions

55. Ibid.

56. Christov, "Being and Existence," 41.

57. First letter of Barlaam to Palamas, as referenced by Христов, "Битие и съществуване," 47; Христов, *Византийското богословие през XIV век*, I.4.

58. Sinkewicz, "The Doctrine of the Knowledge of God," 190.

accepted by one's opponent. This, however, was impossible since there was no agreement between the Latin and the Greek positions on the procession of the Holy Spirit.[59]

The ontology underlying Barlaam's way of using Aristotelian logic

Barlaam's way of using Aristotelian logic is based on an ontology in which being is the same as existence. The sources of this ontology can be found in a neo-Platonic interpretation of Aristotle's *Metaphysics* where the concept of substance has a central place[60] and God's essence is believed to coincide with God's existence.[61] The substance is that essence which is the foundation of the existence of every being. "Substance, then, is the key to being."[62] The unity between essence and existence is the core of this interpretation of the Aristotelian philosophy of substance which is trying to move away from the division between beings and ideas. From this substantialist perspective the essence of a being is also its existence, i.e., every being contains the foundation of its existence in itself. However, "If something is a natural essence—indeed an essence of any kind—it must have a definition (*horismos*). For essences are the ontological correlates of definitions that are themselves the epistemological first principles of sciences. The fact that the sciences are structures of *demonstrations*, therefore, must be reflected in the definitions, and so in the essences they define."[63] Therefore syllogisms and proofs must possess a clearly expressed ontological meaning, i.e., apodictic proofs must reveal the essence of beings.

59. Ibid.

60. Reeve, *Substantial Knowledge*.

61. Most medieval theologians agreed that God's essence coincides with God's existence. See Kassim, *Aristotle and Aristotelianism*, 46: "Beginning with Plotinus and especially Proclus this distinction becomes blurred, either because of the futile attempt to overcome it or due to the fact that the import of Aristotle's connection was not understood properly. Later in the Middle Ages, especially with the interpretation of Aristotle's teachings by al-Farabi and Avicenna in Muslim Philosophy, whom Thomas Aquinas in Christian Philosophy and Maimonides in Jewish Philosophy followed, we find a radical departure from Aristotle's predicative mode of metaphysical inquiry which created a different brand of philosophy that is what one should characterize as Medieval Philosophy in spite of the assimilation of Aristotelian thoughts with modifications and different interpretations of Aristotelian concepts."

62. Reeve, *Substantial Knowledge*, 1.

63. Ibid., 70.

The ontological presuppositions of Barlaam's particular choice of the characteristics of an apodictic syllogism can be then summarized as follows. First, since the essence is something positive, the syllogism which expresses the essence should be affirmative. Second, since a syllogism must reveal in its definition the essence of things, the structural principle of the syllogistic forms should be the genus/species hierarchy. This is the reason for the specific epistemological value of syllogisms in the first figure, where the positioning of the major, middle, and minor terms is based on this hierarchy.[64]

The ontological presuppositions of St. Gregory Palamas's argumentation

The polemic of St. Gregory Palamas with Barlaam follows two main directions. First, St. Gregory in his own turn was trying to refute Barlaam in what he believed to be his strength by accusing him of ignorance of Aristotelian logic. The second direction focuses on another articulation of the ontological foundations of Aristotelian logic which leads to a radical transformation of the nature of the syllogistic proof. The distinction between essence/being and existence provides the ontological foundation for the development of a different teaching on the use of syllogistic proofs. It is not the Divine essence anymore that is the subject of syllogistic proofs but those aspects of the Divine being that are open for participation—the act of being, the Divine life, Wisdom, and Providence. These participations and participatory potentials represent the pre-eternal an approachable Divine essence in its openness towards all creation. In their totality, they offer the essential ground for participation of all beings in the ultimate Divine source of their existence. The existential finitude of the totality of participatory aspects of the Divine essence allows St. Gregory Palamas to call it and refer to it as "nature."[65] This nature is the source of the energies making possible the knowledge and experience of God and opening the possibility for a theological syllogistics. The causality in theological syllogisms pertains to the things around God, i.e., it is based on the Divine energies. This is why their premises and terms are positioned not according to human understanding but according to their own (Divine) nature.

This is the way St. Gregory addresses Barlaam's major arguments against the possibility of using apodictic syllogisms in theology. Theological

64. Христов, "Битие и съществуване," 47; Христов, *Византийското богословие през XIV век*, I.4.

65. Ibid. Gregory Palamas, *The Triads*, III, 2.12, 97.

proofs are not about singulars but about the One singular Who is the source of everything that is general. For the same reason, one cannot really speak of a purely quantitative subordination or positioning of the syllogistic terms since they all express the Divine energies and can be characterized by the same "general" uniqueness. In addition, the cause of the theological conclusions is nothing external to God and one cannot speak of anything that is ontologically and temporally prior to the Divine nature.[66]

The ontological presuppositions of St. Gregory Palamas are not an innovation. In the articulation of the distinction between essence and existence and between essence and energies he is following St. Maximus the Confessor with his distinction between the *logos* of essence and the *tropos* of existence.[67] The fact that this did not clearly come out of the temporal development of the discussions may be only due to the dominating role of Aristotelian syllogistic terminology.[68] It, however, provides the background for the understanding of St. Gregory's ontological presuppositions, epistemology, and overall logic during the debate.

St. Maximus the Confessor—Essence, Energies, and the *Logoi* of Creation

The *logos* of essence and the *tropos* of existence in St. Maximus the Confessor

The fundamental relationship between essence and energy is linked in St. Maximus the Confessor with the distinction *logos-tropos* which constitutes one of the major axes of his theological system.[69] The *logos-tropos* relationship was widely used before him for the articulation of the distinction between the essence and the hypostases of the Trinity.[70] St. Maximus, however, applies it more universally and moves it out of the purely Trinitarian

66. Ibid.

67. As we have already seen, some scholars may argue that in his articulation of the distinction between being and existence St. Gregory is actually following Aristotle himself. See Kassim, "Existence and Essence," Ch. 2, in *Aristotle and Aristotelianism*.

68. As we have seen earlier, in his first letter to St. Gregory, Barlaam accused him of ignorance of Aristotelian logic and philosophy. St. Gregory, on his turn, was trying to refute Barlaam's reasoning by attacking what Barlaam believed to be his strength—exactly, Aristotelian logic.

69. This section follows closely the analysis of Kapriev, *Philosophie in Byzanz*, 56–65.

70. Larchet, *La divinisation de l'homme selon saint Maxime le Confesseur*, 146.

context. This universality is considered as one of the main characteristics of his Christian philosophy.[71]

The doctrine of the *logoi* ("reasons") of creation is at the theological foundation of the Maximus' teaching on the knowledge of God. The *logos* of a thing is its formative cause, the principle of its beginning and purpose in terms of its being.[72] Every created reality has its associated *logos* corresponding to the inner law of its nature.[73] The *logos* is the carrier of the definition of the essence. Any change of the *logos* of an essence would destroy its nature and create a new nature corresponding to a new essence. The *logoi* of creation correspond to God's activity through which He creates, sustains, and guides all things towards Himself. The *logoi* pre-exist eternally in unity as models, goals or purposes of all creation in God Himself—the one *Logos*. Without loosing their unity in the Divine *Logos*, the *logoi* of creation become dynamic and differentiated when they are brought from potentiality into actuality at the creation of the world from nothing. Every created thing bears with it the manifestation or rather manifests its *logos*, and without this manifestation its *logos* cannot be made known.[74] The *logoi*, therefore, have both ontological and existential dimensions that are inseparable. The ontological dimension of the *logos* of a thing corresponds to its existential cause and nature. The existential dimension corresponds to the Divine thought, intention, and goal associated with the creation of that thing and directed towards the believer. The many *logoi* of the one *Logos* make the world a meeting place for Divine-human dialogue reflecting and manifesting God's thoughts and personal activity. "By seeking the *logoi* inherent in creation, man communes with the thoughts and intentions of God, which are directed towards him personally."[75] In this way the *Logos/logoi* relationship provides a personal dimension, a common meaning to every created reality. The common meaning of all things is the one Person of the *Logos* of God, i.e., "Jesus Christ is the 'bridge' to God on all levels of existence, not only through human nature (which He united to the divine in His hypostasis), but also as the one *Logos* of all the *logoi* which are found in all things."[76]

71. Ibid., 144.

72. Maximus the Confessor, "Ad Thalassium 64," in *On the Cosmic Mystery of Jesus Christ*, 145.

73. Louth, *Maximus the Confessor* (Difficulty 31, 1113BC), 101.

74. A detailed synthesis of the patristic understanding of the doctrine of the *logoi* of creation including Dionysius the Areopagite, Maximus the Confessor and Gregory Palamas, was provided in the works of Fr. Dumitru Stăniloae. See Berger, *Towards a Theological Gnoseology*, 191–232.

75. Ibid., 192.

76. Ibid., 196.

The *tropos* (the way) of existence is the mode of the natural activity. It is the carrier of any variation, modification or innovation on the background of the unchangeable *logos*.[77] The *tropos* is the form of the various manifestations of nature, it is the way in which the essence exists and functions. The transition from *logos* to *tropos* is a change from the essential to the existential order. The possession of a *logos* of essence and a *tropos* of existence is a prerequisite for the existence of every being.[78]

St. Maximus relates the *logos* to the essence of a being and the *tropos* to its hypostasis or person.[79] However, the mode of existence is a concept that is not immediately identified with the hypostasis or with the way of hypostatic existence.[80] For St. Maximus the term "existence" does not refer only to the hypostasis and the dyad essence-hypostasis has nothing to do with the medieval coincidence between essence and existence that will be later associated with Thomas Aquinas and that was found as an epistemological premise in Barlaam the Calabrian. St. Maximus does not associate the hypostatic mode of existence directly with the essence.[81] The *tropos* of existence is the way in which any nature actually exists. It denotes nature in its concrete reality. It is true that the *tropos* of existence is realized in a hypostasis, but this is only because there is no nature without a hypostasis.[82] A nature could be present in reality only as enhypostatic, where the hypostasis provides the format in which the way of existence of the enhypostatic nature is actualized.[83] The *tropos* of existence should be always considered in relation to the volitional disposition and choice of particular persons in which the variability of each essence or nature is actualized through a specific way of being.[84] The specific way of being manifests itself in accordance to, or against, the *logos* of nature which constitutes the foundational principle of a nature and defines the authentic destiny of everyone according the Divine ideas or wills. It is therefore through the tropos of existence and the specific way of being that someone could be judged to be just or unjust, to be closer or farther from his or her authentic Divine-given nature. According to Fr. N. Loudovikos,

77. Maximus the Confessor, "Ambiguum 42," *On the Cosmic Mystery of Christ*, 89–90 (1341D); Karayannis, *Maxime le Confesseur*, 206.

78. Ibid.

79. Larchet, *La divinisation de l'homme*, 145.

80. Ibid.

81. Maximus the Confessor, "Ambiguum 42," *On the Cosmic Mystery of Christ*, 91 (1344D); see also note 16 on p. 89.

82. Larchet, *La divinisation de l'homme*, 146.

83. Ibid.

84. Ibid., 147.

> By the *logoi* . . . God creates, that is proposes to beings their own essences and an ontological dialogue follows. If essence is thus given, its "mode of existence" is only the result of this dialogue between the logos word of God and the logos-word of man. That means that the final *esse* of created beings is unknown, indeterminate, because it is the eschatological result of a long dialogue between God and man, a dialogue which culminates in the cross and the resurrection of Christ. . . . So our participation in the divine energies is simply the way of our participation in the crucified and resurrected Christ.[85]

The manifestation of the essence is through its natural energy. Without it neither being, nor existence, would be possible.[86] It is exactly the *logos* of the essential energy that is the limit and the definition of the entire nature.[87] In this sense the energy reveals itself in two different aspects. As far as it is immanent, it is identified completely with the movement that is proper to the essence and, therefore, with the essence itself. But, in so far as it is transitive and directed outwards, it goes beyond that movement. These two aspects of the Divine energy are related to each other within the perspective of the *logos-tropos* relationship.[88] The immanent essential energy is beyond any existence (super-existential) and impossible to be expressed and understood. The (other) transitive energy represents the way of Divine existence. It is manifested outside of the essence and can be known to some extent. This is the energy that is active in all creation.[89] In this sense the *logos-tropos* relationship represents the ontological bridge opening the possibility for the direct knowledge of God through His uncreated energies.

Divine energies and the **logoi** of creation

The doctrine of the *logoi* has three distinctive aspects that could make it look complicated: i) the *logoi* are uncreated realities which are manifested in created things; ii) the *logos* of a thing has multiple ontological and existential dimensions; iii) the *logoi* have a parallel relationship and role with the

---

85. N. Loudovikos, "Ontology Celebrated," 147–48.

86. Maxime le Confesseur, "Ambigua à Thomas 5," in Maxime le Confesseur, *Ambigua*, 112.

87. Ibid. "Ambigua à Thomas 2," 103; "Ambigua à Thomas 5," 112.

88. Kapriev, *Philosophie in Byzanz*, 56–65.

89. Maximus Confessor. "Chapters on Knowledge," First century, Ch. 4, in Maximus Confessor, *Selected writings*, 129.

Divine uncreated energies.[90] The last aspect is of particular relevance for us here. "The primary purpose of the *logoi* reveals the attributes, thoughts, or intentions of God through created things, whereas the primary purpose of the uncreated energies is to bring about direct interpersonal communion. It could be said that the *logoi* reveal God as personal reality indirectly, whereas the uncreated energies reveal Him directly."[91] The *logoi* could be "seen" as uncreated energies only in their created effects. The uncreated energies, however, are not bound to any specific aspect of reality as are the *logoi* of things. The distinction between the *logoi* and the energies can be also seen in the fact that the vision of the *logoi* requires the assistance of grace, i.e., the intentional Divine energies assist in the uncovering of the *logoi* which are reflected in and seen though the created things: "The *logoi* in things are nothing but *logoi* from God, reflected in the mirror of things by intentional divine energies. From the *logoi* mirrored in imperfect ways in things, perspectives of ascent through the divine energies to the *logoi* from God are opened."[92] The role of the Divine energies in uncovering the *logoi* of creation shows that they are interrelated as a cooperative expression of the Divine will—an insight that could be found in St. Maximus the Confessor as an inheritance from Dionysius the Areopagite.[93] For St. Maximus the ultimate goal of the Divine economy is the deification of man and rational creatures are deified insofar as they move and act in accordance with their *logoi*[94] becoming, in this way, their own co-creators.[95]

The similarity between the *logoi* and the energies in St. Maximus does not mean their identification. "In places where Maximus uses both terms he clearly regards them as differing in reference. It would be more faithful to his usage to say that he splits the Cappadocian conception of the divine *energeiai* into three: one part relating to creation (the *logoi*), another to God's eternal attributes ("the things around God"), and the third to the activity an energy of God that can be shared by creatures (for which he tends to reserve

---

90. Berger, *Towards a Theological Gnoseology*, 217–29; Some other recent discussions of the relationship between the *logoi* of creation and divine energies in St. Maximums the Confessor and St. Gregory Palamas can be found in: Tollefsen, *The Christocentric Cosmology of St. Maximus the Confessor*; Kapriev, *Philosophie in Byzanz*; Bradshaw, *Aristotle East and West*, 201–7; Van Rossum, "The *logoi* of Creation and the Divine 'Energies,'" 213–17.

91. Berger, *Towards a Theological Gnoseology*, 222.

92. Ibid., 223 (a quotation from Dumitru Staniloae).

93. Bradshaw, *Aristotle East and West*, 205.

94. Maximus the Confessor, "Ambiguum 7," in *On the Cosmic Mystery of Christ*, 61 (1085A).

95. Bradshaw, *Aristotle East and West*, 206; Alexander (Golitzin), *Et Introibo ad Altare Dei*, 86; Larchet, *La divinisation de l'homme*, 120.

the name *energeia*). The point in using the term *logos* rather than *energeia* is to emphasize that God is present in creatures, not only as their creator and sustainer, but as their meaning and purpose."[96] Tollefsen suggests a similar way of interpreting the difference between the Divine *logoi* of creation and Divine energies in St. Maximus:

> one aspect of the divine operation ad extra is the activity, but the relation between the activity and the creatures in the created and in the redeemed status is regulated by another aspect of God's operation, i.e., by the diverse logoi, expressed as acts of wills instituting essences. By the logoi God diversifies the possible relations that creatures might have to Him, because through these logoi He regulates participation according to nature, according to merit and according to deifying grace. This is an important structure in Maximus' ontology of the cosmic drama which takes place 'between' procession and conversion.[97]

In what it concerns St. Gregory Palamas, it should be pointed out that there is a clear difference in context between his theology of the Divine energies and the St. Maximus doctrine of the *logoi* of creation:

> Palamas' theology is in fact a *doctrine of God*, while Maximus' doctrine of the *logoi* deals with the *world* which is anchored or rooted in God. In other words, Maximus' theology of the *logoi* deals with *cosmology*, while Palamas' theology of the divine "energies" deals with theology proper (*theologia*).[98]

In this sense, the Maximian doctrine of the *logoi* could be used as another starting point for the development of a dialogical platform between physics and theology.

Divine Energies, Personal Dynamism, and the Reality of Divine-Human Communion

The reality of mystical experience

In a way similar to the situation in quantum physics, where Bohr's defense of the dynamic non-local aspects of quantum objects was used to accuse

96. Ibid.

97. Tollefsen, *The Christocentric Cosmology of St. Maximus the Confessor*, 174.

98. Van Rossum, "The *logoi* of Creation and the Divine 'Energies,'" 216.

him of antirealism, St. Gregory Palamas was found by some to be excessive
in the way he articulated the reality of mystical experience:

> The stress Palamas places on the light as not being created and
> as eternal, having no end and no beginning, is developed with
> special reference to the defense of the Divine light that appears
> to the Hesychast in prayer. If this light—which was supposed to
> be equal to the light that was present at the Transfiguration of
> Christ, and hence often referred to as the "Tabor-light"—was a
> *real* manifestation of God, then, one must ask, should it not be
> co-existent with God, who is eternal? The discussion about the
> energies of God and His essence thus emerges quite naturally
> from the previous statements about the Divine light. It is these
> statements of Palamas, stressing that the light that presents itself
> to the Hesychasts *is* God, which bring the question about the
> ontological properties of the light to its head.[99]

For St. Gregory the Divine energy is not a Divine function which exists
on account of creatures. Even if creatures did not exist, God would manifest
Himself beyond His essence. Indeed, as Vladimir Lossky pointed out, "expressions, such as 'manifest Himself' and 'beyond' are really inappropriate,
for the 'beyond' in question only begins to exist with the creation, and 'manifestation' is only conceivable when there is some realm foreign to Him Who
is manifested. In using such defective expressions, such inadequate images,
we acknowledge the absolute, non-relative character of the natural and eternal expansive energy, proper to God."[100] The Divine energies provide the
personal dynamics of the Divine-human relationship but "God is infinitely
beyond all his operations—both essentially and as a personal reality."[101] In
his discussion of the Transfiguration St. Gregory follows St. Maximus pointing out that it was not Christ who was transfigured when he was seen in
glory but the disciples, who were momentarily enabled to see him as He
truly and eternally is. "They passed over from flesh to spirit before they had
put aside this fleshly life, by the change in the activities of sense that the
Spirit worked in them, lifting the veils of the passions from the intellectual
power that was in them."[102] There are several important messages here: i) the
divine energies are both relational (intentionally directed towards us) and
non-relative (existing beyond any relation and independently of us), ii) the
perception of the Divine presence in the world is a Divine initiative but

99. Gunnarsson, *Mystical Realism in the Early Theology of Gregory Palamas*, 233.

100. Lossky, *The Mystical Theology of the Eastern Church*, 74.

101. Berger, *Towards a Theological Gnoseology*, 221.

102. Louth, *Maximus the Confessor* (Difficulty 10, 1128A), 109.

requires cooperation, ascetical struggle and liberation from the passions, iii) the personal relationship between God and man could be described as synergy—a two-fold understanding of the Divine and human energies as an activity that can be shared, and as the natural accompaniment and manifestation of the inner personal being of the one who acts, iv) the synergetic understanding of the Divine energies could explain both our potential for deification and our inability to reach deification on our own or without proper spiritual preparation.

The personal dynamism of Divine-human communion

It is important to underline the personal dynamic nature of the Divine energies. Although God affects things and persons on each occasion through a particular energy or operation, it is always Him personally acting and wholly present in it:

> The operations which produce the attributes of the world are, therefore, bearers of certain attributes found in God in a simple and incomprehensible way. The operations, therefore, are nothing other than the attributes of God in motion—or God Himself, the simple One, in a motion which is, on every occasion, specific, or again, in a number of different kinds of motion, specified and unified among themselves. God Himself is in each of these operations or energies, simultaneously whole, active, and beyond operation and movement. . . . We only know the attributes of God in their dynamism and to the extent that we participate in them. . . . [W]e only know them through the prism of the effect they produce in the world. God Himself changes for our sake in His operations, remaining simple as the source of these operations and being wholly present in each one of them.[103]

The nature of the Divine energies cannot be grasped except dynamically, as a result of God's personal activity and will. It is exactly this Divine personal dynamics that makes the invisible God visibly present in the world. In a way similar to the situation in quantum physics, these dynamic personal (hypostatic) presence and manifestations cannot be considered apart from us. We are co-participants in this inter-action to the measure of our personal participation and humble cooperation which are borne within the specific context and status of our spiritual sensitivity and the

---

103. Staniloae, *Orthodox Dogmatic Theology*, Vol. 1, 125–26.

authenticity of our sacramental life. The personal character of Divine-human communion and "energetic cooperation" bears the signs of personal specificity, historicity, and spiritual conditioning. The Divine energies are "God for us" as persons to the measure of each and every one's personal response and receptivity, ascetic struggle, humility, and love. Bishop Kallistos Ware, one of the distinguished Orthodox theologians today, provides important additional details:

> But God's energies, which are God himself, fill the whole world, and by grace all may come to participate in them. The God who is "essentially" unknowable is thus "existentially" or "energetically" revealed. This doctrine of the immanent energies implies an intensively dynamic vision of the relationship between God and world. The whole cosmos is a vast burning bush, permeated but not consumed by the uncreated fire of the Divine energies. These energies are "God with us." They are the power of God at work within man, the life of God in which he shares. Because of the omnipresence of the Divine energies, each of us can know himself as made in the image of God. Through the Divine energies, Jesus Christ ceases to be for us an historical figure from the distant past, with whose story we are familiar from the books, and he becomes an immediate presence, our personal Saviour. Through the Divine energies we know him not merely as a human teacher but as the pre-eternal *Logos*.[104]

It is important to point out that one of the fundamental reasons for using the distinction between essence and energies in Orthodox Theology is to underline the reality of the personal relationship between God and man and the deeply ontological nature of the human participation in the Divine:

> Cette distinction veut suggérer deux choses: d'une part, que Dieu n'est pas un objet qui se présenterait de soi et indépendamment de son libre vouloir aux intelligences créées, et que celles-ci ne pourront jamais le connaitre comme il se connait lui-meme, ni fusionner avec lui. Toute connaissance de son Être et toute participation sont entièrement dépendantes de sa libre initiative, mesurée a la capacité actuelle de la créature, et tendant à élever celle-ci a un plus haut degré de participation, sans que soit jamais épuisé l'abîme sans fond de la divinité. D'autre part, cette distinction entre l'essence divine et les énergies signifie que l'homme peut participer réellement à une réalité incréée, au rayonnement de l'Être divin, à ce que l'Écriture appelle sa gloire.[105]

104. Ware, "God hidden and revealed," 125–36.
105. Deseille, *Certitude de l'Invisible*, 64.

Divine energies and space-time

God as personal reality exists on multiple planes including both eternity and our time.[106] His personal relations with us on both these planes are effectuated through His uncreated energies and activities. "The plane of time and the plane of eternity are two modes of existence which are inter-related, and not only can the person exist on both, but the very planes themselves would not be understood outside of the person."[107] God gives real being to all created things and persons, and sustains their develop-ment through His uncreated energies. In this sense, time came out of His eternity and He is present in it by opening the realm of His eternity to man. Time began simultaneously with the created world. "Creation of the world is not a temporal act. The world was not created *in time*, the world is created *with time*."[108] When there was no world, there was no time and without the world there is no time. "And the genesis of the world is the beginning of time. This beginning, as St. Basil the Great explains, is not yet time, nor even a fraction of time, just as the beginning of a road is not yet the road itself."[109] Time is "a kind of ladder" extended by God towards the created world in anticipation of its rejoining and deification through the synergetic cooperation with the Divine.

> Saint Gregory Palamas, quoting Saint Maximus, also says that one who has been deified becomes "without beginning" and "without end." He also quotes Saint Basil the great who says that anyone who shares in the grace of Christ "shares in his eternal glory"; and Saint Gregory of Nyssa who observes that man who participates in grace "transcends his own nature, he who was subject to corruption in his mortality, becomes immune from it in his immortality, eternal from being fixed in time—in a word, a god from a man."[110]

God created man and the world for eternity. But eternity is won through a movement towards God which comes about in time and implies the need of both space and time.[111] Time is the ladder extended by the eter-nity of God placed at our disposal, according to each one's own measure,

106. See the sections focusing on the discussion of eternity in "The Super-Essential Attributes of God," Ch. 8 in Stăniloae, *Orthodox Dogmatic Theology*, Vol. 1, 150–71.

107. Berger, *Towards a Theological Gnoseology*, 177.

108. Heller, "Where Physics Meets Metaphysics," 243.

109. Florovsky, "Creation and Creaturehood," 43.

110. Quoted by Stăniloae, *Orthodox Dogmatic Theology*, Vol. 1, 154.

111. Ibid.

through the Divine energies which are carried out on each one's proper level. It becomes the condition for the dynamic interpersonal relationship and union with the eternal God as well as a road towards eternity. In relation to us the eternal God takes a position of anticipation and expectant waiting.[112] There is therefore a remaining distance between us and Him. This distance, however, has a place within the plan of salvation as an expression of the Divine love. "The distance is time understood both as an expectant waiting for an eternity that is directed towards creatures and the hope of the creature towards eternity. This distance will be overcome only in the full final union between us and God."[113] On this road to eternity God shares with us the experience of the expectant waiting and the experience of time, putting on one single plane His energies and our relationship with Him. Time, therefore, cannot be thought on a plane other than the plane of his inter-personal Divine energies.

God is beyond any system of reference and transcends space as He transcends time:

> Since God is spirit, he is incorporeal, but the incorporeal is not situated in place, nor circumscribed by spatial boundaries. Therefore, if someone says that God must be worshipped in some definite place among those in all earth and heaven, he does not speak truly nor does he worship truly. As incorporeal, God is nowhere; as God, he is everywhere. For if there is a mountain, place, or creature where God is not, he will be found circumscribed in something. He is everywhere then, for he is boundless. How then can he be everywhere? Because he is encompassed not by a part, but by the whole? Certainly not, for once again in that case he will be a body! Therefore, because he sustains and encompasses the universe, he is in himself both everywhere and also beyond the universe, worshipped by true worshippers in his spirit and truth.[114]

Space is the form of the relation between God and man, that spiritual "metric" which makes possible the attraction, interaction and movement between persons including the movement towards the Divine persons of the Trinity.[115] It emerges in association with Divine action or is rather defined by the field of Divine action. The following text of St. John Damascene is particularly relevant here:

112. Ibid., 158.

113. Ibid.

114. Gregory Palamas, *One Hundred and Fifty Chapters*, Ch. 60, 155.

115. Stâniloae, *Orthodox Dogmatic Theology*, Vol. 1, 171.

God is not in place, for He is the place of Himself, filling all things and being above all, and holding together all things. When, however, He is said to be in place, this place of God clearly specifies where His energy is at work. This is because He pervades all things without mingling, and is in all through His own energy according to the fitness and receptivity of each.[116]

Therefore, the "places of God are those in whom God's energy is clearly manifested to us."[117] In other words, "the noetic (i.e., spiritual and not somatic) energy of God embraces and transcends the somatic space-time parameters of the universe and refashions them. . . . For Theology the basis of the universe is the uncreated energy of God and the will of God which transcends nothingness, the empty space that lacks existence and on which the limited existence of the created universe is established and floats."[118]

Final Reflections

In concluding this section, I will focus on discussing the potential value of this exploratory study, i.e., its relevance for the science-theology dialogue. In a recent insightful essay Michael Heller offered an answer to the question whether science and theology can nowadays interact with profit for both sides. His insights will be useful in articulating the final reflections concluding this section.

> The profit for theology is obvious; the question at stake is to become relevant for men and women in our times. To see the profit for science is less obvious, but we should take into account the fact that much of Western science, such as for instance Newton's ideas, are imbued with things taken ultimately from theology, and it is better to be aware of this than not. To understand science is a part of the understanding of the world.[119]

Heller has pointed out the delicate nature of the matter, arguing that the interface between science and theology must be based on extremely "fine-tuned" principles. This is because the "so-called 'building bridges' between science and theology without any balanced methodological care easily results in doctrinal anarchy, and even deepens the existing conflict

116. John of Damascus, *Orthodox Faith*, I, XIII, 197.

117. Ibid.

118. Ibid.

119. Heller, "Where Physics Meets Metaphysics," 246.

between them."[120] I could not agree more with Michael Heller and believe that one of the dimensions of the potential value of the present study within the context of the science-theology dialogue is exactly methodological. I believe that in exploring the parallels between the uses of two similar terms in two different fields, it is important to see *first* how these two terms operate in *their own* natural conceptual environment and *then* let the differences or parallels in their meaning and context of use emerge on their own. This is why I have focused on the exposition of the concepts of energy in physics and theology guided by the analogical isomorphism method without forcing a speculative interpenetration between them. One simple conclusion from the application of this method could be the realization that in the way they are using the concept of energy, both physicists and theologians are trying to deal with very similar issues. An example of such an issue is making the limits of our knowledge become part of our knowledge itself. Another example is the articulation of the visible manifestations, properties, and nature of invisible realities.[121]

A second aspect of the potential value of the present study is related to the establishment of a common exploratory ground—epistemology. As we shall see later in this book, this is a subtle epistemology that is effectuated by a dynamic apophatic realistic ontology. I have already pointed out that the epistemological aspects of the concept of energy are clearly articulated in Orthodox theology and not so much in physics where the concept plays a more descriptive and (through the energy conservation law) more operational role. It is true that these aspects become significantly more relevant in modern quantum physics, but still they appear in between the lines, rather than in a straightforward manner. Whether or not theology could inspire a better focus on the epistemological aspects of the concept of energy in physics is an open question. The identification of the common exploratory ground however, is considered as having value on its own.

A third aspect of the potential value of this study is the identification or the emergence of specific cross-disciplinary insights. In what concerns the physics → theology direction, it seems to me that an appropriation of the century-long insights of quantum mechanics, quantum electrodynamics, space-time physics, and gravitation (with the fundamental place of the concept of energy in them) could be particularly valuable to theology.[122] Here I

---

120. Ibid., 241.

121. For example dark matter and dark energy appear to be perfectly invisible and transparent. They interact with ordinary matter only very feebly, if at all. The only way they have been detected is through their gravitational influence on the orbits of ordinary stars and galaxies, the things we do see. See Wilczek, *The Lightness of Being*, 203.

122. And, as a matter of fact, for the social sciences and humanities in general.

do not mean just the value coming from a conceptual cross-fertilization of theology that would help the enrichment of the apophatic language used in the description of the mysteries of faith. What I do mean is the value coming from the opportunity to open an illuminating window to the richness of the theological "space-time insights" themselves. (I cannot stop being amazed by the words of St. John of Damascus: ". . . this place of God clearly specifies where His energy is at work.")

Another cross-disciplinary insight could be found in the realization that modern quantum physics cannot operate without the immersion of the observer into the experiential realm of the dynamic processes emerging from observer's interaction with a quantum object or system. This view has become part of the philosophy of physics and has been continuously affecting the way people reason in general. The experiential nature of Orthodox theology is revealed by grace, in the life in Christ. We are led to truth by experiencing the Truth and this is accomplished not by learning "dry legalistic facts but by entering into the interactive processes within the whole Body of Christ."[123] Orthodox theology understood and adopted this concept long before the "mind of science" perceived it. "The connection between the two: the processes of science and the processes of our theology are not identical in essence, but in a real sense, they are related in concept."[124] It should be possible to utilize this fact in a positive way expounding the existential insights of Orthodox theology to those outside the Church.[125]

In what concerns the theology → physics direction, one of the clearest insights that comes from Byzantine theological history is the affirmation of the hypostatic nature of any energetic manifestations—energy is always the energy of something or someone and there are no anhypostatic energies flying in the world in the anticipation of being enhypostasized by selected people. In all of its history Orthodox theology has firmly rejected all attempts to talk about anhypostatic presences and manifestations. Its theological message could be formulated as a warning with respect to some of the current interpretations of dark energy in the universe which tend to consider it as the energy of nothing (or energy of the absolute vacuum, whatever that means). Theology will not explain what the hypostatic source of dark energy in physics is. It could, however, keep pointing out that there must be one, promoting at the same time a kind of terminological hygiene that would resists the introduction and use of terms such as "energy of nothing," "God

---

123. Puhalo, *The Evidence of Things Not Seen*, 33.

124. Ibid., 34.

125. Ibid.

particle,"[126] and even "dark energy," which, as we have seen, has nothing to do with darkness.[127]

The last aspect of the potential value of this essay is the identification of the major differences in the use of the concepts that could potentially, due to methodological negligence or excessive enthusiasm, harm the creation of bridges between science and theology. There are two important points here. *The first one* is about the difference between personal and impersonal realities. The concept of energy in physics deals with the articulation of our experiences with physical objects and systems. It helps in describing the manifestations of the inner nature of invisible physical realities. To actualize these manifestations we need to bring them up by interacting with the object or system under study and, ultimately, disturbing these the objects or systems in a way that will lead to the manifestation of their specific natural response. The concept of energy in theology is associated with the nature, personal manifestations, and will of a living and loving God. The Divine energies impregnate the language describing our personal relationship with God. "God descends into the world—and unveils not only his countenance to man but actually appears to him. Revelation is comprehended by faith and faith is vision and perception. God appears to man and man beholds God. The truths of faith are truths of experience, truths of a face."[128] We cannot, however, consider our relationship with God in terms of a communicative mastership on our part but within the context of a humble attitude, ascetic discipline, and spiritual life of prayer. We are seeking God's love and will eventually experience it only because He was the first One to find us and open Himself to us. We pray and glorify Him, but his loving answers to our prayers may be "yes," "no," and "not yet."

The second point is about the ultimate goals of physics and theology that are at stake here. We can easily understand that physics ultimately deals with the beauty and the comprehensibility of the world around us and our place in it. It is an expression of our honest appreciation of the fundamental context of human existence. Physics, however, does not deal with questions concerning the purpose and meaning of life. Hoping that physics will provide answers to these questions means to look for answers to questions that physics has never asked. Theology is "the science" dealing with the purpose and ultimate goal of human life, human authenticity, and eschatological destiny. This is why the authenticity of our theological worldviews is so

---

126. http://en.wikipedia.org/wiki/Higgs_boson

127. Dark energy is "a term that has caught on broadly, but is just a mask to hide our ignorance of what is going on." See Wheeler, *Cosmic Catastrophes*, 282.

128. Florovsky, "Revelation, Philosophy and Theology," 21–40.

important—it is ultimately a question about life and death, it is about life eternal which, according to the Gospel of John, is to know God Himself. Interestingly enough, the distinction between Divine essence and energies has emerged in Christian theology to deal exactly with the articulation of our experience and knowledge of God. The difference in the two contexts is crucial and should be always kept in mind.

Chapter 8 _____

The Language of Orthodox Theology & Quantum Mechanics— St. Gregory Palamas & Niels Bohr[1]

Introduction

The terminological or linguistic aspects of Orthodox theology are highly relevant within the context of post-modernity which is posing challenges to both, the mission of the Orthodox Church today and her attitude towards scientific progress in general. Christos Yannaras points out that one of the key characteristics of post-modernity is the emergence of a new language in dealing with ontology and reality, a language emerging from two different scientific disciplines—quantum mechanics and post-Freudian psychology.[2] Christos Yannaras sees the post-modern duty of the Church in the creative appropriation (and not simply adoption) of this new language aiming at linking the salvific message of the gospel to linguistic categories that could be more efficient in the interpretation of "the reality of existence, the appearance and disclosure of being,"[3] and more specifically, in the articulation of the experiential mode of the relationship between God, world, and man.[4] According to Yannaras, such appropriation could become the source of a

---

1. The original text of this chapter was presented at the International Conference "St. Gregory Palamas: The Theological and Philosophical Significance of his work," March 7–15, 2012, Thessaloniki, Greece. A modified version was published in: Dragas, Pavlov and Tanev, *Orthodox theology and the Sciences*.

2. Yannaras, "Christos Yannaras in a conversation with Kalin Yanakiev."

3. Yannaras, *Elements of Faith*, Ch. 6.

4. Yannaras, "Christos Yannaras in a conversation with Kalin Yanakiev."

new proposal coming from the Church to deal with post-modernity and not just to modernize herself.

I am not sure if I agree (or how much exactly I agree) with Yannaras. I would however agree with him that our present situation might be able to provide a greater advantage, as compared to the age of the Church Fathers, who were very much proficient in the sciences of their own time, but still did not have the amazing access to scientific information that is openly accessible today and that could be found helpful for a better articulation of the distinction between what is real and unreal, between reality and its deceiving reflected image—the "idol."[5]

According to others, the challenge of post-modernity is related to the apparent failure of the post-modern epistemological project to secure a secular basis for philosophy by transforming the metaphysical search for the ultimate ground of reality into a quest for its epistemic foundations.[6] According to Scott Pentecost, it is exactly this failure that constitutes post-modernity.[7] It resulted into a shift of focus from exploring and partaking of reality to an obsession with the methodological correctitude of the knowing process, thus detaching, or emptying, language from its inherent link to reality and from its eventful ontological resourcing. Unfortunately, a very similar "post-modern" trend can be found also in everyday Church life where many of the words appear to have lost their authentic meaning and power.[8] This is a danger with significant theological and ecclesial implications since one can formally adopt the dogmatic articulation of the faith, and even turn it into a linguistic idol, without really encountering or partaking of the sacramental events. According to Yannaras, this could not be called a real heresy, but it is a real tragedy.[9] According to the late Fr. John Romanides, the detachment of spiritual life from the cognitive content of contemplative experience is exactly the point where belief turns into superstition and Orthodoxy turns into a religion.[10]

The objective of this chapter is to provide an analytical framework that would enable the comparison of the ways of using words and language in the cases of St. Gregory Palamas and Niels Bohr.[11] The main motivation

---

5. Ibid.

6. Pentecost, *Quest of the Divine Presence*, 1, referring to Dupre, *Metaphysics and Culture*.

7. Ibid.

8. Yannaras, "Christos Yannaras in a conversation with Kalin Yanakiev."

9. Ibid.

10. Romanides, *Patristic Theology*, 45.

11. Tanev, "Essence and Energy," 89–153.

will be to explore Christos Yannaras' point about the opportunity of using quantum mechanics as a source of a new language that could be useful in enhancing the power of theological statements. It is important to point out that the main goal here is to use the insights from existing studies to provide a preliminary comparative analysis. The novelty in such an approach should be sought in the possibility of using the comparison to identify common linguistic themes, the discussion of which could become a source of insights for both theology and physics. On one hand, such an approach could be methodologically beneficial for the ongoing science-theology dialogue. On the other hand, it could be highly relevant within the context of Christian homiletics and apologetics and it is precisely this aspect that is of greatest interest here. The discussion will necessarily focus on epistemological issues, touching on the nature of the relation between the meaning of words and the reality they represent. The focus on epistemological issues could be justified by the fact that both St. Gregory Palamas and Niels Bohr have been acknowledged for their epistemological insights.

St. Gregory Palamas

The controversy between Barlaam the Calabrian and St. Gregory Palamas

The controversy between Barlaam the Calabrian and St. Gregory Palamas has become the subject of multiple recent studies.[12] The goal of this section is to emphasize one particular perspective[13] which focuses on some of the linguistic aspects of the debate. The key charge of Barlaam against the Hesychasts was their claim about the vision of the Divine light. He did not dispute the experience itself but its interpretation. According to him the interpretation could be based on one out of two possible options: the monks are speaking either about a sensible light, or about the *ousia* of

12. Meyendorff, *A Study of Gregory Palamas*; *Byzantine Hesychasm*; Sinkewicz, "The Doctrine of Knowledge of God"; Христов, "Битие и съществуване"; Христов, Византийското богословие през *XIV* век; Стоядинов, Божията благодат; Христов, "Естествения разум и свръхестественото озарение," 125–34; Gunnarsson, *Mystical Realism in the Early Theology of Gregory Palamas*; Konstantinovsky, "Dionysius the Areopagite versus Aristotle?"; Tanev, "Essence and energy," 89–153; Танев, Ти, Който си навсякъде и всичко изпълваш; Gerogiorgakis, "The Controversy between Barlaam of Calabria and Gregory Palamas," 157–69.

13. This section follows the logic and some of the references suggested in the insightful work of Pentecost, *Quest of the Divine Presence*. The author is grateful to Dr. Pentecost for pointing out the linguistic perspective of the debate between St. Gregory Palamas and Barlaam the Calabrian.

God. And since, according to Barlaam, the Divine *ousia* is unknowable, there is one single option left—the light that was seen by the monks and by the Apostles on mount Tabor is a sensible creaturely phenomenon.[14] According to Barlaam, there can be no contemplation of a divine light per se because the only light that can be contemplated by the intellect is related to the knowledge of creatures or "the knowledge expressed in words."[15] And the knowledge possessed by the mind remains always associated with rational discourse.[16] This relationship between Divine knowledge, knowledge about creatures, and the words expressing them was a point that became the subject of Palamas' criticism.

"By my words I stand against other words and not against the one who speaks"

It is important to point out that from the very beginning of the controversy St. Gregory puts an emphasis on the discursive format of their discussion by asking Barlaam to put his thoughts in writing and by engaging into a written defense of the Hesychasts. As the controversy develops, St. Gregory makes it clear that the discussion between them is not a personal issue and he does not oppose Barlaam himself but his words[17] and it is precisely Barlaam's words (i.e., his written and defended opinions) that become the source of his concerns. St. Gregory points out that in his opposition he is not arguing for himself but has taken the burden to speak on behalf of his less illiterate fellow brothers monks. Thus, the discussion moves into the context of the spiritual practices of the Church. "It ought to have sufficed to tell this man who fights about words and presents himself combatively that it is

---

14. Pentecost, *Quest of the Divine Presence*, 43–89.

15. Gregory Palamas, *The Triads*, II, 3.71. Most of the quotations from the *Triads* provided here use the translation of Scott Pentecost in his *Quest of the Divine Presence*. Scott Pentecost provides both the Greek text and the English translation of a quotation. Here we shall use Pentecost's translations of the *Triads* by referring to Gregory Palamas, *The Triads*, followed by a Roman numeral for one of the three books of the *Triads*, and two Arabic numbers designating, respectively, the specific treatise and chapter, all of these separated by periods. The Greek text and a French translation by Fr. John Meyendorff could be found in Grégoire Palamas, *Défense des saints hésychastes*. In the same way as Pentecost, whenever Nicholas Gendle's translation of the *Triads* is used, reference will be made to the *Triad* with a parenthetical remark that it is Gendle's translation.

16. Gregory Palamas, *The Triads*, II.3.35.

17. Ibid., II.1.14.

neither our custom, nor that of God's Church, to be guided by idle words."[18] According to St. Gregory, the Calabrian is satisfied with mere words and fails in seeking the truth of things which is acquired through experience and manifested in deeds. "We think that," he says, "that true opinion is not the knowledge discovered through words and reasonings, but that which is demonstrated through both deeds and life, and which alone is not only true, but also certain and immutable."[19]

Barlaam's failure to go beyond words to reality underlies one of the key concerns of Palamas: "Every word contests another."[20] Words, once given a status independent of that which they signify, are subject to the will and to the specific context of their users.

> Not only are the vices set alongside the virtues, but also impious words seem to be so near to pious ones that by a slight addition or subtraction they easily transform into each other and change entirely the meaning of the words. In this way, for those unable to detect the slightest omission or addition, nearly every false opinion wears the mask of truth.[21]

Barlaam, according to St. Gregory, hides himself in complication, conundrums and ambiguities about the different meanings of words seeking to mislead "by his fair use of words."[22] In contrast, "We are not deceived," St. Gregory says, "nor we deceive others by the sound of words, but entering into the inner meaning of words we are guided by the truth of things."[23] Things are not to be altered because of names, "but the meaning of that which is thought should be changed or transposed according to things. For things are the cause of names and not names of things."[24]

Going beyond the words to the reality they represent

In the debate over the nature of the light seen by the Hesychasts, St. Gregory charges Barlaam with holding that "there is nothing above knowledge"[25]

---

18. Ibid., II.2.10.

19. Ibid., I.3.13.

20. Ibid., II.1.1; I.3.13; II.1.9.

21. Ibid., I.3.1.

22. Ibid., III.2.20.

23. Gregory Palamas, "Contra Akindynos," 5.17.71. In Chrestou, *Syngrammata* III, 340. Translation by Pentecost, *Quest of the Divine Presence, 60.*

24. Ibid., "Contra Akindynos," 5.17.68.

25. Gregory Palamas, *The Triads,* II.3.11.

and that it is only "spoken knowledge" that is light.[26] With respect to that St. Gregory claims that there are two philosophies, a philosophy in words and another in deeds, and that there are "many and various differences" between them.[27] He sees Barlaam's philosophy as being strictly discursive, bounded by language, and ultimately incapable of true knowledge of reality. The danger of such philosophy is found in the restriction of the activities of the mind to discursive reasoning alone which makes the cognitive aspects of contemplation merely impossible. Whenever Barlaam speaks of contemplation, he reduces it to the level of the knowledge of created beings[28] and the monks "did not think it fit to call him a contemplative."[29] The focus on discursive knowledge alone "evidences a denial that one can go beyond words to the reality they indicate. That is, we can speak about God but, since he is transcendent, cannot encounter God himself."[30] And "it is not the same to say something about God as it is to possess and see God. For apophatic theology is a word, whereas contemplation surpasses words."[31] "The intellect, theologizing apophatically, thinks those things that are different from God, and thus acts by discursive reasoning. But in the other case there is union. . . . Contemplation is not simply abstraction and negation, but union and deification."[32] The light seen by the Hesychasts is a pledge of union with God and a true encounter with Him. The light of Barlaam's contemplation is restricted to the realm of concepts, to discursive thought and to words related to natural phenomena.[33] "The philosopher teaches that the knowledge we have from creatures is the most perfect vision of God"[34] but the knowledge of natural phenomena cannot be the measure of human progress towards the likeness of God. "Such knowledge is trapped by a superficial consideration of phenomena—paralleling the superficiality of words—since 'every being that knows is established and remains in that which it knows.'"[35]

26. Ibid., II.3.71.
27. Ibid., II.1.21.
28. Pentecost, *Quest of the Divine Presence*, 61.
29. Ibid.
30. Ibid., 62.
31. Gregory Palamas, *The Triads*, I.3.17.
32. Ibid., II.3.15.
33. Pentecost, *Quest of the Divine Presence*, 63.
34. Gregory Palamas, *The Triads*, II.3.67.
35. Pentecost, *Quest of the Divine Presence*, 69, referring to *The Triads*, II.3.76.

The meaning of symbols

A true philosopher should recognize the symbolic transparency of beings and this recognition acknowledges that the Wisdom of God is fulfilled in creatures and every symbol should be able to open up the One Who is being symbolized. The opening up of the One Who is being symbolized makes it possible for man to see Him. "But, Barlaam says, this light was a sensible light, visible through the medium of the air, appearing to the amazement of all and then at once disappearing. One calls it 'divinity' since it is a symbol of divinity."[36] We can see how the question about the created nature of the light on Mount Tabor brought in the discussion about the nature and meaning of symbols.[37]

"For Barlaam a symbol could only be something other than the reality it represented."[38] "What saint," asks St. Gregory, "has ever said that this light was a created symbol?"[39] "When all the saints agree in calling this light true divinity, how do you dare to consider it alien to the divinity, calling it 'a created reality,' and 'a symbol of divinity,' and claiming that it is inferior to our intellection?"[40] St. Gregory admits the challenges of using the term symbol. "This is why the choir of inspired theologians have almost all been chary of calling the grace of this light simply a symbol, so that people should not be led astray by the ambiguity of this term to conclude that this most divine light is a created reality, alien to the divinity. Nevertheless, the phrase 'symbol of divinity', wisely and properly understood, cannot be considered absolutely opposed to the truth."[41]

> For every symbol either derives from the nature of the object of which it is a symbol, or belongs to an entirely different nature. . . . As to signs which are not connatural in this way, and which have their own independent existence, they are sometimes considered symbols: thus, a burning torch could be taken as a symbol of attacking enemies. If they do not possess their own natural existence, they can serve as a kind of phantom to foretell the future, and then the symbol consists only in that. . . . A natural symbol always accompanies the nature which gives them being, for the symbol is natural to that nature; as for the symbol

36. Gregory Palamas, *The Triads*, III.1.11, (p. 72 in Gendle's translation).

37. For a more recent publication on the meaning of signs and symbols in Orthodox theology see Velimirovich, *The Universe as Symbols & Signs.*

38. Russell, "Theosis and Gregory Palamas," 367.

39. Gregory Palamas, *The Triads*, III.1.12 (p. 73 in Gendle's translation).

40. Ibid., 74 (Gendle's translation).

41. Ibid., III.1.13 (p. 74 in Gendle's translation).

which derives from another nature, having its own existence, it is quite impossible for it constantly to be associated with the object it symbolises, for nothing prevents it from existing before and after its object, for that is impossible; as soon as it has appeared, it at once is dissolved into nonbeing and disappears completely. Thus if the light of Thabor is a symbol, it is either a natural or a nonnatural one.[42]

And if someone says that this light is an independent reality, separate from the nature of Him Whom it signifies, of Whom it is only a symbol—then let him show where and of what kind this reality is, which is shown by experience to be unapproachable, and not only to the eyes . . . and which alone shone forth only from the venerated face and body of Christ. For otherwise, if it were an independent reality, eternally associated with Christ in the Age to Come, He would be composed of three natures and three essences: the human, the divine and that of this light. So, it is clearly demonstrated that this light is neither an independent reality, nor something alien to the divinity.[43]

The Taboric light was not simply an external phenomenon, but an "enhypostatic" symbol, which means that it was real even if it did not have an independent existence, or hypostasis, of its own. "Clearly, this term is not used to affirm that it possesses its own hypostasis."[44] "Enhypostatic reality occupies a place in between the self-subsistent and the accidental. In the case of the Taboric light, it both symbolizes and is divinity. It is accessible to perception yet transcends it. As 'enhypostatic' symbol it enables the beholder to participate in the divine."[45]

The modes of knowledge and the role of the passions

The real problem for St. Gregory Palamas in the approach of Barlaam and his followers is not in the pursuit of knowledge of beings but in their limitation to remain voluntarily trapped into what is merely an introductory knowledge of God without recognizing that "God established the principles of nature as material for the soul's discursive power, but did this in order

42. Ibid., III.1.14 (p. 75 in Gendle's translation).

43. Ibid., III.1.17 (p. 77 in Gendle's translation).

44. Ibid., III.1.18, (p. 78 in Gendle's translation).

45. Russell, "Theosis and Gregory Palamas," 367.

that they could lead it to a higher knowledge."[46] There is no conflict between these higher and lower modes of knowledge but there must be a right epistemological ordering. Following this epistemological order provides an ascetic with a contemplative approach to thought that is characteristic of all true knowledge, and it is exactly this true knowledge that is most intensively pursued by the Hesychast monks.[47] Ignoring the right epistemological order makes the Barlaamites blind to the higher mode of knowledge and makes them think that "they know everything in the abundance of their wisdom"[48] without recognizing that the possession of universal knowledge belongs to God alone. St. Gregory relates such epistemological arrogance to the ancestral sin of Adam, i.e., to the prideful desire to be equal to God which includes the ignorance of the ascetical dimension of true knowledge.[49] This ascetical dimension is related to a humble approach to knowledge, which is expressed in the fact that the process of knowing should allow both for the object to determine the appropriate mode of knowing and also for the activity of the knowing subject to co-operate by anticipating and contributing to this determination.[50] It is in this co-operation that the God-given inner intelligibility and the Divine principles of all things are manifested. They are not given in advance and have to be allowed to emerge on their own. And the problem does not consist in the human inability to know the Divine principles in created beings, but in the fact that they are being obscured by the human passions.

> Our passions lower an obscuring veil over the soul's eyes, rendering it incapable of seeing the principles. Thus the lustful man gazing at a woman and the glutton slavering over the food do not truly understand what it is that is before them. They see only objects fit for their passions. Thus, when beings in general are understood as, for example, utilitarian objects, they are not understood as they are. While such impassioned comportment towards beings can give rise to the appearance of a knowledge of them, it is in fact merely the projection of one's passions into that which can satisfy them.[51]

46. Pentecost, *Quest of the Divine Presence*, 69, referring to *The Triads*, II.3.75.

47. Pentecost, *Quest of the Divine Presence*, 70.

48. Gregory Palamas, *The Triads*, I.1.1

49. Pentecost, *Quest of the Divine Presence*, 71.

50. Torrance, *Reality and Scientific Theology*, 23.

51. Pentecost, *Quest of the Divine Presence*, 72, referring to Gregory Palamas, *The Triads*, I.1.1 and I.3.42.

The purification of the soul vs. a focus on method

The way to deal with such confusion is to develop the ability to seek the true knowledge of beings as they are by the purification of the soul from the passions and the abandonment of evil. In this way asceticism, humility and the purification of the soul become a key component of the process of knowing. Barlaam, however, replaces asceticism with method. This is why in his *Triads* St. Gregory Palamas attacks those who rely on logical demonstrations, which, according to him, constitute the art that is concerned with words[52] and do not go beyond the words to reality. The difference between ascetical spiritual exercises and the methods championed by Barlaam is that the former seek to transform the soul by opening it to receive the truth, while the latter seek to produce discursive knowledge, and especially knowledge that is set forth in treatises.[53] Scot Pentecost identifies this difference with the difference that lies between activism and active receptivity[54] since for Barlaam acquiring wisdom is a human work while for Palamas it is a gift that can be received only by a properly-prepared soul. Scot Pentecost also points out that these are two completely different attitudes towards true knowledge and towards the sciences in general. The difference uncovers Barlaam's non-ascetic, methodological and discursive approach to thought as an early expression of naturalism. But most interestingly,

> Barlaam represents not merely a revival of decidedly secular studies, but the introduction into Byzantine thought of the principles that make possible the modern scientific attitude. . . . Thus, although the Byzantine Empire would not survive to see the full implications of Barlaam's thought, there is reason to see in this 'knowledge without love' an affinity to modern science.[55]

An example from the homilies of St. Gregory Palamas

It is worth pointing out that St. Gregory Palamas addresses the question about the use of words and their relationship to wisdom in his homilies as well. In one of his homilies on Palm Sunday he points out how the reading from Christ's Gospel shows that "those exalted in honour, wealth, and power, and those who concern themselves with words and the acquisition

52. Ibid., 75.
53. Ibid., 76.
54. Ibid., 77.
55. Ibid., 78.

of wisdom by means of them, even if they wish to be saved, are in need of greater force and diligence, since they are less obedient by nature."[56]

The miracle performed on Lazarus openly proved the one who did it to be God. But whereas the people were convinced and believed, the rulers of that time, that is to say, the scribes and Pharisees, were so far from being persuaded that they raged against Him even more, and resolved in their madness to hand Him over to death, although everything He had said and done plainly declared Him to be the Lord of life and death. No one can say that the fact that the Lord lifted up His eyes at that time and said, "Father, I thank thee that thou hast heard me," was an obstacle to their regarding Him as equal to the Father, since He went on to say, "I knew that thou hearest me always: but because of the people which stand by I said it, that they may believe that thou has sent me" (John 11:41–42). So that they might know He was God and came from the Father, and also that He did not work miracles in opposition to God, but in accordance with God's purpose, He lifted up His eyes to God in front of everybody and spoke to Him in words which make it clear that He who was speaking on earth was equal to the heavenly Father on high. . . . Notice that the Father and the Son are of equal honour and have the same will. The words are in the form of a prayer for the sake of the crowd standing by, but they are not the words of prayer but of lordship and absolute authority. "Lazarus come forth" (John 11.43). And at once the man who had been dead four days stood before Him alive. Did this come about by the command of the life-giver or His prayer? He cried with a loud voice, again on account of the bystanders, since He could have raised him not only by using His normal voice, but just by His will alone. In the same way, He could have done it from afar and with the stone in place. But instead He came to the grave and spoke to those present, who took away the stone and smelt the stench. Then He cried with a loud voice. He raised him in this manner so that by means of their sight (for they saw Him standing at the grave), their sense of smell (for they were aware of the stench of the man four days dead), their sense of touch (for they used their own hands to take away the stone beforehand from the grave, and afterwards to loose the grave-clothes from his body and the napkin from his face), and their hearing (for the Lord's voice reached the ears of all), they all might understand

56. Saint Gregory Palamas, "Homily Fifteen delivered on Palm Sunday," In Gregory Palamas, *The Homilies*, 108–14. Available also at: http://www.pravoslavie.ru/english/92790.htm.

and believe that it was He who called everything from non-being into being, who upheld all things by the word of His power, and who in the beginning by His word alone made everything that exists out of nothing. The simple people believed Him in every respect, and did not keep their faith quiet, but began to preach His divinity by deeds and words.[57]

One could easily let the words of St. Gregory speak on their own. However, one could make two observations. The first one is about the deeply theological nature of the argument, which is based on the equality of honor and the identity of will of the Father and the Son: "Notice that the Father and the Son are of equal honor and have the same will." The second point is about the rather good example of how the same words could mean two different things to two different kinds of people—the simple ones who believed the Lord in every respect and the ones who concern themselves with words and the acquisition of wisdom by means of them. These second ones, according to St. Gregory, are less obedient by nature which makes them missing the authentic reality of the events described in the Gospel.

Niels Bohr

Keeping the words without keeping the meaning of the words

The philosophical legacy of Niels Bohr has been received in controversial ways. Even his own followers shared a general feeling of uneasiness with respect to his use of words and wide disagreements with respect to what he really meant to say. For example, Paul Ehrenfest wrote to him in a letter from July 17, 1921: "Now, dear Bohr, every person I know wails only over the fact that you write your things so briefly and compactly that one always has the greatest trouble fetching all of the ideas out of the fruit cake."[58] The point here seems to be that Bohr appears to have struggled with language. He was missing words. One could however look at Bohr's struggle in another way. Heisenberg noted several times that Bohr did not have a problem with language but was in the process of creating a new one. In this process he "tried to keep the words and the pictures without keeping the meaning of the words and of the pictures, having been from his youth interested in the limitation of our way of expression, the limitation of words, the problem of

---

57. Ibid.
58. Chevalley, "Niels Bohr's Words," 33.

talking about things when one knows that the words do not really get hold of the things."[59] Bohr's "obsession" with questions of terminology and his struggle with language point to a problem of a much deeper character and this is the use of ordinary language in scientific language. The motivation for the entire epistemological approach of Niels Bohr can be summarized in what he called the epistemological paradox of quantum theory:

> On the one hand, there is an apparent incompatibility between ordinary language and the requirements for an unambiguous description of the atomic processes; on the other hand, we need ordinary language to communicate, specifically we need classical concepts to "relate the symbolism of the quantum theory to the data of experience."[60]

The key question was how to use classical concepts in the description of quantum processes by taking into account: i) the impossibility to have a visual image of quantum realities, ii) the discontinuity introduced by the quantum of action—the fact the energy for quantum objects can take only specific discrete values, iii) the probabilistic nature of quantum laws, iv) the principle of uncertainty, which does not allow for the simultaneous accurate measurement of some coupled physical quantities such as the position and the momentum of a particle,[61] and v) all the resulting epistemological challenges. Bohr's answer was that: i) the outcomes of measurements have to be described and communicated through the concepts of classical physics, and ii) these classical concepts should no longer be interpreted as referring to "absolute attributes" or "intrinsic properties" of quantum objects. In Bohr's works these two points are always associated with the idea that the language of quantum mechanics is a *symbolic scheme* which is in deep contrast to the intuitive description of physical quantities provided by classical concepts. Bohr wrote that the QM formalism "represents a purely *symbolic scheme* permitting only predictions as to results obtainable under conditions specified by means of *classical concepts*" and that it "defies unambiguous expression in words suited to describe classical physical pictures."[62]

59. Ibid.

60. Ibid., 39.

61. The more precisely the position (momentum) of a particle is given, the less precisely can one say what its momentum (position) is.

62. Ibid., 35

The meaning of symbols in Niels Bohr

Bohr used the word "symbol" in several contexts. One of his main points was that the discontinuity introduced in classical physics by the quantum of action cuts out the access to the possibility for a visual representation and, from this point of view, the link between the "symbol" and the "visualizable," as representative of the bridge between the everyday view of reality and the quantum view of reality, is left to the symbolic realm alone. Bohr's more general concern was "to emphasize the impossibility of the claim that 'words' can represent 'reality' precisely and completely."[63] According to him, words only "orientate us in reality by their immediate or derived reference to demonstrable circumstance."[64] There are no quantum concepts, Bohr says, but only classical concepts and quantum symbols. All our ordinary verbal expressions are a reflection of our customary forms of perception from the point of view of which the existence of the quantum of action is completely irrational. "In consequence of this state of affairs, even words like 'to be' and 'to know' lose their unambiguous meaning. And if nature thus escapes the grasp of words, how can we say anything at all except through the symbolic language of quantum theory?"[65] Bohr often repeated that "reality" is also a concept meaning that when we discuss what is real in the quantum world, we are trying to learn how to use the concept "reality" correctly. The challenges associated with this learning process come from the fact that quantum objects are non-visualizable. The non-visualizable character of quantum objects justifies the need for the adoption of a symbolic representation of the quantum world. "The word 'representation' indicates that there is something real, i.e., something mind-independent is being presented. The word 'symbolic' indicates that the representation does not look like the reality represented for the simple reason that nothing can look like non-visualizable entities."[66] At the same time, when asked whether the language of quantum mechanics could be considered as somehow mirroring an underlying quantum world, Bohr's answer was that "There is no quantum world. There is only an abstract quantum physical description. It is wrong to think that the task of physics is to find out what nature *is*. Physics concerns what we could say about nature."[67] The last statement does not imply that there are no mind-independent quantum objects since, ultimately, there is a

63. Honner, *The Description of Nature*, 158.

64. Ibid.

65. Bohr, *Atomic Theory and the Description of Nature*, 90.

66. Favrholdt, "Niels Bohr and Realism," 92.

67. Petersen, "The Philosophy of Niels Bohr," see quotation on p. 12.

"quantum reality" that becomes the object of study in any quantum physics experiment. "One may say that the aim of experimentation is to put questions to nature"[68] and the answers to these questions will depend on the way the questions were asked.

Complementarity

In the description of quantum experiments the classical concepts of particle and wave remain indispensable. "One of the two conceptual clusters can be adapted to any experimental situation. Neither fits every experimental situation. . . . When this conflict is reduced to an explicit statement such as: 'the electron is a wave and the electron is a particle,' one seems to be countenancing explicit contradictions."[69] Bohr's answer to this emerging contradiction is the principle of *complementarity*. Complementarity was introduced as a way of using intuitive classical concepts within the context of the new quantum physics. It is an attempt to dissolve and not to promulgate contradictions. It makes it possible "without leaving common language, to create a framework sufficiently wide for an exhaustive description of new experience."[70] Complementarity is definitely something that allows one to remain inside of the realm of classical concepts. However, by dealing with classical concepts, complementarity sets the stage for the overcoming of their natural limitations as well as for the emergence of a new relationship between phenomena and objects.

> The language of classical physics is an extension of ordinary language that has incorporated new categorical and quantitative expressions and, by a painstaking historical process, fashioned these concepts into coherent system for representing physical reality. . . . Here we bump our heads against the limits of language. Yet we cannot simply abandon this language. It supplies an indispensable basis for reporting and communicating information concerning experimental results.[71]

---

68. Cited by Favrholdt, "Niels Bohr and Realism," 93.
69. MacKinnon, "Complementarity," 264.
70. Chevalley, "Niels Bohr's Words," 40.
71. MacKinnon, "Complementarity," 265.

A genuine quantum realism

Here we touch on two points that were considered as a basis for accusing Niels Bohr of antirealism. First, this is the fact that by adopting the framework of complementarity, we are dealing with the limits of knowledge of quantum reality, and that the limits of knowledge become part of knowledge itself. It should be pointed out, however, that Bohr never used such statements. Instead of speaking of the limits of knowledge, he was more inclined to simply say that's all that it is to be known.[72] Second, this is the answer to the question of whether reality existed independently of the observer. In relation to the first point one could highlight a statement by Heisenberg, who in a conversation with Albert Einstein, after referring to what Bohr had taught him about our inability to describe processes in time and space with our traditional concepts, also added that "With that, of course, we have said very little, no more in fact than that we do not know."[73] In a similar manner Charles P. Snow, a physicist and a novelist-laureate of the scientific community, "diagnosed the same conviction as he let scientists speak of what had just been achieved by the discoverers of quantum mechanics: 'They had found the boundary of knowledge, something would remain unknown forever.'"[74] "One of the results of this new representation of matter was to tell us what we could not know as well as what we could. We were in sight of the end."[75] Considering the limits of knowledge as part of knowledge itself necessarily affects the way of using concepts and words in quantum mechanics. The fact that words and concepts do not exhaust the reality they represent cannot be easily accepted by scientists who keep looking at the world with a classical physics attitude:

> In addition to his inconsistency in using the word *nature* unambiguously, Bohr also seemed to forget that since no expert in quantum mechanics could ever claim to have observed nature as such, let alone nature as a whole, it could not be part of any discourse on quantum mechanics as long as its Copenhagen interpretation was true. But there was a far greater problem, a sinister trap, in Bohr's unfolding of the ultimate consequences of his interpretation of quantum mechanics. "We here come," he declared, "upon a fundamental feature in the general problem of knowledge, and we must realize that by the very nature of the matter, we shall always have last recourse to a word picture,

72. Jens Hebor, private communication.
73. Jaki, "The Horns of Complementarity."
74. Ibid.
75. Ibid.

in which the words themselves are not further analyzed." Astonishingly, Bohr did not seem to suspect the self-defeating nature of his utterance. For if words were impervious to further rational probing, then the end of philosophy was not merely in sight but on hand.[76]

One can see the unfortunate misunderstanding of Fr. S. Jaki in interpreting Bohr's statement in terms of giving up scientific realism for some sort of agnostic subjectivism as well as in interpreting Bohr's focus on the subtlety of the bridge between words and the reality they represent in terms of giving up philosophical reflection in general. In relation to the second point one could also highlight a statement by Erwin Schrödinger:

> A widely accepted school of thought maintains that an objective picture of reality—in any traditional meaning of that term—cannot exist at all. Only the optimists among us (and I consider myself one of them) look upon this view as a philosophical extravagance born of despair in face of a grave crisis. We hope that the fluctuations of concepts and opinions only indicate a violent process of transformation which in the end will lead to something better than the mess of formulas that today surrounds our subject.[77]

According to Fr. Jaki,

> the possibility for Bohr consisted in restricting discourse to *aspects* of reality while barring questions about reality itself, and especially about its objective existence. In Bohr's case this was all the more laden with further problems because the *aspects* in question were more opposite, nay mutually exclusive, than merely distinct. He tried to hold them together by offering the idea of complementarity.[78]

> These aspects could *really* complement one another only if they inhered in a deeper reality, about which Bohr could only be agnostic. A harmony of relations or aspects, complementing one another, such was Bohr's epistemological message, a message void of reference to the ontological reality of anything harmonious. About the entity which embodied the harmony of

76. Ibid.
77. Ibid.
78. Ibid.

relations he was not permitted by his own premises to make any claim and he carefully avoided doing so.[79]

One can easily detect again Fr. Jaki's unwarranted mistrust of Bohr's epistemological message, including its relationship to the way words and concepts are used in relation to quantum realities. According to Jens Hebor, the main reason for the existence of similar judgments is the confusion of questions of realism with questions of ontology[80] or what he calls the ontology-realism fallacy. "[C]lassical concepts of realism, objectivity, completeness, etc., are only redefined within a highly integrated conceptual framework called *classical ontology.*" It is exactly the presuppositions of classical ontology that is discarded in quantum mechanics, which means that "the very concepts of realism, objectivity, completeness, etc., have to be redefined in the quantum context."[81] All presumed problems in quantum mechanics, such as the one expressed in Stanley Jaki's statement about Bohr's overall epistemological attitude, are largely produced by the illegitimate imposition of classical ontology onto the quantum domain.[82] Without going into too much detail, one could just emphasize that questions about Bohr's *genuine quantum realism* (a term suggested by Jens Hebor) are the subject of an ongoing scholarly discussion[83] as well as point out the position expressed in the insightful works of David Favrholdt[84] and Jens Hebor[85] as the one that appears to be the most relevant within the context of the present discussion. One should note that the comments of Fr. Jaki were made before some of the decisive experiments in quantum physics. These experiments demonstrated that his suspicions about Bohr's epistemological viewpoint were ungrounded.[86] According to Richard Muller,

> Most physicists today accept the Copenhagen interpretation. Einstein continued to dispute it up to his death in 1955. Meetings are still held in which the few and the proud debate the reality of quantum physics, with long mathematical and esoteric discussions of possible alternatives, but most physicists ignore

79. Ibid.

80. Hebor, *The Standard Conception as Genuine Quantum Realism*, 8.

81. Ibid.

82. Ibid.

83. See for example the contributions in Faye and Folse, *Niels Bohr and Contemporary Philosophy.*

84. Favrholdt, *Filosofen Niels Bohr.*

85. Hebor, *The Standard Conception as Genuine Quantum Realism.*

86. Groblacher et al., "An Experimental Test of Non-local Realism," 871.

those meetings. Quantum physics works; that's good enough for the silent majority of physicists.[87]

The latest developments in quantum physics suggest that

we can no longer assume that the properties we measure necessarily reflect or represent the properties of the particles as they really are. As Heisenberg had earlier argued: ". . . we have to remember that what we observe is not nature in itself but nature exposed to our method of questioning." This does not mean that quantum particles are not real. What it does mean is that we can ascribe to them only an *empirical* reality.[88]

Comparative Analysis

In the comparative analysis of the linguistic aspects of the theology of St. Gregory Palamas and the philosophy of physics of Niels Bohr one should clearly point out that this is not an attempt to examine the religious views of Niels Bohr, neither an attempt to compare two different religious worldviews. It is well known that Bohr, in his scarce references to God, was very careful in avoiding any traditional religious connotation. According to David Favrholdt, "Planck was religious and had a firm belief in God; Bohr was not . . ." According to Fr. Stanley Jaki,

Bohr, never sympathetic to anything genuinely transcendental, let alone supernatural and Christian, was most careful not to give unwitting respectability to the idea of a God who can choose with respect to nature. Much less would Bohr have tolerated the reintroduction of God into rational discourse through the mediation of quantum mechanics. The haste with which he tried to dispel the indirect appearance of God on the scene spoke for itself. Moreover, when it came to dispelling the remote flicker of God, Bohr was ready to forget that his own premises permitted him to perform only ambiguously a feat which he meant to be an unambiguous philosophical exorcism. There was not even a trace of ambiguity in the manner in which Bohr now set up the idea of nature against the beckoning of the notion of God.[89]

87. Muller, Richard A. *Now: The Physics of Time*. Kindle Edition. Locations 2719–22.

88. Baggott, *The Quantum Story*, 356.

89. Jaki, "The Horns of Complementarity."

At the same time, however, Bohr was very deeply interested in the relation between language and the unambiguous description of the world by making the point that "physics and linguistics are both part of man's age-old endeavours to clarify his position in that nature of which he is himself a part."[90]

The clarification about Bohr's religious attitude was needed in order to point out that the comparison between the linguistic aspects of the theology of St. Gregory Palamas and the philosophy of physics of Niels Bohr should focus on their epistemological insights by taking into account the difference in the nature of the realities they were discussing. It is important therefore to be fully aware of the challenges that could emerge during the application of comparative approaches in domains as different as Orthodox theology and quantum mechanics. One of the ways to deal with these challenges is to adopt the principles of analogical isomorphism.[91] Analogical isomorphism presupposes the existence of two sets of terms from two different conceptual systems and neither affirms nor denies similarity between them. What it does assert is that the network of relations in one set of terms is similar to the network of relations in the second one. The method concentrates on the structural similarity of the two sets of terms and not on their specific meanings. It examines the ways the two sets of terms operate in their proper context. The analogy therefore is sought between the two ways of operation and between the two types of relationships. The advantage of such an approach can be found in the opportunity to use existing knowledge from two different domains to develop insights of potential benefit for both domains. In our case the expected outcome of such an approach is the articulation of new insights from the identification of specific common themes, issues or patterns of use emerging from the examination of the relationships between words, concepts, language, and reality in Orthodox theology and physics.

A focus on experiential epistemology

One of the obvious points of similarity between St. Gregory Palamas and Niels Bohr is the fact that they deal with the challenges of using words, concepts, and language within the context of an empirical epistemology. Although this is quite a general statement, it helps in opening up a number of emerging common thought patterns. One of these issues concerns the nature of the unknown and the shift from known to unknown. St. Gregory

90. Faye and Folse, "Introduction," 20.
91. Lonergan, "Isomorphism of Thomist and Scientific Thought," 133.

Palamas is concerned with the true knowledge of God and the challenge of using human words and thoughts in expressing the experience of acquiring such knowledge. The problem comes from the fact that the uncreated qualities of God cannot be expressed through human concepts. In this sense every attribution of names and words to God is, strictly speaking, inappropriate. There are no words that could adequately express God. In the experience of *theosis*, concepts about God have to be put aside since this experience discloses the fact that no created concept corresponds to the uncreated reality of God.[92] Focusing on discursive knowledge about created beings as a way of progressing towards the knowledge of God is doomed to failure.

> The Fathers stress that all the expressions and concepts that a person can have are products of human thought. Concepts and expressions do not come down from heaven and God did not personally create concepts and expressions in the human mind. The Fathers base this teaching on their experience of *theosis*, which leads them to stress that every human language is a human invention. Man is the creator of the language with which he communicates with his fellow man. There is no divine language. God does not have His own language that He gave to man and He does not even communicate with man via some special language that He gives to those with whom He communicates. Language is the result of human needs. People formed it in order to help them communicate and interact.[93]

The biggest challenge then consists in defining the criterion for choosing words in referring to God. However, there is "no way to discern which words are appropriate for theology and which are not. There is no unambiguous distinction between acceptable and unacceptable terminology."[94] The only criterion that we can use for choosing a specific terminology when speaking about God is the criterion of reverence, which is based on experience. The experiential basis of the criterion for a proper relationship between specific human words and God is another point of similarity. There are words that are not good to be used in reference to God and other words that are respectful enough to be used in reference to God. "In this context, the epistemology of the Fathers, which is clearly empirical, is in its entirety

92. Romanides, *Patristic Theology*, 69.
93. Ibid., 80.
94. Ibid., 81.

quite useful at least for Orthodox Christians, and perhaps for other Christians as well. You could even call it quite modern."[95]

Niels Bohr deals with the knowledge of quantum objects and the challenge of using classical concepts to describe the quantum world. There are no other than classical concepts and there is no quantum language. We need the concepts of classical physics, but these classical concepts could no longer be merely attributed to quantum objects. It becomes inappropriate to assign words and concepts to quantum objects outside of the context of our interaction with them. In addition, these words should be able to provide an unambiguous description of the experience in a way that we could communicate to each other. The language of quantum mechanics cannot be considered as somehow mirroring an underlying quantum world. It is in this sense that, according to Bohr, there is no quantum world. The task of physics is not to find out what nature *is* but what one could say about nature by keeping the words and the pictures from classical physics without keeping the meaning of the words and of the pictures. There is a fundamental limitation in our way of using words and our ways of expression since we are faced with the problem of talking about things knowing that the words do not really get hold of the things. This is the source of the epistemological paradox of quantum theory: there is no compatibility between ordinary language and the requirements for an unambiguous description of quantum processes, however, we need ordinary language and classical concepts to relate the symbolism of the quantum theory to the data of experience. And the only and ultimate criterion of doing this properly is the lack or the minimum level of ambiguity in the process of communicating our experiences.

Going beyond classical logic:
using opposites vs complementary terms

St. Gregory Palamas points out that there are no concepts in the created world that could be attributed to God as a way of identifying Him.

> So, on the one hand, we do attribute a name to God, but only if, on the other hand, we take it away from Him. For example, although we say that God is Light, we negate this at the same time by saying that God is also darkness. We do not add this qualification because God is not Light, but because God transcends light. . . . But when the Fathers speak about God and attribute opposites to Him, they negate Aristotle's law of

95. Ibid.

contradiction and in so doing overturn the entire edifice of Aristotelian philosophy. This means that the Fathers do not follow
the rules of logic when they deal with theological matters or talk
about God.[96]

This is because the rules of logic are valid, in so far as they are valid, only
for God's creation.

According to Niels Bohr, all our ordinary verbal expressions are a
reflection of our customary forms of perception from the point of view
of which the existence of the quantum of action is completely irrational
and illogical according to classical physics standards. The adoption of the
principle of complementarity seems to be contributing to this "quantum ir-
rationality." However, by dealing with classical concepts, complementarity
sets the stage for the overcoming of the limitations of using classical words
and concepts by allowing for limited mutually incompatible extensions of
classical physics language. The type of extension depends on the question
we put to nature and the experimental setups that embody these questions.
One can use either the wave or the particle cluster to describe a particular
experiment and interpret the results. One cannot use any fusion of these
to describe reality as it exists objectively. The principle of complementarity
therefore does not conform to classical logic[97] and Bohr was among the first
to realize that a proper understanding of the relationship between the two
complementary aspects of a single reality requires the use of a new logical
framework. Here it is important to clarify in what sense exactly the principle of complementarity does not conform to classical logic. The problem
does not consist in the fact that two profoundly opposed models (wave vs.
particle), that preclude one another in a given situation, are both necessary
to achieve a complete understanding of a quantum object.[98] The principle
of complementarity ensures that we never apply both models to the same
entity at the same time, i.e., to the same experimental configuration or measurement. It is only if we tried to apply both models to the same entity at the
same time that contradictions would arise. In order to clarify the emerging
problems of complementarity in relation to classical logic, I will use a comment made by Bohr during the discussion period of a lecture delivered by
him at a conference on New Theories in Physics in Warsaw, May 30–June

96. Romanides, *Patristic Theology*, 85.

97. Birkhoff and von Neumann, "The Logics of Quantum Mechanics," 823–43.

98. I have really appreciated a fruitful discussion with Jim Edwards at the St. Gregory Palamas conference in Thessaloniki, Greece, which helped me clarify my thoughts
and demonstrated the need to clearly emphasize this point.

3, 1938.[99] One of the positions expressed by von Neumann after the lecture was that a complete derivation of quantum mechanics is only possible if the traditional calculation of logics is so extended, as to include the so-called transitional probabilities—probabilities that account for the possibility of particles to switch from one complementary state to another and not only for the probabilities of being in one or the other of two complementary states. In other words, von Neumann was arguing for the need of a quantum upgrade of classical logic. Here is the summary of Bohr's reply:

> Professor Bohr expressed his admiration for the skill with which Professor von Neumann has treated the fundamental problems of quantum theory from the mathematical and logical point of view. He pointed out at the same time how the very simple experimental cases which he alluded to in his paper showed, in more elementary form, the same essential points as those which appeared in the mathematical analysis. We must also notice that the question of the logical forms which are best adapted to quantum theory is in fact a practical problem, concerned with the choice of the most convenient manner in which to express the new situation that arises in this domain. Personally, he compelled himself to keep the logical forms of daily life to which actual experiments were naturally confined. The aim of the idea of complementarity was to allow of keeping the usual logical forms while procuring the extension necessary for including the new situation relative to the problems of observation in atomic physics.[100]

In this statement Niels Bohr clearly points out that, by introducing the principle of complementarity, his main intention was to deal with the problems of logic and not to create them. Interestingly, he emphasizes the need for dealing with *a new situation*. What is that new situation? There was a reason to speak about a new situation since, before the emergence of quantum physics, all physical objects were known to exist in one out of two forms—as a particle or as a wave, i.e., some of the physical objects existing in nature possessed the properties of a particle and others possessed the properties of a wave. They were either particles or waves and there was no way for a particle to become a wave or vice versa. After the emergence of quantum physics, scientific experiments clearly showed that for one and the same physical object it was possible to manifest the properties of either particles or waves. In other words, it became possible for physical objects to

99. Bohr, "The Causality Problem in Quantum in Atomic Physics," 94–121.
100. Ibid., 115–16.

drastically alter their manifested properties depending on the intention and the specific design of the experimental setup of the observer. In a way, one cannot speak anymore of some objectively existing properties of quantum objects independently of observer's experimental intervention. The properties of a quantum object emerge within the context of the experimental setup and observer's mind behind it. This contradicts classical logic which assumes that physical entities have well defined properties and all logical statements refer to these well defined properties. The role of the principle of complementarity was to allow for such a new situation.

It is important to point out the difference between the concepts of complementarity in quantum mechanics and "using of opposites" in Orthodox theology. The principle of complementarity helps in representing two profound oppositions that preclude one another in a specifically given situation. It is, however, impossible to talk about the coexistence of two different natures of one and the same quantum object but only about its two complementary natural manifestations. This is quite different from the situation in theology where, for example, one could call God both Light and Darkness at the same time, without identifying Him with either of them. In addition, we never stop worshiping Christ as a personal or hypostatic unity of a human and a divine nature. He always acts in His single hypostasis as the God-man. The hypostatic union of His two natures is fundamentally important for the Orthodox understanding of salvation. In this sense, the concept of complementarity does not appear to be directly applicable to Orthodox theology.[101] However, there seems to be a potential for the application of the concept of hypostasis in quantum mechanics.

An opportunity to apply the concept of hypostasis in quantum mechanics

This section will focus on pointing out the potential value of the theological understanding of the term "hypostasis" to quantum mechanics. In Niels Bohr's words:

---

101. Meyendorff, *Christ in Eastern Christian Thought*, 21. A remark by Fr. John Meyendorff with respect to the theology of St. Cyril of Alexandria is particularly interesting: "It is clear that *physis* and *hypostasis*, according to Cyril, do not designate a 'substance.' In that case the substance of the God-man would be a new substance, resulting from a mixture of divinity and humanity, *complementary* realities from which the one hypostasis of the incarnate Word would be made. The idea of complementarity constituted Apollinarius's main error, as Diodore of Tarsus perceived, and there was nothing of that in Cyril."

> Information regarding the behavior of an atomic object obtained under definite experimental conditions may . . . be adequately characterized as complementary to any information *about the same object* obtained by some other experimental arrangements excluding the fulfillment of the first conditions. Although such kinds of information cannot be combined into a single picture by means of ordinary concepts, they represent indeed equally essential aspects of any knowledge of *the object in question* which can be obtained in this domain.[102]

What exactly is Bohr trying to convey by using the expressions "about the same object" and "the object in question"? What Bohr appears to be doing is to make a distinction between the unique identity or hypostasis of a specific quantum object and the specific complementary way of its energetic manifestations. This distinction is crucial for Bohr in insisting on the reality of the quantum world while at the same time accepting that it does not make sense to speak about its "being in a certain way" independent of any interaction with our experimental arrangements. Such view goes beyond the classical understanding of realism by pointing to the role of the observer for the adoption of a much more subtle way of looking at reality allowing for a self-subsisting object to manifest mutually exclusive, i.e., complementary, types of natural properties depending on the specific circumstances of the interaction between the observer and the object.

It would be highly valuable to find an example from theology referring to a similar linguistic situation. It seems that such an example can be found in the developments after the Third Ecumenical Council in Ephesus (431). Nestorius denied the fact that He who was born of the Virgin is consubstantial with God the Father according to Divinity and thus by nature God.[103] Nestorius denied the two births of the *Logos* and the double consubstantiality of the one and the same *Logos*, Son of God and the selfsame also son of Mary. In this way he jeopardized the Orthodox meaning of salvation. The Third Ecumenical Council ended with a theological misunderstanding between the Alexandrian and Antiochian participants who were chiefly represented by St. Cyril of Alexandria and John of Antioch, respectively. The controversy was formally ended in 433 by the reconciliation between St. Cyril and John of Antioch where the latter confessed the double consubstantiality of "our Lord Jesus Christ, the only-begotten Son of God," i.e., the very doctrine that was violently rejected by Nestorius. In

---

102. Bohr, "Natural Philosophy and Human Cultures," 23–31.

103. Romanides, "St. Cyril's 'One Physis or Hypostasis of God the Logos Incarnate' and Chalcedon," 84.

his confession, John of Antioch declares that the only begotten Son of God was "before the ages begotten from the Father according to his Divinity, and in the last days the *Self-same* [*ton auton*] for us and for our salvation, (begotten) of Mary according to his Humanity, the Self-same [*ton auton*] consubstantial with the Father according to Divinity and consubstantial with us according to Humanity." The double use of the expression "*Self-same*" here emphasizes the reference to the single hypostasis of the only-begotten Son of God and not to the union of two natures used by Nestorius to deny the two births of the *Logos* and the double consubstantiality of the one and the same Logos. For St. Cyril John's confession was fully acceptable since this was exactly what Nestorius denied, in spite of the fact that John also spoke of "a union of two natures, whereby we confess One Christ, One Lord, One God."[104] To the objection that speaking of two different natures after the union means a predication of two separate kinds of names, divine and human, i.e., of two separate natures, Saint Cyril replies that the division of names does not mean necessarily a division of natures, hypostases, or persons, since all names are predicated of the one *Logos*.[105] It is not by accident that the Fathers of the Fourth Ecumenical Council in Chalcedon (451) intentionally used eight times the same type of "self-same" expression in order to underline "the unity of *subject* in all actions, whether divine or human, of Christ."[106]

An apophatic realism vs. antirealism

It was already pointed out that Niels Bohr was accused of being an antirealist. First, he was emphasizing that the limits of our knowledge become part of knowledge itself. Second, he was restricting discourse to *aspects* of reality while barring questions about reality itself, and especially about its objective existence, i.e., about its possession of properties or attributes independent of the specific circumstances. Here again one can easily find the need for a proper fruitful application of the term "hypostasis" in quantum mechanics since it allows considering a hypostatically single quantum object in its multiple natural manifestations. Using a hypostatic terminology could underline the fact that the reality of the quantum object is unquestionable. However, the knowledge about it goes together with its own natural limitations and there are no words that are able to exhaust it. In addition, the

---

104. Ibid., 85.

105. Ibid., 86, referring to PG 77:193–97.

106. Meyendorff, *Christ in Eastern Christian Thought*, 27.

degree and the way of the manifestation of the quantum reality is contingent on the specific circumstances providing the conditions for its proper actualization. In a way similar to the situation in quantum physics where Bohr's defense of the dynamic non-local nature of quantum objects was used to accuse him of antirealism, St. Gregory Palamas was found to be excessive in his mystical realism:

> The stress Palamas places on the light as not being created and as eternal, having no end and no beginning, is developed with special reference to the defense of the Divine light that appears to the Hesychast in prayer. If this light—which was supposed to be equal to the light that was present at the Transfiguration of Christ, and hence often referred to as the "Tabor-light"—was a *real* manifestation of God, then, one must ask, should it not be co-existent with God, who is eternal? The discussion about the energies of God and His essence thus emerges quite naturally from the previous statements about the Divine light. It is these statements of Palamas, stressing that the light that presents itself to the Hesychasts *is* God, which bring the question about the ontological properties of the light to its head.[107]

In both cases the questions about realism bring in the discussion of the nature of symbols. Both St. Gregory Palamas and Niels Bohr point out the genuine link between symbols and reality, although St. Gregory appears to be much more comprehensive in his elaboration than Bohr is. They both defend the reality of symbols and not a symbolic realism. The similarity of the two approaches opens up the possibility for quantum mechanics to adopt a form of apophatic realism in a way similar to Orthodox theology. Here some of the theological insights that could be found in a recent study by Haralambos Ventis are quite relevant:

> Palamite apophatism . . . signifies a realist theory of knowledge, marked by a strongly pronounced epistemological reserve toward truth. The reserve is best exemplified in apophatism's categorical downplay of linguistic essentialism and all ontologisms of language, premised on the assumption of an *asymmetrical* relation between reality and language, and the prioritization of the former over the latter.[108]

---

107. Gunnarsson, *Mystical Realism in the Early Theology of Gregory Palamas*, 233.

108. Ventis, *Toward Apophatic Theological Realism*, 80.

Such an apophatic approach emphasizes the fact that the reality of things lies independently of our linguistic or conceptual conventions.[109] The theological roots of Orthodox apophatic realism emerge out of an epistemological effort to arrive at an authentic vision of the being of God with an exclusive reference to the Trinitarian mode of existence and not to the divine essence.[110] These roots suggest the potential contemporary relevance of apophatic realism, including its potential relevance for quantum mechanics. It "consists in its *personalism* and the gnosiological novelty that the latter introduces: by considering all 'existents' in relational terms, apophatism fosters a participatory understanding of truth and knowledge, which teaches us to approach the most ordinary objects in *personal* terms, as entities capable of being known, but still immune to crass objectification."[111] The ontological integrity of the existents "is safeguarded by means of a cognitive ban of their *essence*, that is, by rendering meaningless (and, indeed, infeasible) all discourse about substances or essences as absolute attributes of the existents."[112] In this view all entities are considered as lending themselves to being known "in terms other than those of substance, if by substance is meant an ultimate metaphysical structure or texture to be known under ideal epistemic conditions."[113]

Final Reflections

The initial motivation for this chapter was based on a statement by Christos Yannaras concerning the opportunity for the Church to appropriate a new language in linking the salvific message of the gospel to linguistic categories that are much more efficient in the articulation of the existential mode of the relationship between God, world, and man; a language emerging from quantum mechanics and post-Freudian psychology. The analysis provided here suggests that Christos Yannaras appears to be quite optimistic about it. It is unquestionable that there is a great value in exploring the similarities in the ways language works in Orthodox theology and quantum mechanics. However, as it was already shown, Orthodox theology and quantum mechanics are both continuously struggling, each on its own, with the challenges of properly using words and concepts in linking human experience to reality. This struggle appears to be part of their existential modes

109. Bulzan, "Apophatism, Postmodernism, and Language," 261–87.

110. Ventis, *Toward Apophatic Theological Realism*, 81.

111. Ibid., 82.

112. Ibid., 83.

113. Ibid.

of operation—probably more so in theology than in quantum mechanics. "The transmission of the dogmas cannot be done without their interpretation, i.e., through explicating old concepts and terms by contemporary concepts." And "[t]he advantage of this resynchronization is existential, not ethical. Orthodoxy must begin to answer cultural questions not with ethics (which has proved unsuccessful) but with dogmas. However, in order to achieve this, it must interpret its dogmas existentially."[114] The nature of this existential interpretation is not a philosophical one since "[e]very word in the mouth of the Church is not only a declaration of the truth, but also an invitation to a free, wholehearted, personal meeting with the truth, since the Truth is not something, but someone: Christ Himself incarnate."[115] It would be therefore unlikely to expect the Church to just start bringing and adopting quantum mechanical concepts into theology.[116] It would be however highly valuable to keep exploring the similarity of the challenges in dealing with the articulation and communication of the human experience of the Divine and quantum realities. I believe that such an approach to the pursuit of a dialogue between science and theology would be most valuable. The emphasis on the challenges would definitely attract scholarly interest. It would be however much more valuable in terms of its potential homiletic and apologetic capacity as a source of human inspiration for the honest pursuit of the Divine. One of its key messages could be the promotion of a cognitive attitude based on the realization that, in order for man to know God, *man must change himself*[117] or, at least, realize that the knowledge of God is contingent on the degree and the authenticity of the personal spiritual struggle and participation in the sacramental life of the Church. One could therefore say that the synergy between science and theology should be ultimately pursued on a personal existential level. It is only personally, as persons, that we could adopt the proper apophatic cognitive attitude that could link any scientific and theological insights.

> Indeed man is a theologian in his relation to God and scientist in his relation to the universe, whilst the universe is the laboratory of God in which man has been placed as custodian. This combination of the theologian with the scientist, i.e., theology and science, is crucial and very significant, because it allows man to bypass falsehood and recover the truth. . . . In other words, he is

114. Vasiljevic, *History, Truth, Holiness*, 131

115. Ibid.

116. Here I am not assuming that Prof. Yannaras is actually suggesting that, I am just using his point as an opportunity to drive a meaningful discussion.

117. Хоружий, "Естественная теология в свете исихастского боговидения."

called to demythologize the world from fanciful theories which do not correspond to reality and to perceive the transparency of the universe, which points in turn to the transcendental basis of its existence in the ceaseless and inexhaustible energy of the Creator Word.[118]

Every man conceptualizes the relationship between theology and science through his or her personal struggles to grasp the natural manifestations and meanings of both Divine and created realities. And this struggle cannot happen outside of the Church because the Church reveals the truest vocation of the world:

> Far from addressing a minority in society, the Fathers spoke boldly and to the whole world. Erudite, cosmopolitan and conversant with contemporary philosophy and culture, the Fathers proclaimed a message of universal import. For them, the world was in the Church, not the Church in the world. By this, of course, they meant that the world was created for the Church and that the Church revealed the truest vocation of the world.

118. Dragas, "The Anthropic Principle: Christ's Humanity," 48.

Chapter 9

Christos Yannaras and the Encounter between Theology and Physics[1]

Introduction

I would like to start this chapter by going back to 2010 when I started my doctoral thesis in theology as an associate scholar in the Faculty of Theology at the University of Sofia "St. Kilment Ohridski." The topic of my thesis was the theology of Divine energies in twentieth-century Orthodox thought. The last chapter of the thesis offers an analysis of the ways of using the concept of energy in physics and theology. I have previously chosen a similar theme for my Master thesis in Orthodox theology in the University of Sherbrooke, Canada, and continued working on it during my PhD studies. When I started my research I expected that there will be lots of literature in physics focusing on energy and much less in theology. After all, the concept of energy has a fundamental place in physics. Yet, it appears that physicists do not like to talk much about energy; for them it is just one of the many quantities helping them to describe specific physical processes. Its way of use is mostly operational and any the discussion of the physical reality behind the concept is considered to be too philosophical and almost irrelevant.

To my surprise the situation it Orthodox theology was exactly the opposite—the concept of energy has a very specific epistemological and ontological loading and it has been used extensively by both Church Fathers and contemporary Orthodox theologians. So, I was in a kind of impasse since it was quite challenging for me to find a common ground to compare theology and physics in that particular aspect. Eventually, I found some of

---

1. The original text of this chapter was presented at the International Conference dedicated to Christos Yannaras: Philosophy, Theology, Culture—St. Edmund's Hall, Oxford, 2—5 September 2013

the works dedicated to the philosophy of Niels Bohr and realized that his epistemological insights would be very useful.

Later on, when I started my PhD project, I knew that in order to articulate the methodological relevance of my work I needed to find a way back from physics to theology. So I struggled again until I found two key insights from two Greek theologians. The first one was in a paper by Marios Begzos titled "The priority of energy in Gregory Palamas and in Modern Physics."[2] The second insight was from Christos Yannaras that I found in an interview with him during his visit as a plenary speaker at a Conference in Sofia in 2002. Some of the ideas in this interview provided me with a very interesting exploratory angle. In this interview Yannaras points out that one of the key characteristics of post-modernity is the emergence of a new language in dealing with ontology and reality, a language that, according to him, emerges from two different scientific disciplines—quantum mechanics and post-Freudian psychology.[3] What is more interesting however is that Yannaras sees the post-modern duty of the Church in the creative appropriation (and not simply adoption) of this new language aiming at linking the salvific message of the gospel to linguistic categories that could be more efficient in the interpretation of "the reality of existence, the appearance and disclosure of being,"[4] and more specifically, in the articulation of the experiential mode of the relationship between God, world, and man.[5] According to Yannaras, such appropriation could become the source of a new proposal coming from the Church to deal with post-modernity and not just to modernize herself.

But what exactly is the problem with post-modernity? According to Scot Pentecost, the challenge of post-modernity is related to the failure of post-modern epistemology to secure a secular basis for philosophy by transforming the metaphysical search for the ultimate ground of reality into a quest for its epistemic foundations.[6] According to him, this failure resulted into a shift from humanity's focus on exploring and partaking of reality to an obsession with the methodological correctitude of the process of knowing which ultimately detaches our language from its inherent link to reality and from its eventful ontological resourcing.

2. Begzos, "The Priority of Energy in Gregory Palamas and in Modern Physics," 357–64.

3. Yannaras, "Christos Yannaras in a conversation with Kalin Yanakiev."

4. Yannaras, *Elements of Faith*, Ch. 6.

5. Yannaras, "Christos Yannaras in a conversation with Kalin Yanakiev."

6. Pentecost, *Quest of the Divine Presence.*

According to Yannaras, a similar trend can be found also in everyday Church life where many of the words appear to have lost the power of their initial authentic meaning.[7] For Yannaras, this is a danger with significant theological and ecclesial implications since one can formally adopt the dogmatic articulation of the faith, and even turn it into a linguistic idol, without really encountering or partaking of the sacramental events. "So, it is possible for a man to hear the language of the Church and give the words different meaning, and perceive them in a totally different context from that of the ecclesial language, as if they were words of any religion."[8] For Yannaras, this could not be called a real heresy but it is a real tragedy.[9]

I was particularly interested to explore the idea of considering quantum mechanics as a source of new language that could be used to the service of the Church in postmodern society. However, I was not sure how exactly is this to be done, especially when I read some of Yannaras' other works where he points out that "language in the Church is not subsumed to the language of science, our everyday language, which is bound by the limits of this world (Wittgenstein). The Church's gospel becomes flesh in our language but it is not contained in the meanings of this language, it cannot be exhausted by the implications of our worldly experience."[10]

I agree with Yannaras that our present situation might be able to provide a greater advantage, as compared to the age of the Church Fathers, who were very much proficient in the sciences of their own time, but still did not have the amazing access to scientific information that is openly accessible to us today, and that could be found helpful for a better articulation of the distinction between what is real and unreal, between reality and its deceiving reflected image—the "idol."[11] In this chapter I would like to make a very small step in exploring this opportunity by using the insights of Christos Yannaras.

7. Yannaras, "Christos Yannaras in a conversation with Kalin Yanakiev."

8. Yanarras, *The Meaning of Reality*, 8.

9. Yannaras, "Christos Yannaras in a conversation with Kalin Yanakiev."

10. Yanarras, *The Meaning of Reality*, 8.

11. Yannaras, "Christos Yannaras in a conversation with Kalin Yanakiev."

Using the Language of Quantum Mechanics for a Better Articulation of the Distinction between What Is Real and Unreal

I should start by pointing out that the way Yannaras speaks about language in quantum physics and theology reminded me very much of the way Niels Bohr spoke about quantum realities. It is a well-known fact that in his works Bohr struggled in the specific choice of words and the articulation of their meanings. According to some, he had an innate sloppiness in expressing himself. However, his student and Nobel Prize Winner Werner Heisenberg noted several times that Bohr did not have a problem with language but was in the process of inventing a new one. In this process he "tried to keep the words and the pictures without keeping the meanings of the words and of the pictures, having been from his youth interested in the limitation of our way of expression, the limitation of words, the problem of talking about things when one knows that the words do not really get hold of the things."[12] In Bohr's own words: "We here come upon a fundamental feature in the general problem of knowledge, and we must realize that by the very nature of the matter, we shall always have last recourse to a word picture, in which the words themselves are not further analyzed."[13]

Here one could identify one of the sources of Yannaras' excitement with quantum mechanics and the potential of its language for theology— this is the apophatic nature of its language and its continuous struggle to find the proper terms in the description of quantum phenomena. In his terminology apophatism refers to a specific linguistic semantics or attitude to cognition "which refuses to exhaust the content of knowledge in its formulation, which refuses to exhaust the reality of the things signified in the logic of the signifiers" and "consequently refuses to verify knowledge merely by controlling the correct representational logic of the signifiers."[14] An apophatic semantic formulation has a relative, indicative and referential character. It suggests reality, but does not necessarily represent it in a definitive and exhaustive manner.

According to Yannaras, "We are unable to speak even one word about the eschatological hope of the Church, if we do not struggle to keep the radical apophatism of the ecclesial language." And the price of losing apophatism is very high since "[i]f we refuse the apophatic word and want to be fair and consistent with the language of common human experience,

12. Ibid.

13. Bohr, *Atomic Theory and the Description of Nature*, 20.

14. Yannaras, *Postmodern Metaphysics*, 84.

then we have to compromise with a modest agnosticism."[15] Yannaras emphasizes that, in a similar way, the interpretation of physical phenomena could be highly complicated in situations when the empirical approach to reality is not directly possible, for example, in the case of phenomena happening at the subatomic scale when all physical entities become practically invisible. In such cases the semantics of the hermeneutic propositions is even further relativized since there is an additional factor—the impossibility of separating the method from the means of the indirect approach to the things under study. According to Yannaras, in such cases whatever the epistemological method is, it should refuse to function and be imposed as a methodologically correct and uniquely valid cognitive code.[16] And this is the second aspect of similarity that was pointed out by him as a way of comparing quantum mechanics and theology—in both cases "methodology functions as a methodical approach to knowledge, free from subjection to the codification of the methodicity" and without claiming exclusive rights to methodological correctness.[17]

In order to make his point Yannaras distinguishes between Newtonian or classical physics and post-Newtonian, modern, or quantum physics. "Newtonian physics pictured the world as a mechanically organized system consisting of given entities correlating to and influencing each other, with the same strict causality and determinism regardless of their number and size." It "maintained that it could attach precise laws to every phenomenon, that it could attribute full and universal validity to mechanistic causality"[18] pretending that it provides a one-to-one correspondence between theory, language and reality. On the other hand, post-Newtonian physics has developed a consciousness of nature at odds with Newtonianism. By post-Newtonian physics Yannaras means

> the understanding of physical reality which begins to take shape with the appearance of Max Planck's quantum theory of energy (1900), Albert Einstein's special theory of relativity (1905), Niels Bohr's establishment of quantum mechanics (1913), Einstein's general theory of relativity (1916), Louis de Broglie's theory of wave-particle duality (1924), Werner Heisenberg's uncertainty principle (1925), Erwin Schrodinger's matter-wave hypothesis of quantum mechanics (1926), the probabilistic understanding of the behavior of matter introduced by Max Born (1928),

15. Yanarras, *The Meaning of Reality*, 9.
16. Ibid., 85.
17. Ibid.
18. Ibid.

Paul Dirac's theory of anti-matter (1930), Richard Feynman's creation of quantum electrodynamics (1950), etc.

For Yannaras modern physics provides a picture of matter and of the world, as a totality of dynamically uncertain active relations. The new picture of the world emerged within the context of an epistemological revolution which is associated with the name of Niels Bohr. It is not by accident that modern philosophers of science agree about Bohr's contribution to human knowledge through the articulation of an epistemological lesson from the development of quantum mechanics—the conviction that the description of nature is dependent on the words we use and, more specifically, on the ways we use these words to unambiguously describe our experience with nature. "We can speak of nature as experienced only, i.e., structured on the basis of those conditions for description (and for thinking as well) which we are subjected to as part of the world."[19]

The source of the epistemological approach of Niels Bohr can be found in what he called the epistemological paradox of quantum theory: "On the one hand, there is an apparent incompatibility between ordinary language and the requirements for an unambiguous description of the atomic processes; on the other hand, we need ordinary language to communicate, specifically we need classical concepts to 'relate the symbolism of the quantum theory to the data of experience.'"[20] All our ordinary verbal expressions are a reflection of our customary forms of perception from the point of view of which the existence of the quantum phenomena is completely irrational. "In consequence of this state of affairs, even words like 'to be' and 'to know' lose their unambiguous meaning."[21] For Bohr even "reality" is also just a concept meaning that when we discuss what is real in the quantum world, we are actually trying to learn how to use the concept "reality" correctly. Nature escapes the grasp of words and the only way to say anything about it is through the symbolic language of quantum theory: "It is wrong to think that the task of physics is to find out what nature *is*. Physics concerns what we could say about nature."[22]

According to Yannaras, the language of modern physics is based on a semantics suggesting a new way of conceptualizing what is real and existing. It demonstrates a reversal to an ontological attitude to existence that is free of rationalistic biases and superstitions. The words, terms, and expressions used by contemporary physics witness about forms of

19. Favrholdt, "Niels Bohr and Realism," 83.

20. Chevalley, "Niels Bohr's Words," 39.

21. Bohr, *Atomic Theory and the Description of Nature*, 90.

22. Petersen, "The Philosophy of Niels Bohr," 8–14, see quotation on p. 12.

existence and reality that do not conform to human rationality and human representational constructions. In such situations it is impossible to clearly distinguish between phenomena of existence and the epistemological acts of approaching them as reality. In other words, modern quantum physics adopts "a middle ground that is neither purely ontological nor purely epistemological. Instead, it may suggest to us that a separation between reality and information, between existing and being known, and between ontology and epistemology, should be abandoned."[23]

In this way reality becomes rooted in the relation between us humans and the logos of the nature of created things which is expressed in their particular mode of existence. The logos of the nature of every single thing should be seen as an invitation-for-relation with human beings. Humanity becomes the only bearer of consciousness in the Universe which is able to turn quantum phenomena into facts of existence. As it was already pointed out, we cannot speak anymore of some objectively existing properties of quantum objects independently of the experimental setup and the intentional cognitive attitude of the human observer. According to Yannaras this is the meaning of the "anthropic principle" which is very often discussed by both theologians and scientists—the idea that the shape of reality presupposes human consciousness.[24]

But how is the analysis of modern physics suggested by Yannaras relevant for theology? The main question for Yannaras is: *What is the potential link between the ontological maturity of the language of modern physics and the language of the answers provided by ecclesial experience to its own ontological questions?* The direct posing of this question is what makes me admire the way Yannaras addresses the relation between physics and theology.[25] For him the ecclesial attitude to the ontological problematics is of particular relevance since it appears to be the only one outside of the scientific domain that works from within an experiential perspective on truth. The ecclesial experience is based on an apophatic attitude to language and reality that is similar to the one that has emerged within the context of modern physics. This is a perspective which makes modern physics and theology co-workers in the field of the human encounter with reality. And it is magnificently expressed in the experiential realism of Church's ontology, which can be

23. Zeilinger, "Quantum Physics: Ontology or Epistemology?" 38–39.

24. Yanarras, *The Meaning of Reality,* 23. The specific chapter in the book is titled "The Reality of the Person in Postmodernity." The present section follows the Bulgarian translation of Yannaras' original paper: Янарас, "Постмодерната актуалност на понятието личност." The original version of the paper in Greek and its Bulgarian translation appear to have some important differences with the English version.

25. Ibid., 64.

summarized in the semantics of the term person (*prosopon*). For Yannaras this is a key word which presupposes the proper ontological interpretation *of any scientific fact* as well as the shaping of both, a systematic cosmology and anthropology.

> Patristic anthropology and postmodernism have crucial points of convergence. For the Fathers a "person" was never a definite reality; persons cannot be defined. The surprising aspect of personhood is the way a person can change absolutely. Person-hood is a reality totally other—it is characterized by "otherness." We know a human person only though relationship. We may describe a person but we can never formulate a precise descrip-tion. . . . There is a patristic apophatism about personhood. . . . The human person is an existential reality approached through the expression of relationship: relationship is a concrete but un-definable event.[26]

I will now focus on using Yannaras' insights about how the concept of person or hypostasis could be applied within the context of modern physics. According to Yannaras, in quantum physics it became evident that the result of the observation of the micro-world is connected with the specific type of instruments, and also with the specific method of observation and descrip-tion. "Quantum theory tells us that nothing can be measured or observed without disturbing it, so that the role of the observer is crucial in the un-derstanding of physical processes."[27] "What this means is that the nature of existing reality is not independent of human action, yet the answer Nature gives us as the result of the individual measurement is random. The result is beyond our control, which indicates an independent physical reality."[28] According to Yannaras, "when we speak of relations in quantum mechanics, we do not refer to predictable correlations . . . , we refer to a mode of correla-tion, referentiality and coordination which has the character of the unpre-dictable, of the probable, of the possible, and which could be compared only with the dynamic freedom of interpersonal human relations."[29] This is a key point suggesting that we may actually get closer to a better understanding of quantum realities if we describe them in terms of the theological termi-nology of essence, nature, hypostasis and energy. As it was already pointed

---

26. Yanarras, *The Meaning of Reality*, 23.

27. Yannaras, *Postmodern Metaphysics*, 90–93.

28. Zeilinger, "Quantum Physics: Ontology or Epistemology?" 38–39.

29. Ibid.

out, the ontology of quantum mechanics will significantly benefit from the adoption of the term hypostasis with its inherent relational connotation.[30]

Niels Bohr appears to make a clear distinction between the unique identity or hypostasis of the quantum object and the specific complementary ways of its energetic manifestation. This distinction is crucial for Bohr in insisting on the reality of the quantum world while at the same time accepting that it does not make sense to speak about its "being in a certain way" independently of the interaction with a specific experimental arrangement. Such a view does not confirm to the classical understanding of realism. It suggests a more subtle way of looking at reality allowing for a self-subsisting object to manifest mutually exclusive but complementary natural properties depending on the specific circumstances of the interaction between the observer and the object.

The Theological Understanding of Space-Time

Christos Yannaras points out that in contemporary physics space and time are revealed as a result of the presence of matter and energy. If space and time are products of the presence of matter and energy, then that which exists materially is not *within* space and time. Space and time do not *contain* what exists, but are consequences of the materiality of what exists. This means that any question related to the fact of existence in itself as well as to the cause of existence—any question to do with ontology or metaphysics—cannot be posed within the presuppositions and associations of space and time. According to Yannaras, this point has a vital significance since it shows that the inclusion of materiality in the assertion of existence may not be necessary. Even the conceptual expansion of space and time to infinity must be excluded from ontology in the proper sense, because it ties us to the bounds of physics and especially of Newtonian physics.

At the same time, the achievements of modern physics have led to the acceptance of a beginning of the universe in time. The interpretation of this origin refers to an initial Big Bang or the explosion of the universe's matter-energy in its primary super-dense state. Albert Einstein's general theory of relativity showed that at this initial moment the density of matter and the curvature of the geometry of space must have been infinite. This prediction is usually expressed by saying that the equations predict a singularity of space-time in which density and curvature become infinite. This singularity describes the Big Bang that is believed to have happened at the beginning

---

30. Tanev, "The Language of Orthodox Theology and Quantum Mechanics." The content of this essay is reproduced in this book.

of the creation of the universe. What is more important, however, is the fact that the theory does not allow us to ask what existed or what happened *before* the Big Bang. We can say that nothing happened and nothing existed before the Big Bang, because before it there was neither space nor time, and consequently there was *no "before."*

It is a metaphysical given of physics that time and space have a specific beginning in conditions negating them, a beginning that is "within" their initial non-temporality and non-locality, that is, in a metaphysical or pre-physical context. This context is *meta*-physical or *pre*-physical, because physics points to it (making it "real") and at the same time excludes the questions posed by physics itself. However, what is most important for Yannaras is that both the specifications of the Big Bang as a founding event of the universe, and the non-local and non-temporal coordinates of the beginning of space and time emerge as existential facts without entailing materiality in the definition of their existence. In his opinion the important contribution of contemporary physics is that it does not a priori exclude a type of dynamic relationship with the world which leads to a recognition of a personal causal principle of the world.

How is the above discussion of space relevant at all to theology?[31] Yannaras provides an insightful theological interpretation of space and time by focusing on personal relationship.[32] For him the consciousness of space is a consciousness of the *other* and the *other* defines a referential separateness which is located as opposite to us and therefore within spatial dimensions. In his own words, "[w]e recognize the person fundamentally as the unique power of 'being-opposite' to other beings, as a presupposition of the referential disclosure of beings and consequently as a presupposition of the cognition of space." In other words, "we recognize space as the accommodation of personal reference, as a fact of relation."[33] However, the replacement of the inherent ec-static referentiality of the person with a purely intellectual sense of the disclosure of beings as objects leads to the objectification of space. The external view of personal relation objectifies space as the distance between the two terms of the relation.

31. The logic of this section follows closely the logic of Yannaras, *Person and Eros*, 116–18.

32. I should point out that Yannaras's understanding of the relation between person and nature has been the subject of criticism by other well-known contemporary Orthodox theologians such as Jean-Claude Larchet and Fr. Nicholas Loudovikos: Larchet, *Personne et nature*, 207–396; Loudovikos, "Hell and Heaven, Nature and Person," 9–32. I will not go into the details of this critique since it does not seem to affect the present discussion.

33. Yannaras, *Person and Eros*, 105.

The objectification of physical reality, however, within the bounds of local dimensions does not negate the experience of space in terms of interpersonal relation. The ecstatic reference of the person is a fact that transcends the categories of measurable space. The second term of a personal relation may be here, as a presence with dimensions, or elsewhere, as an absence with dimensions, defining always the same space of personal reference—a space without dimensions. The power of personal relations negates the measurable dimensions of here and there, of nearer and farther, and points to both presence and absence as the experience of non-dimensional nearness.[34]

Yannaras points out that Byzantine theologians saw in personal energy the non-dimensional place both of the human person and of the Person of God. He refers to John of Damascus who defines the space of God's disclosure of his personal energy as the place of God: "What is called the place of God is where his energy becomes manifest."[35] And God's personal energy becomes manifest primarily in the space of cosmic reality. In this way the world is revealed to humanity as the non-dimensional place of Divine personal energy. Cosmic space acquires its meaning only as a Divine place. It is then not measured as conventional distance (*apo-stasis*) from humanity or as the interval (*dia-stasis*) between objects.

The world "is far removed from God" by an infinite and indeterminable natural distance, but at the same time the world is the "substantiation" of God's personal will, the place of the disclosure of his personal energy. The divine Will or energy does not remain unrealized and without hypostasis, but is "immediately substantiated" "in the hypostasis and form of creation." It is "substantiated" outside God, although at the same time it discloses the non-dimensional proximity of God in a particular location or place. So it is not the world that accommodates God or his personal energy, but the divine will and energy which accommodates or gives space to the world, a space outside God which is simultaneously God's place, the disclosure of the non-dimensional immediacy of his personal energy. Just as humanity's own personal creative energy preserves the immediacy of personal uniqueness and dissimilarity, so too the distinction between the nature and the energies of God, without denying the reality of the natural distance of God from the world, preserves the world as a space of the immediate personal nearness of God and manifests God as the place of the universe: "For God is not contained, but is himself the place of all."

34. Ibid., 107.

35. John of Damascus, *Exposition of the Orthodox faith*, 1.13.

Final Reflections

Before concluding, it is rather tempting for me to provide an example of how some of the insights of Christos Yannaras could be used to compare two different readings of a biblical story—the story of the two disciples of Christ on the road to Emmaus (Luke 24:13–27).[36] The first reading of the story is by Fr. John Behr, the Dean of the St. Vladimir's Orthodox Theological Seminary in the USA:

> Neither the Crucifixion, nor the empty tomb, nor even the ap-
> pearances of the risen Christ are in themselves the starting point
> for Christian faith: the leader of the apostles denied Christ; the
> myrrh-bearing women did not understand the significance of
> the empty tomb; and the disciples on the road to Emmaus did
> not recognize the risen Lord. Rather, only when the disciples
> finally understood the Passion 'in accordance with scripture' are
> they ready to encounter the risen Christ in the breaking of the
> bread, and once they recognize him, he disappears from sight.
> Thereafter, the disciples, and those following them, always stand
> in the shadow of the Cross: we stand stretching towards the
> coming Christ, looking back to the Cross as the last publicly
> visible image in this world (the tomb being empty, after all, only
> seen by a few and needing interpretation).[37]

At another other occasion Fr. John Behr elaborated a bit more on his comments on the same story[38] by focusing again on the primary role of the opening of scripture and the breaking of the bread, i.e., of the Divine Liturgy, in recognizing the Lord. In addition, Fr. John suggests an interpretation that gives a very specific meaning of the disappearance of the Lord by emphasizing that the earthly mission of the Lord did not help the Apostles to recognize Him and it was only the opening of the scriptures and the breaking of the bread that made it clear to them that He truly was the

---

36. The Apostle Luke places the story on the evening of the day of Jesus' resurrection. The two disciples had already heard that the tomb of Jesus was found empty earlier that day. They were discussing the events of the past few days when a stranger asked them what they were discussing but "Their eyes were kept from recognizing him." The stranger then opened the Scriptures and reminded them the prophecies about the Messiah. On reaching Emmaus, the two disciples asked the stranger to join them for the evening meal. When he broke the bread "their eyes were opened" and they recognized him as the resurrected Lord. Right after that the Lord immediately disappeared from their sight.

37. See Behr, *The Mystery of Christ*, and especially the Postscript "A Premodern faith for a postmodern era."

38. Behr, "Standing by the Cross, Putting on Christ."

Lord. However, the moment of his recognition was also the moment of his disappearance. They lost Him from sight and the only option left to them was the option they handed over to us: always standing in the shadow of the Cross and stretching towards the coming Christ by looking back to the Cross as the last publicly visible image in this world. Christ is still the coming One and, as Fr. John points out, in the Orthodox Church one could not properly talk about a "first coming."[39]

The second interpretation is by Archimandrite Vasileos, the former Abbot of the Iveron Monastery on Mount Athos.[40]

> And during *the breaking of the bread* their eyes are opened. They recognise Him. And he vanishes. After so much labour and pain of soul and body, the time has come for Him to reveal Himself truly by vanishing. He vanishes in a physical sense and manifests Himself in a way that is Divine. He is within them for ever. He sets His seal on their being. He illumines and fills all things. And they leave. They cannot stay. They have to tell of what has happened (that is theology).[41]

> When we live in Christ, we have present before us all that has gone before and all that is yet to come. . . . When we live in Christ, we long for that which we have and remember that which we await. Through Him, all things have come together in one: while we are unaware of Him, He is beside us, giving us strength. And when we recognise him, He vanishes, in order to fill all things by His grace: presence and absence, sorrow and joy, knowledge and ignorance, life and death, heaven and earth and all that is under the earth.[42]

One can easily see how a specific interpretation of the term "disappearance" may significantly influence the interpretation of a biblical passage and apophatism appears to play an important role in the interpretation.

In conclusion I should briefly emphasize some of the key dimensions of the encounter between theology and physics in the works of Christos Yannaras—language, method, and the particular commitment to ontological problematics. Modern physics and Orthodox theology have both contributed to supporting the authenticity of the human encounter with reality. More importantly, they have both contributed to the understanding

39. Ibid.
40. Vasileios, *I Came that They May Have Life*.
41. Ibid., 25.
42. Ibid., 22.

of what is it to be human. They do not use the same language but share the same attitude to language which provides the basis for a fruitful interaction. The Church in particular has contributed to this encounter by elaborating the semantics of the term person (*prosopon*). The apophatic nature of the language of modern physics and Orthodox theology has become the source of a true encounter and dialogue between them and the price of losing apophatism is very high. It is expressed in Yannaras' warning that "If we refuse the apophatic word and want to be fair and consistent with the language of common human experience, then we have to compromise with a modest agnosticism."[43]

43. Yanarras, *The Meaning of Reality*, 9.

The Concept of Energy in Thomas F. Torrance and Orthodox Theology

Introduction

This distinction between the essence and energy of God is a basic principle of the Trinitarian thinking of the Eastern Church.[1] While some tend to associate it exclusively with the works of St. Gregory Palamas and the theological controversies of fourteenth century Byzantium, Gregory himself considered his theological efforts as a direct elaboration on the dogmatic definitions of the Sixth Ecumenical Council (Constantinople III, 680/681), referring back to the works of Sts. Athanasius and Cyril, the Cappadocian Fathers, St. Cyril of Alexandria, St. Maximus the Confessor, and St. John of Damascus. Recent scholarship has demonstrated the link between Palamas' teaching and the Greek Fathers before him, as well as the early Christian appropriation and transformation of Hellenic philosophical understandings of *energeia*.[2] The fall of Byzantium to the Ottoman Turks initiated centuries of struggle during which Orthodox theology, and the teaching on the Divine essence and energies in particular, did not find a strongly articulate voice. However, the theology of Palamas was "rediscovered" in the first half of the twentieth century. The rediscovery was initiated by the theological controversies associated with some Russian monks on Mount Athos who were accused of claiming that the name of God is God Himself (the so-called Name-worshipers or *Imiaslavtzi*), and whose teaching was associated with the theology of St. Gregory Palamas.[3] This rediscovery, together with

---

1. Amphiloque (Radovic), *Le Mystère de la Sainte Trinité selon Saint Grégoire Palamas.*

2. Larchet, *La théologie des énergies Divines*; Bradshaw, *Aristotle East and West.*

3. Evtuhov, *The Cross and the Sickle*; Alfeev, *Le Mystère sacré de l'Église*; Tanev, "ΕΝΕΡΓΕΙΑ vs. ΣΟΦΙΑ"; Танев, Ти, Който си навсякъде и всичко изпълваш.

the controversy revolving around the sophiology of Fr. Sergii Bulgakov,[4] is of particular interest, as it initiated a renewal of Orthodox theology by reopening some key theological themes, including the essence-energies distinction, which have impacted Orthodox theology to the present.[5]

In parallel to the Orthodox theological renewal in the first half of the twentieth century there were ongoing inter-confessional debates (predominantly between Orthodox and Roman Catholics) focusing on the relevance of the theology of St. Gregory Palamas. These debates emerged within theological circles associated with the Russian diaspora in France and clearly contributed to the rediscovery and the appropriation of the teaching on the distinction between Divine essence and energies.[6] This distinction has become a quite sensitive topic in inter-confessional discussions ever since, due to its relation to all-important chapters of Christian theology as well as to such controversial issues as the *filioque*. According to Duncan Reid, the distinction between essence and energies runs "directly contrary, it seems, to one of the basic principles of the Western Trinitarian tradition, viz. 'that we have no formula for the being of God in Godself other than the being of God in the world.'"[7] In Reid's view, the Western position is an "*a priori,* though not always acknowledged, methodological principle," while the Eastern position is "a recognized doctrine, confirmed by ecclesiastical synods, that has in turn certain methodological ramifications."[8] Here Reid refers to the relevance of the Church councils in fourteenth-century Byzantium that provided the most explicit doctrinal articulation of this teaching. The importance of these councils for Orthodox theology is well expressed by a statement of Fr. George Florovsky:

> This basic distinction (i.e., between Divine essence and energies) has been formally accepted and elaborated at the Great Councils of Constantinople in 1341 and 1351. Those who would deny this distinction were anathematized and excommunicated. The anathematisms of the council of 1351 were included in the

---

4. For a summary of Bulgakov's sophiological doctrine see Bulgakov, *The Wisdom of God.*

5. Флоровский, "Тварь и тварьность"; Florovsky, "L'idée de la création dans la philosophie Chrétienne"; Кривошеин. Аскетическое и богословское учение св. Григория Паламы; Staniloae, *Life and teachings of Gregory Palamas*; Lossky, Essai sur la théologie mystique de l'Église d'Orient; Meyendorff, *Introduction à l'Etude de Grégoire Palamas*; Romanides, *The Ancestral Sin.*

6. Larchet, "Intorduction" to *La théologie des énergies Divines.*

7. Reid, *Energies of the Spirit,* 3, referring to Schleiermacher, *Der Christliche Glaube,* Vol. 2, 589.

8. Ibid., 4.

rite for the Sunday Orthodoxy, in the Triodion. Orthodox theologians are bound by this decision.[9]

The motivation to focus on this theme of Divine energy in a text
dedicated to the theological insights of Thomas F. Torrance and their relation to Orthodoxy is fourfold. *First*, it is to emphasize the fact that this
teaching is an integral part of Orthodox theology, and *second*, to provide
an initial analysis of why Torrance did not adhere to it. *Third*, I hope that
the discussion suggested here will help in correcting certain erroneous per-
ceptions regarding Orthodox theology put forward by scholars who have
already discussed Torrance's view on the essence and energies distinction
in its relation to deification or theosis. *Fourth* and finally, the motivation for
the present chapter is to suggest an analysis demonstrating the correlation
between Torrance's engagements with particular themes in modern physics
and the content of his theological positions. This last analysis is of particular
relevance since it is directly associated with his interpretation of the distinction between essence and energies.

Torrance against dualisms

Before going into the details of Torrance's views on the essence-energies
distinction, it is worth highlighting one major aspect of his theological
preoccupations—his passion for addressing theological and scientific dualisms. This is a major point since, as it will be shown later, it provides a
key for understanding Torrance's view on the relationship between science
and theology. Torrance repeatedly highlighted the struggle of the Church
throughout all her history with cosmological and epistemological dualisms
that threaten to destroy the meaning the gospel. The Christian doctrine of
the incarnation was articulated against a philosophical background characterized by a fundamental disjunction between the real world of the intelligible and the shadowy, less real world of phenomenal or sensible.[10] In
Torrance's own words:

> The Church found itself struggling with two powerful ideas that
> threatened to destroy its existence: *(a)* the idea that God himself
> does not intervene in the actual life of men in time and space for

9. Florovsky, "St. Gregory Palamas and the Tradition of the Fathers," 105–120.

10. Torrance, *Theology in Reconstruction*, 34, 175, 211; Torrance, *Space, Time and
Incarnation*, 15, 43; Torrance, *The Trinitarian Faith*, 47, 275; Torrance, *Theology in Rec-
onciliation*, 224. For more insights on Torrance's view on dualisms, see Purves, "The
Christology of Thomas F. Torrance," 52.

he is immutable and changeless, and *(b)* the idea that the Word
of God revealed in Christ is not grounded in the eternal Being
of God but is detached and separated from him and therefore
mutable and changeable.[11]

According to Torrance the split between God and the world in modern
thought has been most damaging following Kant's arguments for an axi-
omatic distinction between unknowable things in themselves and what is
scientifically knowable, i.e., the things as they appear to us. In other words,
for Kant knowledge was limited to the appearances of things without any
grounding in their inner dynamic nature and the lack of grounding severed
the connection between science and faith, depriving faith of any objective or
ontological reference and emptying it of any real cognitive content.[12]

According to Colin Gunton, Torrance's concern with dualism has two
distinct aspects.[13] *First*, there is the division between the world of sense and
the world of intellect, which deprives modern intellectual life of its basis in
material being. The continuity of the human mind with the material world
is essential for the integration of thought and experience, without which
neither natural nor theological science can operate. According to Gunton,
Torrance's approach generates a realist parallel to Kant's essentially ideal-
ist epistemology, since for Torrance all theological concepts must have a
corresponding empirical grounding if they are not to detach into a theology which is not rooted in the gospel. *The second* aspect of dualism with
which Torrance concerned regards the relation between being and act of
God.[14] Interestingly, Torrance associates this dualism with what he calls "the
Latin Heresy": "for in theology at any rate its roots go back to a form of
linguistic and conceptual dualism that prevailed in Patristic and Mediaeval
Latin theology."[15] According to Torrance, this heresy has entrenched in the
tradition the breach between the act of God (what he does) and his being
(what he is) leading to a radical distinction between the person and work of
Christ. Torrance seeks to avoid this dualism and its resultant external, trans-
actional notion of redemption through the adoption of an incarnational
model of atonement.[16] Further, Torrance's Trinitarian theology appears to
be a continuous effort to overcome the same dualism. For him the danger

11. Torrance, *Theology in Reconstruction*, 261.

12. Torrance, *Ground and Grammar of Theology*, 26–27.

13. Gunton, "Eastern and Western Trinities: Being and Person. T. F. Torrance's
Doctrine of God," 34.

14. Ibid., 35.

15. Torrance, "Karl Barth and the Latin Heresy," 461–82.

16. Habets, *Theosis in the Theology of Thomas F. Torrance*, 50.

of the dualistic disconnect between God and man requires a knowledge of Jesus Christ on his own ground as he reveals Himself to us and according to His nature *(kata physin)* within the objective frame of meaning that he has created for the Church, through the apostolic testimony to him. Here Torrance follows the basic Barthian axiom that God's being is known only through his act, and that the person and work of Christ are inseparable.[17] In Torrance's own words, "Christ is what he does, and does what he is."[18] If the identity and mission of Jesus Christ form a coherent whole, then it is both the person and the work that have redemptive significance. "The Redemption is the Person of Christ in action; not the action itself thought of in an objectivist impersonal way."[19]

One should point out that the above statements manifest Torrance's unwarranted preoccupation with the danger of a potential disjunction between person and agency, as if personal acts and activity may exist somehow independently of the person itself. Such preoccupation may be explained with Torrance's predominant focus on the theology of St. Athanasius and the Christian theological debates of the fourth and the fifth centuries, when the distinction between essence *(ousia)*, nature *(physis)*, person *(hypostasis* or *prosopon)*, and activity *(energeia)* was not fully articulated yet. It is undisputed that Torrance's argumentation against dualism never loses its basis in the Arian controversy and Nicene theology.[20] For Torrance the coexistence of the Divine and human natures in the person of Christ is not a dualism but "the only way to safeguard a real, dynamic, and open (that is, free of deterministic causalities) relationship between God and the world."[21] For him dualism does not consist in a mere appearance of two poles but in the specific understanding of the nature of the relation between the two poles involved. His emphasis on the *homoousion* is an expression of a realism that could be applied to both theology and science: "what is observed is of the same being with reality itself so that an observation does not relate to a superficial phenomenon only but to reality in its ontological depth. Apparent phenomena and reality, then, do not live their own separate lives but are actually one and the same."[22] In this way the link between theology and science in Torrance's thought emerges not as mere academic endeavor but as part of an integrated vision of God, man and the world. This point should

---

17. Torrance, *The Doctrine of Jesus Christ*, 150.

18. Ibid., 150, 165.

19. Ibid., 151.

20. Luoma, *Incarnation and Physics*, 90.

21. Ibid.

22. Ibid., 91.

help later in clarifying part of the motivation for his critique of the distinction between essence and energies.

The Distinction between *Theologia* and *Oikonomia*

Torrance equates the distinction between the being of God (what he is) and his act (what he does) with the patristic distinction between *theologia* and *oikonomia,* and emphasizes that this distinction should not be understood dualistically: "Due to the epistemological dualism (*chorismos*) pervading Hellenistic thought the Church had constantly to struggle against a threat to *sever* 'economy' from 'theology' (*oikonomia* from *theologia*), for it would have done away with the ontological reference of the Gospel and of faith to any real ground in the being and activity of God."[23] Here Torrance refers positively to Florovsky's essay "The Concept of Creation in Saint Athanasius" for support; yet it is interesting that in this paper Florovsky expresses exactly the *opposite* concern.[24] In Florovsky's words:

> In fact, St. Athanasius carefully eliminates all references to the *oikonomia* of creation or salvation from his description of the inner relationship between the Father and the Son. This was his major and decisive contribution to the Trinitarian theology, in the critical situation of the Arian dispute. And this let him free to define the concept of creation properly. *Theologia*, in the ancient sense of the word, and *Oikonomia* must be clearly and strictly distinguished and delimited, although they could not be separated from each other. But God's 'Being' has an absolute and ontological priority over God's action and will. . . . There are two different sets of names which may be used of God. One set of names refers to God's deeds or acts—that is, to His will and counsel—the other of God's essence and being. St. Athanasius insisted that these two sets of names had to be formally and consistently distinguished. And, again, it was more than just a logical or mental distinction. There was a distinction in Divine reality itself. God is what He is: Father, Son and the Holy Spirit. It is an ultimate reality, declared and manifested in the Scriptures. But Creation is a deed of the Divine will, and this is common to and identical in all Three Persons of the One God. . . . The actual mystery is double. There is, indeed, the mystery of the Divine Being. But there is another mystery of the Divine *oikonomia*. No

23. Torrance, *The Christian Doctrine of God, One Being Three Persons*, 7.
24. A similar point was made by Baker, "The Eternal 'Spirit of the Son,'" 402.

real advance can be achieved in the realm of "Theology" until the realm of "Oikonomia" had been properly ordered.[25]

Florovsky points out here that the differentiation between Divine generation, as an effect of nature, and creation, as an effect of will, is one of the distinctive marks of Eastern theology, which was systematically elaborated later especially in the theology of St. Gregory Palamas. St. Gregory's emphasis that "unless a clear distinction had been made between the 'essence' and 'energy' of God, one could not distinguish also between 'generation' and 'creation'. . . was a true Athanasian motive," says Florovsky. "Not only do we distinguish between 'Being' and 'Will'; but it is not the same thing, even for God, 'to be' and 'to act.' This was the deepest conviction of St. Athanasius."[26] In his earlier essay "Creation and Creaturehood," Florovsky elaborated on this theme even further, pointing out that the "life-giving acts of God in the world *are God Himself*—an assertion which precludes separation but does not abolish distinction."[27] One can see how in Florovsky the fear of dualism is replaced by a subtle understanding of the important distinction between *theologia* and *oikonomia*, Divine nature and will, Divine being and act, Divine essence and energies. It is the perception of this subtlety that provides a hint of the dynamic apophatic realism[28] of Divine-human communion.

Torrance's concerns, however, go in the opposite direction, stressing the identity of *oikonomia* and *theologia*:

> While for Athanasius *economy* and *theology* (*oikonomia* and *theologia*) must be clearly distinguished, they are not to be separated from each other. If the economic or evangelical Trinity and the ontological or theological Trinity were disparate, this would bring into question whether *God himself* was the actual content of his revelation, and whether *God himself* was really in Jesus Christ reconciling the world to himself. . . . The economic Trinity and the ontological Trinity overlap with one another and belong to one another, and can no more be separated than the Act of God can be separated from his Being or his Being from his Act. It is in that interrelation between the two that the

25. Florovsky, "The Concept of Creation in Saint Athanasius," 48, 54.

26. Ibid., 56–57.

27. Florovsky, "Creature and Creaturehood," 65–66 (a careful examination of part III and IV of Florovsky's essay will illustrate its relevance to the present topic and its relation to the teaching on the divine essence and energies).

28. The term was discussed in greater detail by Ventis, *Toward Apophatic Theological Realism*.

redemptive significance and evangelical relevance of the Holy Trinity become disclosed.[29]

What is important here for the present study is that Torrance directly associates the discussion of the distinction/identity of the ontological and economic Trinity to the distinction between Divine essence and energies; as he writes:

> The question must be asked how far the Byzantine elaboration of the distinction between the uncreated energies (*energeiai, dunameis*) and the Being (*ouisia*) of God retreats from the Athanasian position as to the real knowability of God, and how far it bars the way in an intelligible movement from the Economic Trinity to the Immanent Trinity. . . . The Byzantine thesis that all we can say positively of God manifests not his Nature but the things about his Nature[30] seems to put a question mark before any doctrine of oneness between the Immanent or Ontological Trinity and the Economic Trinity.[31]

Torrance on the Teaching Regarding Divine Essence and Energies

The theological insights of Thomas Torrance can be closely associated with his inspiration from two major theologians: Karl Barth and St. Athanasius of Alexandria. According to Colin Gunton, "Athanasius served Torrance as a theologian of God's being as Barth served as a theologian of his act (though the greatness of both is that they integrated the two) and it would be difficult to exaggerate the importance for him, in all aspects of his work, of the principle of the *homoousion*."[32] It is against this background that one should examine Torrance's comments about the distinction between Divine essence and energies.

Discussing John of Damascus' use of Athanasius, Torrance points out that "God is so wonderfully and transcendentally free in his own eternal Being that he can do something new without changing in his *ousia* and can

29. Torrance, *The Christian Doctrine of God, One Being Three Persons*, 7, 8.

30. This is a reference to a comment by John of Damascus, *Exposition of the Orthodox Faith*, 1.4, of Gregory Nazianzen's words in his "Oratio 38.7" (see *Nicene and Post-Nicene Fathers*, Vol. VII). Torrance considers this interpretation as inappropriate and misleading.

31. Torrance, *Theology in Reconciliation*, 222, 237.

32. Gunton, "Being and Person: T. F. Torrance's Doctrine of God," 116.

go outside of himself in the Incarnation without ceasing to be what he is eternally in himself in his own ineffable Being, for his *energeia* inheres in his eternal *ousia*." In Athanasius, the Greek notion of *energeia* was Christianized under the transforming impact of the biblical conception of the creative and providential activity of the living God:

> The Athanasian view of God was one in which activity and movement were regarded as intrinsic to his very being as God. God is never without his activity, for his activity and his being are essentially and eternally one. The act of God is not one thing, and his being another, for they coinhere mutually and indivisibly in one another. Hence far from God being inactive in his inner being, it belongs to the essential and eternal nature of his being to move and energise and act.[33]

However, according to Torrance, this "is an entirely different conception of God from that which developed in later theology when the *energeia* of God was distinguished from his *ousia*,"[34] as, for instance, in the Cappadocians and in St. John of Damascus. Torrance is fully aware of the evolution of Greek philosophical terminology, in which the "meanings of *ousia* and *hypostasis*, *logos* and *energeia*, underwent a radical change through the use to which they were put in the hermeneutical and theological activity of the Church." In particular he believes that the Nicene *homoousios* marked a significant redefinition of *ousia*:

> The *homoousios to Patri* was revolutionary and decisive: it expressed the fact that what God is "toward us" and "in the midst of us" in and through the Word made flesh, he really is *in himself*; that he is in the *internal relations* of his transcendent being the very same Father, Son and Holy Spirit that he is in his revealing and saving activity in time and space toward mankind. In precise theological usage *ousia* now refers to being not simply as that which is but to what it is in respect of its internal reality. . . . If God is in himself what he is in the Person and activity of his incarnate Word and Son, then the being or *ousia* of God must be understood in a very un-Greek way. Applied to God *enousios logos* and *enousios energeia* express the fact that the being of God

---

33. Torrance, *Trinitarian Faith*, 74–75. It is worth comparing this last statement to a statement by Florovsky, *The Concept of Creation in Saint Athanasius*, 56–57: "Not only do we distinguish between 'Being' and 'Will'; but it is not the same thing, even for God, 'to be' and 'to act.'" As we have already seen, according to Florovsky "this was the deepest conviction of St. Athanasius."

34. Torrance, *Divine Meaning*, 187–88.

is not intrinsically empty of word or activity, not mute or static,
but is essentially eloquent and dynamic.[35]

Moreover, Torrance repeatedly points out that "If the Word (*Logos*)
and activity (*energeia*) of God manifest in the gospel are not inherent (*enou-
sioi*) in his eternal being, as Athanasius had insisted, then we cannot relate
what God is toward us in his economic self-revelation and self-giving to
what he ever is in himself or *vice versa*." However, in Torrance's view, this
was precisely "the danger that lurked in the Basilian distinction between the
Divine being and the Divine energies, which had the effect of restricting
knowledge of God to his Divine energies, and ruling out any real access to
knowledge of God in the intrinsic relations of his eternal triune being."[36]
According to Torrance, the approach of St. Athanasius was quite different:

> In speaking of the being or *ousia* of God, Athanasius used the
> term in its simplest sense as that which *is* and subsists by itself,
> but allowed that to be changed and transformed by the nature of
> God. Thus the *ousia* of God as Athanasius understands it is both
> *being* and *presence,* presence in being, and *being* and *activity,*
> activity in being, the transcendent Being of God the Creator
> who is actively, creatively present in all that he has made, up-
> holding it by the Word of his power and by *his* Spirit.[37]

Here one clearly finds articulated one of Torrance's main concerns
with the essence-energies distinction, the introduction of which he blames
on St. Basil the Great and St. Gregory of Nyssa. For Torrance, the distinction
restricts the knowledge of God to his energies, which are something else
than what God is in himself, i.e., not God himself. The distinction therefore
rules out any real access to the knowledge of God in the intrinsic relations of
his eternal triune being. This opinion of Torrance again goes against some of
the key points of Florovsky in his papers "The Concept of Creation in Saint
Athanasius"[38] and "Creature and Creaturehood,"[39] where it is stressed that
the Divine essence is God's inherent self-existence and the energies are his
relations towards the other:

> God *is* Life, and *has* life; *is* Wisdom, and *has* wisdom; and so
> forth. The first series of expressions refers to the incommuni-
> cable essence, the second to the inseparably distinct energies of

35. Ibid., 130–32.
36. Ibid., 335–36.
37. Ibid., 182.
38. Florovsky, "The Concept of Creation in Saint Athanasius," 36–57.
39. Florovsky, "Creature and Creaturehood," 43–78.

the one essence, which descend upon creation. None of these energies is hypostatic, nor hypostasis in itself, and their incalculable multiplicity introduces no composition into the Divine Being. The totality of the Divine "energies" constitutes His pretemporal will, His design—His good pleasure—concerning the "other," His eternal counsel. This is God Himself, not His Essence, but *His will*. The distinction between "essence" and "energies"—or, it could be said, between "nature" and "grace" [φύσις and χάρις]—corresponds to the mysterious distinction in God between "necessity" and "freedom," understood in a proper sense.[40]

"Translating" the distinction between essence and energies to the distinction between necessity and will could be helpful in identifying the hidden dangers in Torrance's terminology. Although emphasizing that understanding Divine *ousia* as being and presence, presence in being, and being and activity in the transcendent being of God the Creator who is actively and creatively present in all that he has made, is a wonderful way of expressing the dynamically active nature and presence of God in the world, it could be misinterpreted as referring to the assignment of necessity and homogeneity to the Divine activity in the world. This danger seems to emerge from the predominant emphasis on preserving the Divine unity expressed in Torrance's energetic terminology. This emphasis explains Torrance's focus on the epistemological and soteriological role of the *homoousion*. However, it leaves open the question about the specificity of the Divine activity within the created order. As Florovsky points out,

> Out of eternity God sees and wills, by His good pleasure, each and every being in the completeness of its particular destiny and features, even regarding its future and sin. . . . "Christ will behold all the numberless myriads of Saints, turning His glance away from none, so that to each one of them it will seem that He is looking at him, talking with him, and greeting him," and yet "while remaining unchanged, He will seem different to one and different to another."[41] . . . God in the counsel of His good pleasure, beholds all the innumerable myriads of created hypostases, wills them, and to each one of them manifests Himself in a different way. And herein consists the "inseparable distribution" of His grace or energy, "myriadfold hypostatic" in the bold phrase of St. Gregory Palamas, because this grace or energy is beneficently imparted to thousands upon myriads of thousands

40. Ibid., 68–69.
41. Here Florovsky refers to St. Symeon the New Theologian.

of hypostases. Each hypostasis, in its own being and existence, is sealed by a particular ray of the good pleasure of God's love and will. And in this sense, all things are in God—in "image" *but not by nature,* the created "all" being infinitely remote from Uncreated Nature.[42]

In this paragraph one may sense the advantage of the essence-energy distinction in providing a more subtle picture of Divine-human communion.

As we have seen, Torrance's main objection to the essence-energies distinction is that it appears to suggest that "we cannot know God through the immediate activity of his Being, or according to what he is in himself, but only through mediating forces emanating from him, and not according to what he is in himself."[43] However, drawing on Florovsky's subtle reading of Athanasius and other Greek Fathers—a reading to which Torrance himself appeals as authoritative—we can also see that Torrance's reading is not quite satisfactory or accurate on this point. To repeat Florovsky's unpacking of the essence-energies distinction: "The life-giving acts of God in the world *are God Himself*—an assertion which precludes separation but does not abolish distinction."[44]

Remarkably, Torrance suggested that the specific use of the "Basilian" distinction between essence and energies by Sts. Maximus the Confessor, John of Damascus and Gregory Palamas had the effect of introducing into Byzantine theology a "damaging dualism of an Augustinian kind."[45] This is a serious and very unfortunate (and un-historical) claim, which only demonstrates that Torrance did not have the chance to seriously engage with later Byzantine thought articulated for example in the dogmatic formulations of the Fifth, Sixth, and Seventh Ecumenical Councils. Unfortunately, by keeping himself so restrictively to the theological legacy of Sts. Athanasius and Cyril, he framed himself within pre-Chalcedonian terminology, missing the opportunity to enjoy the subtleties of its later theological refinement in the works of Maximus the Confessor, John of Damascus, and Gregory Palamas. Undoubtedly, there were understandable reasons for this, since his main audience consisted of fellow Reformed Christians, and he may have used his interaction with the Orthodox Church as a way for the careful initiation of a respectful and very much needed renewal of

42. Florovsky, "Creature and Creaturehood," 72–73.

43. Torrance, "The Doctrine of the Holy Trinity in Gregory Nazianzen and John Calvin," 38.

44. Florovsky, "Creature and Creaturehood," 65–66.

45. Ibid., 38.

his own tradition.[46] Perhaps it was some awareness of this limitation that allowed him on occasion to be soberly insightful about the value of the Orthodox teaching on the Divine essence and energies, as in one place he admits, reflecting a more accurate understanding:

> Yet Orthodox theology does not rest content merely with an Economic Trinity, for the uncreated energies through and in which God makes himself known to us are proper to and inseparable from the Divine Being who nevertheless remains unapproachable and unknowable in his innermost essence. The distinction is intended to reject any surrender of God's transcendence, while maintaining an ontic relation between God's economic self-revelation and what he is inherently in himself. . . . It is the essence of the Being (or Essence) of God that we can never know, but in *God* the Son and in *God* the Spirit we really are given to know God in his Being or *Ousia*, for in them God really reveals *himself through-himself.*[47]

A Science and Theology Interlude

One of the most popular and passionate themes in Torrance's works is related to theological importance of the relational understanding of space. Why is the relational notion of space so important for Torrance? The reason is that, according to him, the Newtonian understanding of space as static and absolute would shut God out of the world in a way that he could not enter into any relation with his creation. For Torrance, therefore, the discussion of the relational character of space has a definite epistemological import, since it is related to his understanding of Divine activity as a way for God to manifest himself and act in the world. "If we are really to have knowledge of God we must be given a point of access to him which is both in God himself and in our creaturely existence."[48] The actuality and the reality of the presence of the incarnate God in space and time enabled the Fathers of the Church to develop relational conceptions of space and time applying them in different ways to God and to created beings: "to God in one way in accordance with his transcendent nature, and to creaturely beings in another way in

46. This was an idea suggested in a private communication by Fr. George D. Dragas, Professor at the Holy Cross Greek Orthodox School of Theology, Brookline, MA, former student and close friend of Thomas Torrance.

47. Torrance, *Theology in Reconciliation*, 222, 237.

48. Torrance, *Trinitarian Faith*, 52–53.

accordance with their contingent natures."[49] The Church Fathers therefore were "able to relate the being and activity of the Son of God to bodily place (*topos*) when he entered into our human space (*hora*) and became man, without leaving God's 'place' and without leaving the universe empty of his presence and rule."[50] Space is regarded here within the context of the creative and redemptive activity of God in Christ; this is not the conception of space understood as infinite receptacle or as infinite substance. There emerges a concept of space in terms of the relations between God and the physical universe established in creation and incarnation: "Space in this formulation is a sort of differential concept that is essentially open-ended, for it is defined in accordance with the interaction between God and man."[51]

For Torrance, however, the emergence of the relational understanding of space was not without problems and difficulties. Torrance comments:

> The rise of these difficulties is particularly clear in the thought of John of Damascus, with whom the two poles in the Nicene concept of space began to draw apart. On the one hand, he appropriated fully the Aristotelian conception . . . which tended to give his notion of place or space a closed or rigid character; on the other hand, however, in order to balance this he had both to develop a concept of "mental place" and to carry his theology much further in an apophatic direction than Athanasius could go, even to claiming, like Basilides, that we cannot know what God is but only what he is not.[52]

One can see again that for Torrance the main issue here is epistemological, and the specific understanding of space entails a specific understanding of the nature of the relation between God and the world.

In Torrance's view, "the Nicene conceptions of space and time have proved more fruitful and adaptable, and certainly have a much closer relation to more modern notions of space and time."[53] For him the relational view of space adopted by the early Church anticipated the later emergence of the view of space expressed in the field theory introduced by James Clark Maxwell and in Albert Einstein's theory of relativity.[54] The new scientific understanding of space-time has emerged as an alternative to Newtonian physics by providing a new ontological status of space-time. Newton made

49. Ibid., 104.

50. Torrance, *Divine Meaning*, 371.

51. Ibid.

52. Ibid., 372–73.

53. Ibid.

54. Torrance, *Space, Time and Incarnation*, 57–59.

the successful hypothesis that space and time are fixed structured back-ground entities underlying material reality, which participate in governing the motion of physical objects. What Einstein discovered is that Newton had mistaken a physical field for a background entity.[55] The two entities hypostatized by Newton, space and time, could be actually considered as a particular local configuration of a physical entity—the gravitational field. Einstein's discovery was that Newtonian space and time and the gravi-tational field were the same entity. To emphasize the relational aspect of space-time one may express the meaning of Einstein's discovery in a radical way by saying that "there are no space and time: there are only dynamical objects. The world is made by dynamical fields. These do not live in, or on, space-time: they form and exhaust reality."[56]

It is a fact that Torrance was a great admirer of the scientific contribu-tions of James Clark Maxwell and Albert Einstein. This fact is quite revealing since it illustrates Torrance's preferences for a relatively narrow spectrum of ideas within modern physics. However, according to John Polkinghorne, although Maxwell and Einstein are among the greatest scientists ever and definitely deserve their status as scientific heroes of Torrance, they are "the last of the ancients rather than the first of the moderns."[57] For Polkinghorne it is quite unfortunate that Torrance did not engage more seriously with the developments of quantum mechanics, which has developed a more subtle sense of reality. Torrance's appreciation of Einstein led him to stay on the same front with him in the debate concerning the possibility of a realist interpretation of quantum mechanics, a fact that evidently prevented Tor-rance from engaging in further dialogue with modern quantum physicists, especially with those who do not adhere to Einstein's interpretation.[58] For example, Torrance expressed multiple times his distrust of the Copenhagen interpretation of quantum mechanics and specifically of the epistemology of Niels Bohr. According to him, there are "difficulties which we still have with quantum theory, particularly as it stems from Bohr, Heisenberg and Born, which may be traced, in part at least, to Kantian presuppositions."[59] He also points out that there is a tension that arises between critical realism and the epistemological presuppositions latent in the Copenhagen inter-pretation of quantum theory.[60] According to Tapio Luoma, "the primary

55. Rovelli, "The Disappearance of Space and Time," 25–36.
56. Ibid.
57. Polkinghorne, *Belief in God in an Age of Science*, 80.
58. Luoma, *Incarnation and Physics*, 67.
59. Torrance, *Reality and Scientific Theology*, 75.
60. Torrance, *Preaching Christ Today*, 41.

reason for Torrance's reluctance to the widely accepted Copenhagen interpretation of quantum physics lies precisely in his view of realism."[61] The
particular feature in Torrance's thought that makes it incompatible with
the Copenhagen interpretation of the behavior of elementary particles is
associated with the problem concerning the real objective existence of the
physical entities observed in quantum mechanical experiments. In Torrance's view the standard interpretation of quantum mechanics remains
agnostic with regard to the existence of an objective reality independently
of the observer. This view is not unique to Torrance. For example, according to Fr. Stanley Jaki—a Roman Catholic priest and theologian whose
ideas Torrance respected very much,[62]

> the possibility for Bohr consisted in restricting discourse to *as-
> pects* of reality while barring questions about reality itself, and
> especially about its objective existence. In Bohr's case this was
> all the more laden with further problems because the *aspects*
> in question were more opposite, nay mutually exclusive, than
> merely distinct. He tried to hold them together by offering the
> idea of complementarity. These aspects could *really* complement
> one another only if they inhered in a deeper reality, about which
> Bohr could only be agnostic. A harmony of relations or aspects,
> complementing one another, such was Bohr's epistemological
> message, a message void of reference to the ontological reality
> of anything harmonious. About the entity which embodied the
> harmony of relations he was not permitted by his own premises
> to make any claim and he carefully avoided doing so.[63]

Unfortunately, the views of both Torrance and Jaki seem to be the
result of a mere misunderstanding of Bohr's position. Bohr made a clear
distinction between the unique identity of a quantum object and the specific
complementary ways of its *energetic manifestation*. This distinction is crucial for Bohr in emphasizing the reality of the quantum world while at the
same time accepting that it does not make sense to speak about its "being in
a certain way" independent of the interaction with a specific experimental
arrangement. Such view does not conform to the classical understanding
of realism; it adopts a more subtle way of looking at reality allowing for a
self-subsisting object to manifest mutually exclusive (or complementary)

61. Luoma, *Incarnation and Physics*, 67–68.

62. I am grateful to Fr. George G. Dragas for pointig out to me Torrance's admira-
tion for the works and ideas of Fr. Stanley Jaki.

63. Jaki, "The Horns of Complementarity."

types of natural properties depending on the specific circumstances of the interaction between the observer and the object.

How can we explain this misunderstanding of Bohr's ideas? One might point out two different reasons. The first one is the fact that both Torrance and Stanley Jaki formed their opinions before some of the most recent decisive experiments in quantum physics which proved the inconsistency of their suspicions about Bohr's epistemological viewpoint.[64] The latest developments in quantum physics suggest that

> [w]e can no longer assume that the properties we measure necessarily reflect or represent the properties of the particles as they really are. As Heisenberg had argued, "we have to remember that what we observe is not nature in itself but nature exposed to our method of questioning." This does not mean that quantum particles are not real. What it does mean is that we can ascribe to them only an *empirical* reality.[65]

According to Christos Yannaras, in quantum physics it became evident that the result of the observation of the micro-world is connected with the specific type of instruments, and also with the specific method of observation and description.[66] The specific model that could be used to describe a physical system depends on the observer and the nature of the apparatus it is interacting with. Our perception of reality can change in accordance with our instruments or our method of observation; conversely, observed reality can be transformed by the fact of observing it. "What this means is that the nature of existing reality is not independent of human action, yet the answer nature gives us as the result of the individual measurement is random. The result is beyond our control, which indicates an independent physical reality."[67]

The second reason for Torrance's misunderstanding of Bohr's realist position is the lack of a proper understanding of the concept of hypostasis. It was already pointed out that Torrance had an unwarranted preoccupation with the danger of a potential disjunction between person/hypostasis and act/agency as if hypostatic acts and activity may exist independently of a specific hypostasis. This preoccupation seems to have been the source of Torrance's sense of dualism in relation to both the teaching on the distinction between essence and energies and Bohr's interpretation of quantum mechanics. It is true that Bohr did not use a well formed terminology

64. Groblacher et al., "An Experimental Test of Non-local Realism," 871.
65. Baggott, *The Quantum Story*, 356.
66. Yannaras, *Postmodern Metaphysics*, 90–93.
67. Zeilinger, "Quantum Physics: Ontology or Epistemology?" 38–39.

allowing him to better articulate the inherent relationship between quantum entities and their specific natural manifestations. However, one may definitely see his struggle with the lack of such terminology. Just as an example, at one place he pointed out that

> information regarding the behavior of an atomic object obtained under definite experimental conditions may . . . be adequately characterized as complementary to any information *about the same object* obtained by some other experimental arrangements excluding the fulfillment of the first conditions. Although such kinds of information cannot be combined into a single picture by means of ordinary concepts, they represent indeed equally essential aspects of any knowledge *of the object in question* which can be obtained in this domain.[68]

Here "the same object" and "the object in question" refer exactly to the quantum entity which triggers its specific natural manifestations during a specific quantum mechanical experiment. Werner Heisenberg noted several times that Bohr did not have a problem with language but was in the process of inventing a new one. In this process he "tried to keep the words and the pictures without keeping the meanings of the words and of the pictures, having been from his youth interested in the limitation of our way of expression, the limitation of words, the problem of talking about things when one knows that the words do not really get hold of the things."[69]

It is quite interesting that Torrance, who had developed a great sensitivity for the ways of using of language in theology and physics, did not show any empathy towards Bohr's efforts to develop a proper language in articulating the subtlety of quantum mechanical realism. On the other hand, the potential for a mutual terminological enrichment between theology and quantum mechanics has been already discussed within the context of Orthodox theology. For example, Christos Yannaras points out that when we speak of relations in quantum mechanics, we do not refer to predictable correlations, but rather "to a mode of correlation, referentiality and coordination which has the character of the unpredictable, of the probable, of the possible, and which could be compared only with the dynamic freedom of interpersonal human relations."[70] This is a key point suggesting that we may actually get closer to a better understanding of quantum phenomena if we describe quantum entities in terms of the theological terminology of

---

68. Bohr, "Natural Philosophy and Human Cultures," 23–31.

69. Ibid.

70. Yannaras, *Postmodern Metaphysics*, 93.

THE CONCEPT OF ENERGY IN THOMAS F. TORRANCE AND ORTHODOX THEOLOGY 211

essence, nature, hypostasis, and energy.[71] The basis for this claim is the fact that, by distinguishing essence or nature from person or hypostasis as well as the energies both from the nature and from the hypostasis, the theology of the Eastern Church has adopted a terminology that is very helpful in interpreting the reality of existence, the appearance and disclosure of being.[72]

What is, however, even more interesting is that Yannaras provides a theological interpretation of space by using the concept of energy within the context of a relational understanding of person (*prosopon*): "we recognize space as the accommodation of personal reference, as a fact of relation."[73] The external view of personal relations objectifies space as the distance between the two terms of the relation and establishes distance as the basis for the measurement of space. The objectification of physical reality, however, does not negate the experience of space in terms of interpersonal relation. The ecstatic reference of the person is a fact that transcends the categories of measurable space. According to Yannaras, the second term of a personal relation may be here or elsewhere, present or absent, but is always referring to the same non-dimensional space of personal reference. "The power of personal relations negates the measurable dimensions of here and there, of nearer and farther, and points to both presence and absence as the experience of non-dimensional nearness."[74] The Byzantine theologians saw in personal energy the non-dimensional place both of the human person and of the Person of God. He refers specifically to John of Damascus (whose understanding of space Torrance considered as problematic), who defined the space of God's disclosure of his personal energy as the place of God: "What is called the place of God is where his energy becomes manifest."[75] This is a statement that provides a link between the relational understanding of space in John of Damascus and modern physics where space and time are considered as a result of the presence of matter and energy. For Yannaras, God's personal energy becomes manifest primarily in the space of cosmic reality and the world is revealed to humanity as the non-dimensional place of Divine personal energy. Cosmic space acquires its meaning only as a Divine place. It is then not measured as conventional distance from humanity or as the interval between objects. The cosmos accommodates or gives space to the mutual relation between God and humanity. Humanity discovers the

71. Tanev, "The Language of Orthodox Theology and Quantum Mechanics." The content of this essay is reproduced in this book.

72. Yannaras, *Elements of Faith*, 43.

73. This section follows very closely the insights of Yannaras, *Person and Eros*, 105.

74. Ibid., 107.

75. John of Damascus, *An exposition of the Orthodox faith*, 1.13.

accessibility of God in the fact of the reality of the world, without this accessibility removing the *natural* distance of God from the world, the distance separating uncreated from created nature. The closeness of humanity to God within the context of the world is not natural but *personal*—a closeness defined by a relationship. In this sense, one could say that it is not the world that accommodates God or his personal energy, but the Divine will and energy which accommodates or gives space to the world, a space outside God which is simultaneously God's place, the disclosure of the non-dimensional immediacy of his personal energy. The distinction between the nature and the energies of God, without denying the reality of the natural distance of God from the world, preserves the world as a space of the immediate personal nearness of God and manifests God as the place of the universe: "For God is not contained, but is himself the place of all" (Theophilus of Antioch, *To Autolycus*, Book II, Ch. III: What has become of the gods?).[76]

The theological understanding of space suggested by Christos Yannaras provides an example of an alternative approach to the encounter between theology and physics. Yannaras develops a comprehensive theological perspective of the world by borrowing ideas from both Albert Einstein (general relativity) and Niels Bohr (quantum mechanics) in combination with a genuinely personal understanding of Divine-human communion which includes the distinction between Divine essence and energies. The comparison of Yannaras' and Torrance's approaches provides an opportunity to demonstrate the correlation between their preoccupations with specific themes in modern physics and their specific theological insights. Thomas Torrance has clearly neglected the epistemological insights emerging from the advances of quantum mechanics in the twentieth century and has ended up with neglecting the value of the Orthodox teaching on the distinction between Divine essence and energies. This neglect seems to be also associated with an underdeveloped understanding of person/*prosopon*/*hypostasis*. The overall result is the appearance of statements that contradict the apophatic character of the distinction between Divine essence and energies and the subtlety of the apophatic realism of Divine-human communion.

Final Reflections

The purpose of this paper was to review and discuss Thomas Torrance's interpretation of the Orthodox teaching on the distinction between Divine essence and energies. As a way of conclusion one could make two final points.

76. http://www.newadvent.org/fathers/0204.htm

First, some of Torrance's main concerns are associated with: (i) the danger of falling into dualistic divisions between what God is in himself and what he is towards us, and (ii) the danger of an understanding of the Trinitarian Monarchy on the basis of the Person of the Father as compared to a Monarchy of the Trinity based on the unity of the Divine essence and agency. Torrance does not accept any ontological ordering within the Trinity starting with the Person of the Father and considers such teaching to be correlated with the distinction between essence and energies. This is one of the reasons for him to be suspicious in his interpretation of the teachings of St. Basil concerning the Divine unity and the possibility to know God through the Divine energies. There are two interesting "moments" in this approach. The first is that it goes directly against the theology of one of the major Orthodox theologians alive today—Metropolitan John Zizioulas.[77] What is even more interesting, however, is that Metropolitan John is himself also quite suspicious about the teaching on the distinction between essence and energies and its role in Orthodox theology in particular.[78] The discrepancy between the two theologians could be (schematically) expressed in terms of their different understanding of the ontological sources of Divine energy or activity. If Divine activity is grounded in the being and essence of God as tri-unity (Torrance), the Divine monarchy cannot be other but Trinitarian and *perichoretic*; on the other hand, if the Divine activity, will and love are grounded in the person or hypostasis (Zizioulas), the Divine monarchy requires a single hypostasis—the hypostasis of the Father, as a guarantee of the Divine unity.

The second "moment" is that Torrance's approach has some interesting similarities with the theological synthesis of Fr. Dumitru Staniloae, for whom the unity of the Trinity is both essential and personal. The essential unity is based on the common *ousia* which is not seen as a separate reality or in separation from the Divine persons. The personal unity is based on the inter-subjectivity of the Persons in their coinherence or *perichoresis*. Interestingly, however, Fr. Dumitru is one of the few Orthodox theologians who have systematically employed the teaching on the distinction between Divine essence and energies to provide probably the most comprehensive synthesis in Orthodox theology today. There have already been some good attempts at a systematic comparison of the theological approaches of Zizioulas and Staniloae.[79] It would be quite relevant for future studies to concen-

77. See for example the relevant sections in Zizioulas, *Communion & Otherness*.

78. Ibid. See the theological context of the references to St. Gregory Palamas.

79. Berger, "Does the Eucharist make the Church?"; Berger, *Towards a Theological Gnoseology*; Танев, *Ти, Който си навсякъде и всичко изпълваш*.

trate on a more comprehensive comparison of the Trinitarian theologies of Torrance and Staniloae.

Second, although Torrance has clearly vocalized his concerns with some key Orthodox theological teachings, his theology has been perceived quite sympathetically by contemporary Orthodox theologians. Without any doubt there will be more studies focusing on exploring his theological contributions. One of the subjects of such explorations should focus on Torrance's approach to the interplay between theology and science. At the same time, the discussion of his specifically theological positions, including his critique of the distinction between Divine essence and energies, should be considered as a fruitful resource in some of the ongoing Orthodox theological discussions.

Chapter 11

Man as Co-creator: The Theological Insights of St. Maximus the Confessor within an Interdisciplinary Context[1]

Introduction

In a discussion of St. Maximus' understanding of the *logoi* as "prede-terminations and divine acts of will," David Bradshaw points out that such understanding could explain St. Maximus' claim that God knows creatures "as His own acts of will."[2] He also points out that according to St. Maximus rational creatures are deified insofar as they move and act in accordance with their *logoi* and it is actually the free choice of human beings that makes them move either toward the state of full being, which is the Creator's intent, or towards non-being. Bradshaw refers to Bishop Alexander Golitzin's work on Dionysius the Areopagite where the human movement in accordance with the *logoi* is considered as a way for human beings to become their own *co-creators*:

> The *logoi* are therefore our personal and foreordained vocations to which we may or may not choose to become conformed, or better—since they remain transcendent by virtue of their source in God—to which we may choose to be ever in process of becoming conformed in order thus to share, as it were, in the eternal process of our own creation.[3]

---

1. The original text of this chapter was presented at the International Colloquium "Maximus the Confessor as a European Philosopher," Berlin, September 26–28, 2014.

2. Bradshaw, *Aristotle East and West*, 206.

3. Alxander (Golitzin), *Et Introibo Ad Altare Dei.*, 86.

Bradshaw also refers also to Jean-Claude Larchet who provides a similar reading of a long passage from the *Ambigua* 7 [1080B].[4] It should be pointed out that St. Maximus offers multiple occasions for such interpretations. One of the most articulated examples is in his *Ascetic Life* where St. Maximus emphasizes that "the Lord bestowed on us the method of salvation and has given us eternal power to become sons of God. So finally our salvation is in our will's grasp."[5]

The reason I referred to the work of David Bradshaw is the fact that it was the first occasion for me to face the use of the term "co-creation" within a specific theological context. I happen to have a particular interest in studying co-creative phenomena since I have spent almost ten years exploring similar concepts in the fields of technology innovation management, participatory design and marketing. In these fields value co-creation has emerged as part of a paradigm shift in the way we look at people as consumers and customers.[6] The old paradigm had assigned designers, inventors and firms with the privileged role of being "the creators" of value for the rest of us, the customers, who were considered to be mere consumers. The new paradigm repositions the creation of value on the interface between the designers/inventors/firms and the customer, transforming customers into co-creators of value. Once a customer acquires the role of a co-creator, his or her contribution to the value creation process becomes personal. The most radical aspect of the new paradigm is the way it changed the dominant twentieth-century understanding of marketing where people were considered statistically, i.e., as personally indistinguishable individuals who were compartmentalized in target market segments that were to be addressed by the same product or service. The repositioning of customers as co-creators of value has also enabled the rediscovery of personhood in the social sciences.[7] This is because the technological advancements in information and communication technologies have made it possible for customers to actively participate in the definition and the *personalization* of the generic market offers that are equally available to everyone. What the technological advancements actually did was to enable the development of customer participation platforms allowing the personal contributions of individual customers. However, the growing relevance of customer *participation* in value

4. Larchet, *La divinisation de l'homme selon saint Maxime le Confesseur*, 119–20, referring to Maximos the Confessor, "Ambiguum 7," in *On difficulties in the Church Fathers*, Vol. I, 97–99.

5. St. Maximus the Confessor, *The Ascetic Life*, 133.

6. Tanev et al. "How Do Value Co-creation Activities Relate to the Perception of Firms' Innovativeness?" 131–59.

7. Smith, *What Is a Person?*

creation was not just a technologically enabled phenomenon. It was also the expression of an emerging trend in design and innovation studies focusing on the participatory role of users as contributors to the actual design of specific new products and services.[8] This trend has helped the emergence of the concepts of participatory design, open and user innovation. It has also enabled the emergence of the unfortunate term "crowdsourcing"—a combination of the words "crowd" and "outsourcing" which was coined more than ten years ago by referring to a specific process used by firms to obtain innovative ideas by soliciting contributions from online user communities, rather than from traditional employees or partners. As some scholars in the business and social sciences have already realized "it is worth being careful with words because the structure of the language chosen determines the penetrative power of the resulting analysis."[9]

The emerging relevance of the various aspects of *personalization* and *participation* in our everyday lives and, respectively, in the social sciences, offers the opportunity of exploring the interdisciplinary potential of the terminological cross-examination of the co-creation concepts in theology and in the social sciences in general. It is a fact that the social sciences are in need of a refinement of the co-creation terminology since the excessive scholarly interest in researching co-creative phenomena has resulted in a kind of semantic pollution which is not really contributing to the relevance of the ongoing research studies.[10] The underlying motivation for such cross-examination is grounded in the fact that Byzantine theology in general and, more specifically, the theological anthropology of St. Maximus the Confessor offer a unique and comprehensive conceptual apparatus that could be highly valuable for the social sciences. The specific choice of an appropriate conceptual apparatus is quite important since the logic to which we rely on in a particular empirical context is directly related the conceptual apparatus that was adopted—"by changing the conceptual apparatus, we change the logic into another one."[11] This present chapter offers a first attempt for a terminological cross-examination with a focus on the reception of the co-creative aspects of the theological anthropology of St. Maximus the Confessor. It will summarize the contributions of several modern Orthodox

8. Schuler and Namioka, *Participatory Design: Principles and Practices.*

9. Spender, *Business Strategy*, 2.

10. Tanev et al., "Value Co-creation as Part of an Integrative Vision for Innovation Management."

11. The notion of conceptual apparatus was introduced by Kazimierz Ajdukiewicz. According to him, the picture of the world one has developed is not coming directly from the data of experience but depends on the specific conceptual apparatus chosen. See Ajdukiewicz, *The Scientific World-Perspective*, 81.

theologians and philosophers who have focused on the articulation of the co-creative role of human beings in shaping their own eschatological future, and conclude by discussing the potential theological value of Actor-Network Theory—an exploratory perspective that emerged in the early 1980s at the Centre de Sociologie de l'Innovation of the École Nationale Supérieure des Mines de Paris, which is usually associated with the names of Bruno Latour, John Law and Michael Callon.[12]

Co-creation and the Legacy of St. Maximus in the Twentieth and Twenty-first Centuries

This co-creative role of human beings as active agents in the process of their own continuous creation, salvation and deification has been emphasized by some of the key Orthodox thinkers in the twentieth and twenty-first centuries with a direct reference to the theology of St. Maximus the Confessor. For example, according to Fr. George Florovsky, "the whole history of Divine Providence is for St. Maximus divided into two great periods: the first culminates in the Incarnation of the Logos and is the story of Divine condescension ('through the Incarnation'); the second is the story of human ascension into the glory of deification, an extension, as it were, of the Incarnation to the whole creation."[13] Following a similar line of thought Fr. George points out that:

> creation is not a phenomenon but a "substance." The reality and substantiality of created nature is manifested first of all in creaturely freedom. Freedom is not exhausted by the possibility of choice, but presupposes it and starts with it. And creaturely freedom is disclosed first of all in the equal possibility of two ways: to God and away from God. This duality of ways is not a mere formal or logical possibility, but a real possibility, dependent on the effectual presence of powers and capacities not only for a choice between, but also for the following of, the two ways. Freedom consists not only in the possibility, but also in the necessity of autonomous choice, the resolution and resoluteness of choice. Without this autonomy, nothing happens in creation. As St. Gregory the Theologian says, "God legislates human self-determination." "He honored man with freedom that good might belong no less to him who chose it than to Him Who planted its

---

12. Latour, *Reassembling the Social*.
13. Florovsky, *"Cur Deus Homo? The Motive of the Incarnation,"* 70–79.

seed." Creation must ascend to and unite with God by its own efforts and achievements.[14]

Another Orthodox theologian who referred to the theology of St. Maximus in order to emphasize the co-creativity of human beings in the pursuit of union with God is St. Justin Popovich. According to Vladimir Cvetkovic "St. Justin relies on St. Maximus" in claiming that,

> taken in the context of our salvation, faith, according to St. Justin, is not only belief in the Divine salvific work, but also belief in our capacity to contribute to our salvation by acquiring the virtues. Thus, by becoming gods, human beings fulfill the purpose of their creation. Since they continue to perfect themselves throughout all eternity by love of God and other virtues, faith as the crown and the perfection of all these virtues does not stop to exist. Faith is transformed then from the belief in our salvation to the belief in the progress "from glory to glory" in the eternal union with God.[15]

The theological insights of St. Maximus have obviously helped St. Justin Popovich in articulating one of the most Christologically theantropic vision of the relationship between man and God in the twentieth century. In his own words:

> In the center of the worlds stands Christ the Theanthropos. He is the axis around which all worlds, both high and low, revolve. He is the mysterious center towards which all souls that hunger for eternal truth and life gravitate. He is both the project and the source of all the creative forces of Orthodox theanthropic culture. Here God works and man collaborates; God creates through man and man creates trough God; here the divine creation is continued through man. To this end, man brings out of himself all that is divine and puts it into action, creation arid life. In this creativity, all that is divine, not only in man but also in the world around him, is expressed and brought into action; all that is divine is active, and all that is human joins in this activity. But, in order to collaborate successfully with God, man must accustom himself to thinking, feeling, living, and creating by God. . . . Man serves God through himself and all creation around him. He systematically, deliberately, brings God and the divine into all his work, all his creativity. He awakens all that is divine in nature around him, so that nature, led by man with

14. Florovsky, "Creation and Creaturehood," 48–49.
15. Cvetkovic, "St. Justin Popović's reception of St. Maximus the Confessor."

his yearning for Christ, can serve God. In this way, all creation participates in the universal, divine service, for nature serves man, who serves God.[16]

Fr. Nicholas Loudovikos is another Orthodox theologian who has most explicitly emphasized the dialogical natural of the relationship between man and God. His emphasis is based on an insightful reading of the Maximian teaching on the Divine *logoi*. According to Fr. Nicholas the term "*logoi* of beings" is not translatable in English.

> *Logos* means "constitutive principle," "inner principle," "essential principle," "rationale," "reason," or simply "word." . . . The uncreated *logoi* are acts (*energeiai*) of the divine loving will in constant dialogue with creation: *logos* means always dia-*logos* (dialogue) in the Greek patristic tradition and particularly in St. Maximus the Confessor's thought. Logos is uncreated but distinct from uncreated divine being. It is personal (*enhypostatos*) not in the sense that it is a being itself, but in the sense that it is the volitive expression of a personal being who moves his essence to act ad extra. . . . By the *logoi* . . . God creates, that is proposes to beings their own essences and an ontological dialogue follows. If essence is thus given, its "mode of existence" is only the result of this dialogue between the logos word of God and the logos-word of man. That means that the final *esse* of created beings is unknown, indeterminate, because it is the eschatological result of a long dialogue between God and man, a dialogue which culminates in the cross and the resurrection of Christ. Christ, the Divine Logos-Son of the Father, is himself in his incarnate composite hypostasis the ontological presupposition of this ontological dialogue. . . . So our participation in the divine energies is simply the way of our participation in the crucified and resurrected Christ.[17]

In another text Fr. Nicholas elaborates further on his dialogical reciprocity theological approach by emphasizing the generically relational and dialogical character of the Divine energies: He points out that for St. Gregory Palamas deification "is neither a sort of natural 'imitation,' nor an 'amelioration of human nature' but the assimilation of God himself through the Divine energies, which descend from the Father and become participable in Christ, through the Spirit."[18] According to Fr. Nicholas,

16. Popovich, *Man and the God-Man*, 49–50.

17. N. Loudovikos, "Ontology Celebrated," 147–48.

18. Ibid., 130.

"[t]he most important thing concerning the Palamite concept of deification, as a participational ascent to God through the Divine energies manifested in Christ by the Spirit, is its *relational* and finally *ecclesial* character. The energies themselves are 'relational and participational,'" which for Fr. Nicholas means that they are dialogical or analogical. And the fundamental reason for this dialogical/analogical aspect of the Divine energies is twofold. *First*, this is the connection, on one hand, between the Divine energies and Divine will and, on the other hand, between the energies and the Dionysian or Maximian Divine processions/participations/*logoi* of beings.

> For Dionysius, as well as for Maximus, the divine processions/
> participations/*logoi*, as expressions of the divine loving will, are
> deeply connected with the concept of analogy (while Maximus
> develops this concept changing it into a mimetical icon). This
> is a term that signifies a deep dialogue of *synergy*, or, better,
> *syn-energy*, since analogy for the above authors refers not to a
> similitude of essences but to an analogous action between two
> different agents in order for them to achieve union. Thus, divine
> energy as a participable expression of divine will, is *dialogical*,
> in the sense that it calls for an energetic/active response on the
> part of its recipients.[19]

In his latest book Fr. Nicholas associates his dialogical theological perspective with the concepts of sophianicity and co-creation:

> The activation by free otherness of this dialogue forms the
> sophianicity of creation and constitutes a co-creation with God,
> making the natures of beings complete in their natural mode of
> existence. Thus the sophianic nature of beings is manifested in
> a sophianic manner in the common will and energy of human-
> kind and God (as free reception of the will and energy of God
> by the will and energy of humankind) and will be revealed, since
> it still remains unknown it its fullness, in the eschatological age.
> What we already know is that the mode of this sophianic, syner-
> gistic becoming of nature is consubstantiality.[20]

The second dimension of the dialogical/analogical aspect of the Divine energies can be found in the ecclesial core of the Palamite understanding of participation. In the words of Fr. Nicholas,

> If energy exists only as an analogical syn-energy, this syn-energy
> does not have to do only with the vertical relation with God, but

19. Ibid., 131.
20. Loudovikos, *Church in the Making*, 209.

also with the horizontal relation between creatures. . . . Any real elevation to God has to happen by the grace/energy of the Holy Spirit, in Christ, and that means that man has to bring with him "every kind of creature, as he himself participates in everything and is also able to participate in the one who lies above everything, in order for the icon (image) of God to be completed." . . . In ecclesiological terms, that means that it is only in the process of the realization of the ecclesial dialogical/analogical synergetic communion, that elevation to God can be achieved.[21]

And, as Fr. Nicholas pointed out, the manifestation of the double participational analogy of such dialogical syn-energy can be found in the Eucharist:

The mode of existence of beings in the state of becoming is consubstantiality, in the manner that this is activated in the eucharistic assembly and embodiment of the faithful and, in the measure in which, by the personal ascetical appropriation of the mystery of the cross, the will, or rather, the gnomic desire of the faithful preserves the grace of the eucharistic mystery of the unity. This mode of existence is therefore through participation uncreated, except that it is activated only by the dialogical assent and synergy of created human freedom.[22]

One can also see how using this dialogical and participational theological perspective helps in emphasizing a very interesting aspect of the Maximian understanding of the Divine *logoi* of creation—the fact that they could explain not only the relationship between the One (Who is uncreated) and the many (who are created) but also the salvific relevance of the relationship between every one (who is created) to the rest of the many (who are created). Fr. Nicholas points out that the Divine *logoi* can be seen as the ontological expression of the entire organization of reality, a term used by Fr. Dumitru Staniloae,[23] inasmuch as, in the words of St. Maximus, "in their substance and formation all created things are positively defined by their own *logoi*, and by the *logoi* that exist around them and which constitute their defining limits."[24]

---

21. Ibid., 132.

22. Ibid., 209

23. Fr. Nicholas Loudovikos refers to Staniloae, "Eisagogi asto ergo tou agiou Maxomou 'Philosophika kai Theologika Erotemata,'" 22. See also Staniloae, "The World as Gift and Word," in *The Experience of God. Orthodox Dogmatic Theology*, Vol. 2.

24. Maximos the Confessor, "Ambiguum 7," in *On difficulties in the Church Fathers*, Vol. I, 101.

The co-creativity of human beings should be considered therefore within the context of the multiplicity of their own *logoi* and the *logoi* that exist around them as co-constitutive principles of their existential field of action. The *logoi* of all co-existing things provide the basis for the communication between entities, because their *logoi* interpenetrate each other and are determined by each other:

> The *logos* of each entity is "threefold," because "if entities have essence and potentiality and energy, it is clear that in this respect they have a threefold *logos* of being." Furthermore, we have *logoi* of races, species, and individuals, *logoi* of time and nature, without which things could not exist, and also *logoi* of bodies and of bodiless beings. We also find a special *logos* of *hypostasis* (substantive existence), because "nature possesses the common *logos* of being, while the *hypostasis* possesses the *logos* whereby something exists in itself."[25]

The multiplicity of the *logoi* is quite important in explaining the contingency of the relationship between man and God, neither in terms of some kind of agential arbitrariness or unpredictability of both, Divine activity and human existence, nor in terms of some kind of fatalistic Divine or impersonal and naturalistic form of predestination that would somewhat secretly shape the ultimate end of human destiny. It is rather in terms of the interplay between the relevance of individual human activities and the specificity, and the interdependence of the Divine providential activities within the creaturely context of the agency of the surrounding human and physical natural environments.

This multifold and composite format of the interactive human and worldly environments providing the context of the relationship between God and man has been also discussed by Georgi Kapriev in his recent book on St. Maximus which, unfortunately, is available only in Bulgarian. Kapriev also refers to *Ambigua* 7 [1081B] to point out that for St. Maximus all created things are positively and entirely defined by their own *logoi*, and by the *logoi* that exist around them and which constitute their defining limits.[26] He however emphasizes in a most explicit way that

> [t]here is no one single *logos* to which each individual thing would uniquely correspond but a multiplicity of *logoi* which synthesize in a coherent way the proper *logos* of each concretely existing thing. And, in a completely symmetrical way, the *logoi* should be seen in their particularizing function due to

25. Loudovikos, *A Eucharistic Ontology*, 72–73.
26. Maximos the Confessor, "*Ambigua 7*," 101.

which each particular being becomes different and independent of all other beings.[27]

Kapriev points out that "[f]rom this perspective the being of the created world becomes 'intelligible' exactly because of the togetherness of its
logoi which come from God and converge together, enter into coherence
and interlink each other in a variety of ways. All differences in terms of
quality depend on the different types of configurations emerging in between
the *logoi*."[28] According to Kapriev,

> When Maximus mentions a certain individual created *logos*,
> he always sees it in the horizon of the manifestation of an-
> other, higher or more general, logos, ultimately relating both
> of them to the highest One *Logos*. . . . The *Logos* actualizes the
> differentiation of the economic and creative Divine energies
> in a way that each individual being acquires in a concrete and
> specific way its individually assigned energies. . . . This is how
> God simultaneously sees and knows both the individual things
> and the entirety of the created order. When considered in itself
> the *Logos* is a purely dynamical reality which translates activ-
> ity, i.e., energy. The dynamism of the reality consists in its in
> permanent correspondence with the entire energetic structure
> of the Divine economy.[29]

In this sense, every individual created thing should be seen as part of
the logi-cal network emerging out of the interactions of its multiple *logoi*.
One should admit however that, "since it is created out of nothing, every
single thing can deviate in a greater or lesser extent from its proper logic
or 'logos-ness' and such deviations should be considered as an expression of its existential autonomy."[30] We should therefore conceptualize the
dialogical and analogical aspects of the *logoi* in a multidimensional way,
extending the uni-directional understanding of the relationship between
God and man by including the interplay between the "logical" variety and
consistency of the world as a gift enabling the communion between the
created and uncreated order.

By referring to the understanding on the world as a gift we can now
focus on discussing the theological insights of Fr. Dumitru Staniloae who
has beautifully discussed the dialogical nature of the relationship between

27. Каприев, Максим Изповедник, 145.

28. Ibid., 147.

29. Ibid., 150.

30. Ibid., 151.

God and man within the context of the specificity and the multiplicity of the Divine reasons/*logoi* of all created things.[31] According to him,

> The world as nature proves itself a rational unitary reality that exists for the sake of the dialogue among human beings and as a condition for the spiritual growth of humans and for the development of humankind. According to the fathers, all things have their inner principles/reasons in the divine Logos or the supreme Reason. . . . The rationality of the world has, however, multiple values. It is malleable and contingent, and the human person is the one who makes use of these characteristics and brings them to light. . . . In the human person alone does the rationality of nature's undefined possibilities acquire meaning or a purpose, or draw even closer to its fulfillment. . . . By discovering and harnessing the manifold rationality of the world— freely and in cooperation with his neighbors—in order to make better use of the world's resources and to grasp its inexhaustible meanings, the human person grows in communion with these. Moreover, this process itself becomes a source that leads to the knowledge of other and still more sublime meanings.[32]

> Through created things God has given humans two gifts: *first*, the possibility to think and speak, for this arises from the very fact that God conceived the inner principles of things and posited them in existence, having created for them beforehand a material covering adapted to the level of humanity; and *second*, the need to conceive and express these inner principles so as to be able to make use of them in reciprocal human relationships and in this way bring about that dialogue between themselves and God, which God himself willed to have with them, so that human beings might respond to God through their own thinking and speaking. It is precisely in this that all things find their meaning. The human person discovers ever new alternative dimensions of creative things not only through his own reason and new combinations and uses of the things themselves, but also trough the feelings and continual new thoughts his body produces in its contact with things and through the ever changing relationships between himself and his neighbors, which use created things as their medium. And this must be

31. In the following section we will refer specifically to Staniloae, "*The World as Gift and Word.*"

32. Ibid., 27–28.

expressed and communicated by means of a language that is continually being enriched.[33]

This enrichment of the human language in dealing with the meaning of created reality is a creative process in itself. Interestingly, one can find similar insights in Wittgenstein's later theory of language and meaning which was articulated in some of his unpublished manuscripts. According to Hans Schneider's interpretation of the late Wittgenstein,

> the peculiarity of this creative process is not that an independent and diversely-formed preexisting reality is projected onto the plan of language, in the course of which some differentiation is inevitably lost, so that the same few forms of speech always appear, regardless of the "content." Rather an existent form of expression is used in a new context of application . . . and is this "projected" onto new kinds of objects. The starting point of projection in *this* sense is not a pre-structured reality, waiting to be articulated in language. . . . Rather, the starting point of a projection is a pre-existing grammatical form, at first necessarily specific to a *particular* area of discourse, which is then carried into *new* areas of discourse in a free, spontaneous act of creative imagination. This act was unforeseen in the previously available ways of speaking (i.e., available rules) of the language, but its freedom is limited, of course, by internal or external constraints of the situation and by the need to be understood.[34]

One can use the above interpretation to describe how human beings configure the world uniquely for themselves by using all of their existing linguistic potential to creatively discover and appropriate the meanings and the interdependencies of the *logoi* of created beings in their ultimate relation to the Divine Logos. In this sense human creativity with respect to the world is always dialogical, configurational and co-creational. According to Staniloae, in the human process of creative reconfiguration or co-creation there is always a meaning which is clearly intuited in association with every individual reality and at the same time remains unknown and undefined in the strict sense.

> The mind, or the reason as understanding, sees this higher meaning and every kind of connection between the different realities and units, and in its grasp of each unit the mind takes into account the other units as well. This shed light simultaneously upon the more complete reason of each thing. Hence

there exists a general *logos* of the *logoi* of all individual realities, but one that transcends the *logos* of all *logoi*. The more general reason is the meaning or the wealth of meanings of one thing joined to the reasons and meanings of all its components and to all other things as well. . . . Their unique supreme meaning is the Divine *Logos*, for within this Logos are found the meanings of all things. The one who believes is particularly the one who grasps this supreme meaning through a general act of intuition, that is, through his spirit.[35]

An Interdisciplinary Interlude

The conceptualization of Divine-human communion as part of a co-creative configurational process could be related to Actor-Network Theory (ANT).[36] Although it is a completely secular theory, it has been already adopted as part of an interdisciplinary project focusing on using Byzantine philosophical and theological insights within the context of the contemporary sociology of action.[37] The reason to mention it here is the opportunity to discuss the interdisciplinary potential of the theological contributions of St. Maximus. It is also an opportunity to explore the analogical potential of ANT's conceptual apparatus for philosophical theology which can be found in the similarity of its linguistic format and struggles to provide a better articulation of the multiplicity of the sources of agency and the contingency of human innovative activity in the world. John Law has recently referred to ANT as a set of "tools, sensibilities and methods of analysis that treat everything in the social and natural worlds as a continuously generated effect of the webs of relations within which they are located. It assumes that nothing has a reality or form outside the enactment of those relations."[38] ANT analyzes how all things—natural, conceptual, textual, social, or technical—could be considered as equally or symmetrically present and equally relevant in the web of relations defining the reality around us. It "advances a *relational materiality,* the material extension of semiotics, which presupposes that all entities achieve significance in relation to others."[39] The *symmetry principle* between human and non-

---

35. Staniloae, *The World as Gift and Word*, 30–31.

36. Latour, *Reassembling the Social.*

37. Kapriev et al., *Le Sujet de l'Acteur*; Kapriev and Tchalakov, "Actor-Network Theory and Byzantine Interpretation of Aristotle's Theory of Action," 207–38; Tchalakov and Kapriev, "The Limits of Causal Action," 389–433.

38. Law, "Making a Mess with Method," 595–606.

39. Crawford, "Actor Network Theory," 1–4.

human entities which is promoted by ANT scholars should be interpreted as a reaction against any *a priori* assumptions about the sources and the nature of agency within a particular human context. The adoption of this principle shifts the focus away from the identity and the nature of all potential actors to the interactions, the associations, and the relationships between them. In a way, ANT dissolves the notion of social force and replaces it either by short-lived interactions or by new associations. In this way it makes it possible to distinguish between what pertains to its durability and what pertains to its substance.[40] The distinction between durability and substance allows to virtually "un-substantiate" all entities and subjects in order to focus on those aspects of agency that could lead to the emergence of durable relationships—a shift that was enabled by the introduction of the concept of "actant." An actant "is any agent, collective or individual, that can associate or disassociate with other agents. Actants enter into networked associations, which in turn define them, name them, and provide them with substance, action, intention, and subjectivity. In other words, actants are considered foundationally indeterminate, with no a priori substance or essence, and it is via the networks in which they associate that actants derive their nature."[41] On the other hand, action is not understood as springing out only from the singular intentionality, will or desire of an already-constituted subject, but rather as the effect of the hybrid association of entities of various ontologies. In ANT's version of action, humans and non-humans coalesce to achieve a kind of delocalized and distributed synergetic interaction that cannot be merely reduced to the intention or activity of either party. ANT follows "the actors themselves" in deciding what the nature, relevance and impact of agency or activity is. The most interesting question is "not to decide who is acting and how but to shift from a certainty about action to an uncertainty about action" by asking "Which agencies are invoked? Which figurations are they endowed with? Through which mode of action are they engaged?"[42]

The main point here is that ANT offers a unique approach to conceptualizing creativity as a dialogical process which is based on the notion of configuration.[43] This approach positions creativity not only in the minds and practices of individual people but also in the effectuation of all surrounding personal human and non-human activity including the struggles and the efforts through which particular relationships emerge and through which a particular human being is constituted as such. The association of

40. Latour, *Reassembling the social*, 66.
41. Crawford, "Actor Network Theory," 1.
42. Latour, *Reassembling the Social*, 60.
43. Bartels and Bencherki, "Actor Network Theory and Creativity Research," 32.

these struggles and creative efforts with the emergence of new courses of action is just one of the interesting aspects here. What is even more interesting is how the human struggles and efforts lead to the invention of new contextual configurations including new actors and new relationships. Such an understanding of creativity reminds of the definition of creation suggested by Gilles Deleuze—the act of making configurations.[44] From this perspective, studying human creativity can be only understood as the study of the way new relations or connections are established between different elements in order to make new things and situations happen. Thus, to be a creative human being is not an optional activity but a kind of necessity because the configurations that a human being builds entangle and constitute him or her as a subject.[45]

Final Reflections

The brief interlude provides a hint about the opportunity for both, a theological upgrade of ANT focusing on including Divine activity as part of its relational approach to reality, and the terminological enhancement of theology through the adoption of ANT's comprehensiveness in addressing the multiplicity and contingency of agency. According to Tchalakov and Kapriev, the Byzantine philosophical tradition (such as articulated in the works of Maximus the Confessor, but also of John of Damascus and Gregory Palamas) could easily agree with many of ANT's basic principles.[46] It offers a unique and original language, which allows describing the way for different acting agencies to mutually influence each other in the course of action. The most important concepts here are *hypostasis, persona/prosopon* and *perichoresis* (interpenetration or co-inherence). The fact that the Byzantine concept of *hypostasis* has a universal meaning (every single being has a hypostasis) is of significant importance here. By emphasizing this point Tchalakov and Kapriev suggested relating the concept of *hypostasis* to ANT's notions of *actant* and *agency*. In turn, the fact that the concept of *perichoresis* denotes the mutual interpenetration and co-inherence of two or more different natures opens the possibility for the description of the multiplied effect of multiple sources of agency appearing as seemingly single actants or composite hypostases. In addition, Byzantine theology has the ability to address such situations by adopting another Aristotelian category

44. G. Deleuze, "Qu'est-ce que l'acte de création?" *Trafic* 27 (1998) 133–42.

45. Ibid.

46. Tanev, "Actor Network vs. Activity Theory," 65–85.

(in addition to *energeia*)—*hexis*, which defines the personal or, rather, the uniquely hypostatic factor in the actualization of the natural energies or actions. As Tchalakov and Kapriev have pointed out, the dominant understanding of *habitus* which is currently used within the context of ANT[47] appears to be unable to incorporate the comprehensiveness of the Greek notion of *hexis*. Last but not least, the theology of St. Maximus offers the potential of its teaching on the relationship between the Divine and created *logoi* and the multi-logi-cal nature of activity as a valuable framework that could be used for the benefit of the social sciences.

In conclusion, one should emphasize that the above reflections should not overshadow the key message in the theology of St. Maximus for whom the Incarnation is the ultimate goal of both Creation and Deification. "Because of this the whole arrangement of created things exists, they abide and were brought into being from nothing."[48]

47. Latour, *Reassembling the Social*, 210–11.
48. Sherwood, "Introduction," 28.

Epilogue

I n this book I have adopted a comparative approach that is based on examining the intellectual encounters of specific theologians and scientists. In
other words, I have used the dynamism and authenticity of the encounters
of specific personal positions as a source of reflection and new insights. In
doing so, I have been critical to the opinions of some of the people involved
in the encounters and supportive of others. I have been also both critical
and supportive towards the opinions of theologians and scholars who have
recently contributed to the discussion of the issues I have been concerned
with. I do not want my critique to be seen as the result of personal attacks and accusations. If I am allowed to use an expression of St. Gregory
Palamas, I would say that "by my words I stand against other words and not
against the one who speaks."

I should emphasize however that a living and vibrant theological
community should not fear engaging in meaningful encounters. I could
not agree more with one of my teachers, a colleague and friend—Tony
Bailetti, Professor at Carleton University in Ottawa, Ontario, Canada—
that a healthy relationship includes trust, encounter, and commitment. In
other words, if people do not trust each other to the extent that they could
not afford to disagree with each other, they will not be able to commit to
each other. I should point out however that, theologically speaking, the
value of any disagreement is in its potential to help in reaching an ultimate
agreement. This is exactly how I have seen the theologians involved in the
encounters and controversies discussed in this book—they were people
who had the courage to openly encounter each other because they were
committed to the Orthodox Church, its Ecclesial experience and theology.
Understanding the nature of and motivations behind their personal encounters is part of our own appropriation of their theological legacy. The
way we "do" theology in the twenty-first century is grounded in the way

they were doing theology before and for us. Going beyond the way they were doing theology in a meaningful way cannot happen without the approrpiation of their key theological insights. It is my firm belief that the ultimate concern of them all was to affirm the reality of Divine-human communion. The existential relevance of this affirmation was the main source of my motivation in writing this book. It should be emphasized that such affirmation is an expression of both theological and anthropological concerns since it is ultimately concerned with the eschatological future of all humankind. The interdisciplinary aspects of my research should be seen in this particular context. In this sense this book is not an academic exploration but a personal invitation aiming at engaging a broader audience in sharing the existential dimensions and richness of Orthodox theology.

Bibliography

Ajdukiewicz, Kazimierz. *The Scientific World-Perspective and Other Essays 1931–1963*. Dordrecht: Reidel, 1977.

Alexander (Golitzin), Hieromonk. *Et Introibo ad Altare Dei: The Mystagogy of Dionysius Areopagita, with Special Reference to its Predecessors in the Eastern Christian Tradition*. Vol. 59 of Analekta Vlatadon Series. Thessaloniki: Patriarchikon Idruma Paterikon Meleton, 1994.

Alfeev, Hilarion. *Le Mystère sacré de l'Église: Introduction à l'histoire et à la problématique des débats athoniques sur la vénération du nom du Dieu*. Fribourg: Academic Press, 2007.

Amphiloque (Radović), Métropolite. *Le Mystère de la Saint Trinité selon Saint Grégoire Palamas*. Traduit du grec par Yvan Koenig. Paris: Cerf, 2012.

Angold, Michael. "Byzantium and the West, 1204–1453." In *The Cambridge History of Christianity*, Vol. 5, *Eastern Christianity*, edited by Michael Angold, 53–78. Cambridge: Cambridge University Press, 2005.

Arjakovsky, Antoine. *Essai sur le père Serge Boulgakov (1871–1944): Philosophe et théologien Chrétien*. Paris: Parole et Silence, 2006.

———. "The Sophiology of Father Sergius Bulgakov and Contemporary Western Theology." *St. Vladimir's Theological Quarterly* 50 (2005) 219–35.

Aspect, Alain, et al. "Experimental Realization of Einstein-Podolsky-Rosen-Bohm Gedankenexperiment: A New Violation of Bell's Inequalities." *Physical Review Letters* 49 (1982) 91–94.

———. "Experimental Test of Bell's Inequalities Using Time-Varying Analyzers." *Physical Review Letters* 49 (1982) 1804–07.

———. "Experimental Tests of Realistic Local Theories via Bell's Theorem." *Physical Review Letters* 47 (1981) 460–63.

Athanasopoulos, Constantinos, and Christoph Schneider, eds. *Divine Essences and Divine Energies: Ecumenical Reflections on the Presence of God in Eastern Orthodoxy*. London: James Clarke, 2013.

Atkins, Peter. *Galileo's Finger: The Great Ideas of Science*. Oxford: Oxford University Press, 2003.

Baggott, Jim. *The Quantum Story: A History in 40 Moments*. Oxford: Oxford University Press, 2011.

Baker, Matthew. Book Panel Presentation on Paul Gavrilyuk's *George Florovsky and the Russian Religious Renaissance* (Oxford, 2014). Paper presented at the Orthodox Studies Group, American Academy of Religion, San Diego, November 2014.

———. "The Eternal 'Spirit of the Son': Barth, Florovsky and Torrance on the *Filioque*." *International Journal of Systematic Theology* 12 (2010) 382–401.

———. "Neopatristic Synthesis and Ecumenism." In *Eastern Orthodox Encounters of Identity and Otherness*, edited by Andrii Krawchuk and Thomas Bremer, 235–60. New York: Palgrave Macmillan, 2014.

Bartels, Gerald, and Nicolas Bencherki. "Actor Network Theory and Creativity Research." In *Encyclopedia of Creativity, Invention, Innovation, and Entrepreneurship*, edited by Elias G. Carayannis, 29–35. New York: Springer, 2013.

Behr, John. *The Mystery of Christ: Life in Death*. Crestwood, NY: St. Vladimir's Seminary Press, 2006.

———. *Standing by the Cross, Putting on Christ*. CD with a plenary talk at the MASI Study days, July 3, 2009. Ottawa, Canada: The Metropolitan Andrey Sheptytsky Institute of Eastern Christian Studies, St. Paul University, 2009.

Berger, Calinic. "Does the Eucharist Make the Church? An Eccesiological Comparison of Stăniloae and Zizioulas." *St. Vladimir's Theological Quarterly* 51 (2007) 23–70.

Berger, Kevin. "An Integral Approach to Spirituality: The Orthodox Spirituality of Fr. Dumitru Staniloae." *St. Vladimir's Theological Quarterly* 48 (2004) 125–48.

———. "Towards a Theological Gnoseology: The Synthesis of Fr. Dumitru Staniloae." PhD diss., Washington, DC: Catholic University of America, 2003.

Begzos, Marios. "The Priority of Energy in Gregory Palamas and in Modern Physics." Άνάτυπον ἐκ τῆς ΕΕΘΣΠΑ, Τόμος ΜΒ, ΑΘΗΝΑΙ (2007) 357–64.

Birkhoff, George, and John von Neumann. "The Logics of Quantum Mechanics." *Annals of Mathematics* 37 (1936) 823–43.

Blane, Andrew, ed. *Georges Florovsky. Russian Intellectual. Orthodox Churchman.* Crestwood, NY: St. Vladimir's Seminary Press, 1993.

Bohr, Niels. *Atomic Theory and the Description of Nature*. Cambridge: Cambridge University Press, 1934.

———. "The Causality Problem in Quantum in Atomic Physics." In *Causality and Complementarity*, Vol. IV of the Philosophical Writings of Niels Bohr, edited by Jan Faye and Henry J. Folse, 94–121. Woodbridge, CT: Ox Box, 1998.

———. "Discussion with Einstein on Epistemological Problems in Atomic Physics." In *Albert Einstein: Philosopher-Scientist*, edited by Paul Arthur Schilpp, 199–241. Evanston, IL: The Library of Living Philosophers, 1949.

———. "Natural Philosophy and Human Cultures." In *Essays 1932–1957 on Atomic Physics and Human Knowledge*, Vol. II of The Philosophical Writings of Niels Bohr, 23–31. New York: Wiley, 1958.

Born, Max, and Albert Einstein. *The Born-Einstein Letters*. Translated by Irene Born. New York: Walker and Company, 1971.

Boulovich, Irenej. *The Mystery of Essence-Energies Distinction in the Holy Trinity according to St. Markus Eugenicus*. Thessaloniki: Patriarchal Institute of Patristic Studies, 1983.

Bradshaw, David. *Aristotle East and West: Metaphysics and the Division of Christendom*. Cambridge: Cambridge University Press, 2004.

———. "The Concept of the Divine Energies." *Philosophy and Theology* 18 (2006) 93–120.

———. "The Concept of the Divine Energies." In *Divine Essence and Divine Energies: Ecumenical Reflections on the Presence of God in Eastern Orthodoxy*, edited by Constantinos Athanasopoulos and Christoph Schneider, 27–49. Cambridge: James Clarke, 2013.

———. "The Divine Energies in the New Testament." *St. Vladimir's Theological Quarterly* 50 (2006) 189–223.

———. "The Divine Glory and the Divine Energies." *Faith and Philosophy* 23 (2006) 279–98.

Bridgman, Percy. *The Nature of Thermodynamics*. Cambridge: Harvard University Press, 1958.

Bulgakov, Sergius. *The Bride of the Lamb*. Translated by Boris Jakim. Grand Rapids: Eerdmans, 2002.

———. *The Comforter*. Translated by Boris Jakim. Grand Rapids, Michigan: Eerdmans, 2004.

———. *The Lamb of God*. Translated by Boris Jakim. Grand Rapids: Eerdmans, 2008.

———. *La philosophie du Verbe et du nom*. Lausanne: L'age de l'homme, 1991. Edition in Russian: Булгаков, С. Философия имени. Paris: YMCA, 1953.

———. *The Wisdom of God: A Brief Summary of Sophiology*. Translated from the Russian by Rev. Patrick Thompson, Rev. O. Fielding Clarke and Miss Xenia Braikevitc. New York: Paisley, 1937.

Bulzan, Daniel. "Apophatism, Postmodernism, and Language." *Scottish Journal of Theology* 3 (1997) 261–87.

Bunge, Mario. "Energy: From Physics to Metaphysics." *Science and Education* 9 (2000) 459–63.

———. *Philosophy of Physics*. Dordrecht: Reidel, 1973.

Chevalley, Catherine. "Niels Bohr's Words and the Atlantis of Kantianism." In *Niels Bohr and Contemporary Philosophy*, edited by Jan Faye and Henry J. Folse, 33–55. Dordrecht: Kluwer Academic, 1994.

Christov, Ivan. "The Natural Reason and the Supernatural Illumination in the Theological Debate between Barlaam and St. Gregory Palamas." *Critics and Humanism* 1 (2001) 125–34.

Chrestou, P. K., ed. *Syngrammata*, Vol. III. Thessalonica: Oikos Kyromanos, 1970.

Colyer, Elmer M., ed. *The Promise of Trinitarian Theology: Theologians in Dialogue with T. F. Torrance*. Lanham, MD: Rowman & Littlefield, 2001.

Crawford, Cassandra. "Actor Network Theory." In *Encyclopedia of Social Theory*, edited by George Ritzer, 1–4. London: Sage, 2004.

Cvetkovic, Vladimir. "St Justin Popović's Reception of St. Maximus the Confessor." Paper presented at the *Fourth International Conference on St. Maximus the Confessor*. Tsageri, Georgia, Oct. 10, 2011. The text was recently published in Serbian: Cvetković, Vladimir. "Sveti Justin Novi (Popovic) kao tumač misli Svetog Maksima Ispovednika" [St. Justin the New (Popovich) as an Interpreter of St. Maximus the Confessor's Thought]. In *Politika, identitet, tradicija (Politics, Identity, Tradition)*, edited by Aleksandar Petrović & Mikonja Knežević, 471–94. Kosovska Mitrovica: Faculty of Philosophy, 2015.

Dear, Peter. *The Intelligibility of Nature: How Science Makes Sense of the World*. Chicago: University of Chicago Press, 2006.

Deleuze, Gilles. "Qu'est-ce que l'acte de création?" *Trafic* 27 (1998) 133–42.

Deseille, Placide. *Certitude de l'Invisible: Éléments de Doctrine Chrétienne.* Paris: Presse Saint Serge, 2002.

Dey, Ian. *Grounding Grounded Theory: Guidelines for Qualitative Inquiry.* San Diego: Academic Press, 1999.

Dragas, George D., "The Anthropic Principle: Christ's Humanity." In *Orthodox Theology and the Sciences,* edited by George D. Dragas et al., 34–50. Sofia: Sofia University Press & NewRome, 2016.

———. Book review of Demetrios G. Koutsourês, *Synods and Theology Connected with Hêsychasm: The Synodical Procedure Followed in the Hêsychastic Disputes.* Athens: Sacred Metropolis of Thebes and Levadeia, 1997. In *The Greek Orthodox Theological Review* 45 (2000) 631–46.

———. "Divine and Human Synergy." In *The Wedding Feast: Proceedings of the Colloquia of Orthodox Theology of the Univeristé de Sherbrooke 2007–2009,* edited by Paul Ladouceur, 35–53. Montreal: Alexander, 2010.

Dragas, George D., et al., eds. *Orthodox Theology and the Sciences.* Sofia: Sofia University Press & NewRome, 2016.

Dupre, Louis. *Metaphysics and Culture: The 1994 Aquinas Lecture.* Milwaukee: Marquette University Press, 1994.

Eunomius. *The Extant Works.* Translated by Richard Paul Vaggione. Oxford: Clarendon, 1987.

Evdokimov, Paul. *The Art of the Icon: A Theology of Beauty.* Translated by Steven Bigham. Crestwood, NY: St Vladimir's Seminary Press, 1990.

Evtuhov, Catherine. *The Cross and the Sickle: Sergei Bulgakov and the Fate of Russian Religious Philosophy.* Ithaca, NY: Cornell University Press, 1997.

Favrholdt, David. *Filosofen Niels Bohr.* Copenhagen: Informations Forlag, 2009.

———. "Niels Bohr and Realism." In *Niels Bohr and Contemporary Philosophy,* edited by Jan Faye and Henry J. Folse, 77–96. Dordrecht: Kluwer Academic, 1994.

Faye, Jan, and Henry J. Folse, eds. *Niels Bohr and Contemporary Philosophy.* Dordrecht: Kluwer Academic, 1994.

———. "Introduction." In *Niels Bohr. Causality and Complementarity,* Vol. IV of The Philosophical Writings of Niels Bohr. Edited by Jan Faye and Henry J. Folse. Woodbridge, CT: Ox Bow, 1998.

Feynman, Richard. *The Character of Physical Law.* New York: The Modern Library, 1994.

———, et al. *The Feynman Lectures on Physics.* Vol. 1. Boston: Addison-Wesley, 1964.

Finch, Jeffrey. "Neo-Palamism, Divinizing Grace, and the Breach between East and West." In *Partakers of Divine Nature: The History and Development of Deification in the Christian Tradition,* edited by Michael Christensen and Jeffery Wittung, 233–49. Madison, NJ: Fairleigh Dickinson University Press, 2007.

Florensky, Pavel. *The Pillar and Ground of the Truth: An Essay in Orthodox Theodicy in Twelve Letters.* Princeton: Princeton University Press, 2004.

Florovsky, Georges. "The Authority of the Ancient Councils and the Tradition of the Fathers." In *Bible, Church, Tradition: An Eastern Orthodox View.* Vol. I of *The Collected Works of Georges Florovsky,* 93–103. Belmont, MA: Nordland, 1972.

———. *Bible, Church, Tradition: An Eastern Orthodox View.* Vol. I of *The Collected Works of Georges Florovsky,* 93–103. Belmont, MA: Nordland, 1972.

———. "The Concept of Creation in Saint Athanasius." *Studia Patristica VI, Papers presented at the Third Conference on Patristic Studies, held at Christ Church, Oxford, September, 1959*, 36–57. Berlin: Akademie-Verlag, 1962.

———. "Creation and Creaturehood." In *Creation and Redemption*, Vol. III of *The Collected Works of Georges Florovsky*, 43–78. Belmont, MA: Nordland, 1976. (Russian edition: Флоровский, Г. „Тварь и тварьность." Православная мысль 1 (1928) 176–212.)

———. "Cur Deus Homo? The Motive of the Incarnation." In *Evharisterion: Hamilcar Alivisatos*, 70–79. Athens, 1957. (Reprinted in *Creation and Redemption*. Vol. III of *The Collected Works of Georges Florovsky*, 310–14. Belmont, MA: Nordland, 1976.)

———. "The Idea of Creation in Christian Philosophy." *Eastern Churches Quarterly* 8 (1949) 53–77.

———. "Patristics and Modern Theology." In *Procès Verbaux du Premier Congrès de Théologie Orthodoxe a Athènes, 29 Novembre–6 Décembre, 1936*, edited by Hamilcar Alivisatos, 238–42. Athènes: Pyrsos, 1939.

———. "Revelation, Philosophy and Theology." In *Creation and Redemption*. Vol. III of *The Collected Works of Georges Florovsky*, 21–40. Belmont, MA: Nordland, 1976.

———. "St. Athanasius' Concept of Creation." In *Aspects of Church History*. Vol. 4 of The Collected Works of Georges Florovsky, 39–62. Belmont, MA: Nordland, 1975.

———. "St. Gregory Palamas and the Tradition of the Fathers." *The Greek Orthodox Theological Review* 2 (1959–60) 119–31. (Reprinted in *Sobornost* 4 (1961) 165–76 and in *Bible, Church, Tradition: An Eastern Orthodox View*. Vol. I of *The Collected Works of Georges Florovsky*, 105–20. Belmont, MA: Nordland, 1972.)

Freedman, Stuart J., and John F. Clauser. "Experimental Test of Local Hidden-Variable Theories." *Physical Review Letters* 28 (1972) 938–41.

Gallaher, Anastassy Brandon. "'Waiting for the Barbarians': Identity and Polemicism in the Neo-patristic Synthesis of Georges Florovsky." *Modern Theology* 27 (2011) 659–91.

Gallaher, Anastassy Brandon, and Irina Kukota. "Protopresbyter Sergii Bulgakov: Hypostasis and Hypostaticity: Scholia to The Unfading Light." *St. Vladimirs Theological Quarterly* 49 (2005) 5–46.

Gavrilyuk, Paul. *George Florovsky and the Russian Religious Renaissance*. Oxford: Oxford University Press, 2014.

Gavrilyuk, Paul. "Georges Florovsky's Reading of Maximus: Anti-Bulgakov or Pro-Bulgakov?" In *Knowing the Purpose of Creation through the Resurrection: Proceedings of the Symposium on St. Maximus the Confessor, Belgrade, October 18–21, 2012*, edited by Maxim Vasiljevic. Kindle ed. Alhambra, California: Sebastian.

Geffert, Bryn. "The Charges of Heresy against Sergei Bulgakov: The Majority and Minority Reports of Evlogii's Commission and the Final Report of the Bishops' Conference." *St. Vladimir's Theological Quarterly* 49 (2005) 47–66.

Gerogiorgakis, Stamatios. "The Controversy between Barlaam of Calabria and Gregory Palamas on Demonstrative and Dialectical Syllogisms Revisited." *Philotheos* 10 (2010) 157–69.

Glaser, Barney, and Anselm Strauss. *The Discovery of Grounded Theory: Strategies for Qualitative Research*. New York: Aldine de Gruyter, 1967.

Grégoire Palamas. *Défense des Saints Hésychastes*. Translated by John Meyendorff. Études et documents 30–31. Louvain: Spicilegium sacrum Lovaniense, 1959.

Gregory Palamas. *The Homilies*. Essex, UK: Stavropegic Monastery of St. John the Baptist, 2014.

———. *The One Hundred and Fifty Chapters*. Edited and translated by Robert E. Sinkewicz, C.S.B. Studies and Texts 83. Toronto: Pontifical Institute of Mediaeval Studies, 1988.

———. *The Triads*. Edited with an introduction by John Meyendorff. Translated by Nicholas Gendle. Mahwah, NJ: Paulist, 1983.

Groblacher, S., et al. "An Experimental Test of Non-local Realism." *Nature* 446 (2007) 871–75.

Gross, David. "Einstein and the Quest for a Unified Theory." In *Einstein for the 21st Century: His Legacy in Science, Art, and Modern Culture*, edited Peter Galison et al., 287–98. Princeton: Princeton University Press, 2008.

Griffiths, David G. *Introduction to Electrodynamics*. 3rd ed. Upper Saddle River, NJ: Prentice Hall, 1999.

Gunnarsson, Håkan. *Mystical Realism in the Early Theology of Gregory Palamas: Context and Analysis*. Göteborg: Skrifter Utgivna vid Institutionen for religionsvetenskap, 2002.

Gunton, Colin. "Being and Person: T. F. Torrance's Doctrine of God." In *The Promise of Trinitarian Theology: Theologians in Dialogue with T. F. Torrance*, edited by E. M. Colyer, 115–37. Lanham, MD: Rowman & Littlefield, 2001.

———. "Eastern and Western Trinities: Being and Person. T. F. Torrance's Doctrine of God." In *Father, Son & Holy Spirit: Toward a Fully Trinitarian Theology*, 32–57. London: T. & T. Clark, 2003.

———. *Father, Son & Holy Spirit: Toward a Fully Trinitarian Theology*. London: T. & T. Clark, 2003.

Habets, Myk. *Theosis in the Theology of Thomas F. Torrance*. Farnham, UK: Ashgate, 2009.

Harrison, David M. *The Concept of Energy*. http://www.upscale.utoronto.ca/PVB/Harrison/ConceptOfEnergy/ConceptOfEnergy.html.

Harman, Peter M. *Energy, Force and Matter: The Conceptual Development of Nineteenth-Century Physics*. Cambridge: Cambridge University Press, 1982.

Hebor, Jens. *The Standard Conception as Genuine Quantum Realism*. Odense, Denmark: University Press of Southern Denmark, 2005.

Hecht, Eugene. *Physics: Calculus*, Vol. 1 & 2. 2nd ed. Pacific Grove, CA: Brooks/Cole, 2000.

Heller, Michael. "Where Physics Meets Metaphysics." In *On Space and Time*, edited by Alain Connes et al., 238–77. Cambridge: Cambridge University Press, 2008.

Hermanns, William. *Einstein and the Poet: In Search of the Cosmic Man*. Wellesley, MA: Branden, 2013.

Hierotheos, Metropolitan of Nafpaktos. *Saint Gregory as a Hagiorite*. Translated by Esther Williams. Levadia, Greece: Birth of the Theotokos Monastery, 1997.

Honner, John. *The Description of Nature: Niels Bohr and the Philosophy of Quantum Physics*. Oxford: Clarendon, 1987.

Horuzhy, Sergey. "The Idea of Energy in the Moscow School of Christian Neoplatonism." *Online publication of the Institute of Synergetic Anthropology*. http://synergia-isa.ru/wp-content/uploads/2011/08/hor_idea_energy.pdf.

———. "Neo-Patristic Synthesis and Russian Philosophy." *St. Vladimir's. Theological Quarterly* 44 (2000) 309–28.

Ierodiaknou, Katerina. "The Anti-Logical Movement in the Fourteenth Century." In *Byzantine Philosophy and its Ancient Sources*, edited by Katerina Ierodiakonou, 219–36. Oxford: Clarendon, 2002.

Jaki, Stanley. "The Horns of Complementarity." In *The Road of Science and the Ways to God*, 197–213. Chicago: University of Chicago Press, 1978.

John of Damascus. *Exposition of the Orthodox Faith*. Translated by Salmond. In *Nicene and Post-Nicene Fathers*, Series II, Volume 9. Edited by Philip Schaff and Henry Wace. Christian Classics Ethereal Library. Reprint. Grand Rapids: Eerdmans, 1984.

———. *Writings*. Translated by Frederick H. Chase Jr. New York: Fathers of the Church, 1958.

Jugie, Martin. "Introduction." *Oeuvres complètes de Gennade Scholarios*, t. III. Edited by L. Petit et al. Paris: Maison de la Bonne Presse, 1930.

———. "Palamas Grégoire." In *Dictionnaire de théologie catholique: contenant l'exposé des doctrines de la théologie catholique, leurs preuves et leur histoire*, Tome XI, Part 2, edited by Alfred Vacant, from 1852 to 1901; Eugène Mangenot, from 1856 to 1922; Emile Amann, from 1880 to 1948, cols. 1735–76. Paris: Letouzey et Ané, 1932.

———. "Palamite (Controverse)." In *Dictionnaire de théologie catholique: contenant l'exposé des doctrines de la théologie catholique, leurs preuves et leur histoire*, Tome XI, Part 2, edited by Alfred Vacant, from 1852 to 1901; Eugène Mangenot, from 1856 to 1922; Emile Amann, from 1880 to 1948, cols. 1735–76. Paris: Letouzey et Ané, 1932.

Kapriev, Georgi. *Byzantica Minora*. Sofia: Lik, 2000.

———. "Gregory Palamas." In *Encyclopedia of Medieval Philosophy: Philosophy between 500 and 1500*, edited by Henrik Lagerlund, 520–30. Dordrecht: Springer, 2011.

———. *Philosophie in Byzanz*. Wuerzburg: Koenigshausen und Neumann, 2005.

———. "Скотисткото различие между същност и енергия при Георги Схолар и собствените ресурси на паламитската традиция" ("The Scotist Distinction between Essence and Energies in Georgios Scholarios and the Internal Resources of the Palamite Tradition"). In *Archiv für Mittelalterliche Philosophie Und Kultur*, Heft XXI, edited by Tzocho Boiadjiev et al., 232–66. Sofia: Iztok-Zapad, 2015.

Kapriev, Georgi, and Ivan Tchalakov. "Actor-Network Theory and Byzantine Interpretation of Aristotle's Theory of Action: Three Points of Possible Dialogue." *Yearbook of the Institute for Advanced Studies on Science, Technology and Society* 57 (2009) 207–38.

Kapriev, Georgi, et al., eds. *Le Sujet de l'Acteur. An Anthropological Outlook on Actor-Network Theory*. Munich: Fink Verlag, 2014.

Karayannis, Vasilios. *Maxime le Confesseur, Essence et Énergies de Dieu*. Paris: Beauchesne, 1993.

Kassim, Husain. *Aristotle and Aristotelianism in Medieval Muslim, Jewish, and Christian Philosophy*. Lanham, MD: Austin & Winfield, 2000.

Klimoff, Alexis. "Georges Florovsky and the Sophiological Controversy." *St. Vladimir's Theological Quarterly* 49 (2005) 67–100.

Konstantinovsky, Julia. "Dionysius the Areopagite versus Aristotle? The Two Points of Reference for Gregory Palamas in Initial Confrontations with Barlaam the Calabrian." *Studia Patristica* XLII, Papers Presented at the Fourteenth International

Conference on Patristic Studies Held in Oxford 2003, edited by Frances M. Young et al., 313–20. Leuven: Peeters, 2006.

Kotiranta, Matti. "The Palamite Idea of Perichoresis of the Persons of the Trinity in the Light of Contemporary Neo-Palamite Analysis." *Byzantium and the North: Acta Byzantina Fennica* IX (1997–98) 59–69.

Krausmuller, Dirk. "The Rise of Hesychasm." In *The Cambridge History of Christianity*, Vol. 5, *Eastern Christianity*, edited by Michael Angold, 101–26. Cambridge: Cambridge University Press, 2005.

Krivoshein, Basil. "The Ascetic and Theological Teaching of Gregory Palamas." *The Eastern Churches Quarterly* 3 (1938–39) 26–84; 138–56; 193–214. (This work was published earlier in Russian: Монах Василий (Кривошеин). Аскетическое и богословское учение св.Григория Паламы. Сборник статей по археологии и византиноведению, издаваемый Институтом имени Н.П.Кондакова, VIII. Прага, 1936, 99–151.)

Lange, Marc. *An Introduction to the Philosophy of Physics: Locality, Fields, Energy, and Mass.* Oxford: Blackwell, 2002.

Larchet, Jean-Claude. *La divinization de l'homme selon Saint Maxime le Confesseur.* Paris: Cerf, 1996.

———. "Исихазам и Шести Васељенски Сабор. Има ли паламистичко богословље о Божанским енергијама основу у VI Васељенском Сабору?" ["Hesychasm and the Sixth Ecumenical Council: Is Palamite Theology of the Divine Energies Founded on the Sixth Ecumenical Council?"]. In *Proceedings of the International Scientific Colloquium "650 Years of the Synodal Tomos (1351–2001)—Saint Gregory Palamas in the Past and Today,"* 66–80. Serbia: Vrnjačka Banja, 2003.

———. "La notion d'*energeia* dans l'Ancien et le Nouveau Testaments." Црквене студије *[Church Studies]* III (2006) 15–22.

———. *Personne et nature: La Trinité–Le Chirst–L'Homme.* Paris: Cerf, 2011.

———. *La théologie des énergies divines: Des origines à saint Jean Damascène.* Paris: Cerf, 2010.

Latour, Bruno. *Reassembling the Social. An Introduction to Actor-Network Theory.* Oxford: Oxford University Press, 2005.

Law, John. "Making a Mess with Method." In *The Sage Handbook of Social Science Methodology*, edited by William Outhwaite and Sephen Turner, 595–606. London and Beverly Hills: Sage, 2007.

Le Grys, James. "Names for the Ineffable God: St. Gregory of Nyssa's Explanation." *The Thomist* 62 (1998) 333–54.

Lindsay, R. B. "The Concept of Energy and its Early Historical Development." *Foundations of Physics* 1 (1971) 383–93.

———. "The Scientific and Theological Revolutions and Their Implications for Society." *Zygon* 7 (1972) 212–43.

Lonergan, Bernard. *Collected Works of Bernard Lonergan—Vol. 4, Collection.* Edited by Frederick E. Crowe and Robert M. Doran. Toronto: University of Toronto Press, Lonergan Research Institute of Regis College, 1988.

———. "Isomorphism of Thomist and Scientific Thought." In *Collected Works of Bernard Lonergan—Vol. 4, Collection.* Edited by Frederick E. Crowe and Robert M. Doran, 133–41. Toronto: University of Toronto Press, Lonergan Research Institute of Regis College, 1988.

Lossky, Vladimir. *Essai sur la théologie mystique de l'Église d'Orient*. Paris: Éditions Montaigne, 1944.

———. *The Mystical Theology of the Eastern Church*. Translated by members of the Fellowship of St. Alban and St. Sergius. 1957. Reprint. Cambridge: James Clark, 2005.

Lot-Borodine, Myrrha. "La doctrine de la deification dans l'Eglise grecque jusqu'au XI siècle." *Revue de l'histoire des religions*, tome CV (1932) 5–43; tome CVI (1932) 525–74; tome CVII (1933) 8–55.

Loudovikos, Nikolaos. *Church in the Making: An Apophatic Ecclesiology of Consubstantiality*. Translated by Norman Russell. Yonkers, NY: St. Vladimir's Seminary Press, 2016.

———. *A Eucharistic Ontology: Maximus the Confessor's Eschatological Ontology of Being as Dialogical Reciprocity*. Translated by E. Theokritoff. Brookline, MA: Holy Cross Orthodox Press, 2010.

———. "Hell and Heaven, Nature and Person: Chr. Yannaras, D. Stăniloae and Maximus the Confessor." *International Journal of Orthodox Theology* 5 (2014) 9–32.

———. "Ontology Celebrated: Remarks of an Orthodox on Radical Orthodoxy." In *Encounter between Eastern Orthodoxy and Radical Orthodoxy*, edited by Adrian Pabst and Christoph Schneider, 141–55. Farnham, UK: Ashgate, 2009.

———. "Striving for Participation: Palamite Analogy as Dialogical Syn-energy and Thomist Analogy as Emanational Similitude." In *Divine Essence and Divine Energies: Ecumenical Reflections on the Presence of God in Eastern Orthodoxy*, edited by Constantinos Athanasopoulos and Christoph Schneider, 122–48. Cambridge: James Clarke, 2013.

Louth, Andrew. *Maximus the Confessor*. London: Routledge, 1996.

Luoma, Tapio. *Incarnation and Physics: Natural Science in the Theology of Thomas F. Torrance*. Oxford: Oxford University Press, 2002.

MacKinnon, Edward. "Complementarity." In *Religion & Science: History, Methods, Dialogue*, edited by W. M. Richardson and W. J. Wildman, 255–70. New York: Routledge, 1996.

Mayor, Joseph B. *The Epistle of St. James: The Greek Text with Introduction, Notes, and Comments*. London: Macmillan, 1892.

Maxime le Confesseur, Saint. *Ambigua*. Translated by Emmanuel Ponsoye. Paris: l'Ancre, 1994.

———. *Opuscules théologiques et polémiques*. Translated by Emmanuel Ponsoye. Paris: Cerf, 1998.

Maximus the Confessor. *The Ascetic Life, the Four Centuries on Charity*. New York: Newman, 1955.

———. *On the Cosmic Mystery of Jesus Christ*. Translated by P. M. Blowers and R. L. Wilken. Crestwood, NY: St. Vladimir's Seminary Press, 2003.

———. *On Difficulties in the Church Fathers. The Ambigua*, Vol. I–II. Edited and translated by Nicholas Constas. Cambridge: Harvard University Press, 2014.

———. *Selected Writings*. The Classics of Western Spirituality. New York: Paulist, 1985.

Meyendorff, John. *Byzantine Hesychasm: Historical, Theological and Social Problems*. London: Variorum Reprints, 1974.

———. *Byzantine Theology*. New York: Fordham University Press, 1974.

————. *Byzantine Theology: Historical Trends and Doctrinal Themes.* Rev. 2nd ed. New York: Fordham University Press, 1983.

————. *Byzantium and the Rise of Russia.* Crestwood, NY: St. Vladimir's Seminary Press, 1989.

————. *Christ in Eastern Christian Thought.* Crestwood, NY: St. Vladimir's Seminary Press, 1987.

————. "Creation in the History of Orthodox Theology." *St. Vladimir's Theological Quarterly* 27 (1983) 27–37.

————. "The Holy Trinity in Palamite Theology." In *Trinitarian Theology East and West: St. Thomas Aquinas—St Gregory Palamas*, edited by Michael Fahey and John Meyendorff, 25–43. Brookline, MA: Holy Cross Orthodox Press, 1977.

————. "L'iconographie de la Sagesse Divine dans la tradition Byzantine." *Cahiers archéologiques* 10 (1959) 259–77.

————. *Introduction à l'étude de Grégoire Palamas.* Collection Patristica sorbonensia 3. Paris: Seuil, 1959.

————. *A Study of Gregory Palamas.* London: Faith, 1964.

————. "Wisdom–Sophia: Contrasting Approaches to a Complex Theme." *Dumbarton Oaks Papers* 41 (1987) 391–401.

Milbank, John. "Sophiology and Theurgy: The New Theological Horizon." In *Encounter between Eastern Orthodoxy and Radical Orthodoxy*, edited by Adrian Pabst and Christoph Schneider, 45–85. Farnham, UK: Ashgate, 2009. http://www.theologyphilosophycentre.co.uk/papers/Milbank_SophiologyTheurgy.pdf.

Murphy, George. "Energy and the Generation of the World." *Zygon* 29 (1994) 259–74.

Nadeau, Robert, and Menas Kafatos. *The Non-Local Universe: The New Physics and Matters of the Mind.* Oxford: Oxford University Press, 1999.

Nicene and Post-Nicene Fathers, Second Series. Edited by Philip Schaff. Reprint. Grand Rapids: Eerdmans, 1982.

Omnès, Roland. *Quantum Philosophy: Understanding and Interpreting Contemporary Science.* Princeton: Princeton University Press, 1999.

Pabst, Adrian, and Christoph Schneider. "Transfiguring the World through the Word." In *Encounter between Eastern Orthodoxy and Radical Orthodoxy*, edited by Adrian Pabst and Christoph Schneider, 1–25. Farnham, UK: Ashgate, 2009.

Papanikolaou, Aristotle. *Being with God: Trinity, Apophaticism, and Divine-Human Communion.* Notre Dame, IN: University of Notre Dame Press, 2006.

————. "Sophia, Apophasis, and Communion: The Trinity in Contemporary Orthodox Theology." In *The Cambridge Companion to the Trinity*, edited by Peter C. Phan, 243–58. Cambridge: Cambridge University Press, 2011.

————. "Sophia! Orthoi! The Trinitarian Theology of Sergei Bulgakov." Unpublished paper presented at Catholic Theological Society of America Conference on June 5th, 2009.

Penrose, Roger. "Causality, Quantum Theory and Cosmology." In *On Space and Time*, edited by Majid, Shahn, 141–95. Cambridge: Cambridge University Press, 2008.

Pentecost, Scot F. *Quest of the Divine Presence: Metaphysics of Participation and the Relation of Philosophy to Theology in St. Gregory Palamas' Triads and the One Hundred and Fifty Chapters.* PhD diss., Washington, DC: Catholic University of America, 1999.

Petavius, Dionysius. *Opus de Theologicis Dogmatibus a J.-B. Thomas Recognitum et Adnotatum.* Bar-le-Duc: Guérin, 1864–70.

Petersen, Aage. "The Philosophy of Niels Bohr." *Bulletin of the Atomic Scientists* 19 (1963) 8–14.

Philotheos, Patriarch of Constantinople. *On the Text of Proverbs: Wisdom Has Built Her House and Set up Seven Columns.* Edited by V. S. Pseutogkas. Thessaloniki: Patriarchal Institute of Patristic Studies, 1981. (Russian edition: Три рѣчи къ Епископу Игантию с объяснениемъ изреченія притчей: Премудрость созда себѣ домъ и проч. Греческій текстъ и Русский переводъ. Новгородъ, 1898.)

Plotnitsky, Arkady. *The Knowable and the Unknowable: Modern Science, Nonclassical Thought and the 'Two Cultures'.* Ann Arbor, MI: University of Michigan Press, 2002.

Podskalsky, Gerhard. *Theologie und Philosophie in Byzanz.* München: Beck, 1977.

Polemes, Ioannes. *Theophanes of Nicaea: His Life and Work.* Vienna: Verlag der Österreichischen Akademie der Wissenschaften, 1996.

Polkinghorne, John. *Belief in God in an Age of Science.* New Heaven: Yale University Press, 1998.

Popescu, Dumitru. "Logos, Trinity, Creation." *International Journal of Orthodox Theology* 1 (2010) 60–64.

Popovich, Archimandrite Justin. *Man and the God-Man.* Alhambra, CA: Sebastian, 2009.

Puhalo, Lazar, Archbishop. *The Evidence of Things Not Seen: Orthodox Christianity and Modern Physics.* 2nd ed. Dewdney, BC: Synaxis, 2004.

Purves, Andrew. "The Christology of Thomas F. Torrance." In *The Promise of Trinitarian Theology: Theologians in Dialogue with T. F. Torrance,* edited Elmer M. Colyer, 51–80. Lanham, MD: Rowman & Littlefield, 2001.

Putallas, François-Xavier. "Audace et limites de la raison." Foreword to Josef Pieper, *Le concept de création: La "philosophie négative" de saint Thomas d'Aquin.* Paris: Ad Solem, 2010.

Randall, Lisa. "Energy in Einstein's Universe." In *Einstein for the 21st Century: His Legacy in Science, Art, and Modern Culture,* edited by Peter G. Galison et al., 297–309. Princeton: Princeton University Press, 2008.

Reeve, C. D. C. *Substantial Knowledge: Aristotle's Metaphysics.* Indianopolis: Hackett, 2000.

Reid, Duncan. *Energies of the Spirit: Trinitarian Models in Eastern Orthodox and Western Theology.* Atlanta: Scholar's, 1997.

Robinson, J. Armitage. *St. Paul's Epistle to the Ephesians: A Revised Text and Translation with Exposition and Notes.* London: Macmillan, 1903.

Rogich, Daniel. *Becoming Uncreated: The Journey to Human Authenticity.* Minneapolis: Light & Life Publishing, 1997.

Romanides, John. *The Ancestral Sin: A Comparative Study of Our Ancestors Adam and Eve according to the Paradigms and Doctrines of the First- and Second-Century Church and the Augustinian Formulation of Original Sin.* Ridgewood, NJ: Zephyr, 2002. (This is the English version of Romanides' doctoral dissertation defended in 1959 at the University of Athens.)

———. "Notes on the Palamite Controversy and Related Topics, Part I." *The Greek Orthodox Theological Review* 6 (1960–61) 193–202.

———. *An Outline of Orthodox Patristic Dogmatics.* Rollinsford, NH: Orthodox Research Institute, 2004.

———. *Patristic Theology.* Tagarades, Greece: Uncut Mountain, 2008.

————. "St. Cyril's 'One Physis or Hypostasis of God the Logos Incarnate' and Chalcedon." *The Greek Orthodox Theological Review* 10 (1964–65) 82–107.

Rosenthal, Bernice. "The Nature and Function of Sophia in Sergei Bulgakov's Prerevolutionary Thought." In *Russian Religious Thought*, edited by Judith Deuitsch Kornblatt and Richard F. Gustafson, 154–75. Madison, WI: University of Wisconsin Press, 1996.

Rovelli, Carlo. "The Disappearance of Space and Time." In *The Ontology of Spacetime*, Vol. 1, edited by Dennis Dieks and Miklos Redei, 25–36. Amsterdam: Elsevier, 2006.

Russell, Norman. *The Doctrine of Deification in the Greek Patristic Tradition.* Oxford: Oxford University Press, 2004.

————. *Fellow Workers with God: Orthodox Thinking on Theosis.* Crestwood, NY: St. Vladimir's Seminary Press, 2009.

————. "Theosis and Gregory Palamas: Continuity or Doctrinal Change?" *St. Vladimir's Theological Quarterly* 50 (2006) 357–79.

Sakharov, Nicholas. *I Love Therefore I Am: The Theological Legacy of Archimandrite Sophrony.* Crestwood, NY: St. Vladimir's Seminary Press, 2002.

Schuler, Douglas, and Aki Namioka. *Participatory Design: Principles and Practices.* Hillsdale, NJ: Erlbaum, 1993.

Sénina, Tatiana. "Un palamite russe du début du XXème siècle: le hiéromoine Antoine Boulatovitch et sa doctrine sur l'énergie divine." *Scrinium. Revue de patrologie, d'hagiographie critique et d'histoire ecclésiastique* 6: *Patrologia Pasifica Secunda* (2010) 400–405.

Schleiermacher, F. D. E. *Der Christliche Glaube,* Vol. 2, 1831 Edited by M. Redeker. Berlin: de Gruyter, 1960.

Schneider, Hans. *Wittgenstein's Later Theory of Meaning: Imagination and Calculation.* Chichester, UK: Willey Blackwell, 2014.

Sergeev, Mikhail. "Divine Wisdom and Trinity: A 20th-Century Controversy in Orthodox theology." *Greek Orthodox Theological Review* 45 (2000) 573–82.

————. *Sophiology in Russian Orthodoxy. Solov'ev, Bulgakov, Loskii and Berdiaev.* Lewiston, NY: Mellen, 2006.

Sherwood, Polycarp. "Introduction." In St. Maximus the Confessor, *The Ascetic Life. The Four Centuries on Charity.* Translated by Polycarp Sherwood. New York: Newman, 1955.

Sinkewicz, Robert E. "The Doctrine of Knowledge of God in the Early Writings of Barlaam the Calabrian." *Medieval Studies* 44 (1982) 181–242.

Smith, Christian. *What Is a Person? Rethinking Humanity, Social Life, and the Moral Good from the Person Up.* Chicago: University of Chicago Press, 2010.

Spender, J.-C. *Business Strategy: Managing Uncertainty, Opportunity, and Enterprise.* Oxford: Oxford University Press, 2014.

Staniloae, Dumitru. *Eisagogi Asto Ergo Tou Agiou Maxomou "Philosophika kai Theologika Erotemata."* Vol. I. Edited by P. Nellas. Athens: Apostoliki Diakonia, 1978.

————. *The Experience of God: Orthodox Dogmatic Theology,* Vol. 1: *Revelation and Knowledge of the Triune God.* Translated by Robert Barringer. Brookline, MA: Holy Cross Orthodox Press, 1998.

————. *The Experience of God: Orthodox Dogmatic Theology*, Vol. 2, *The World: Creation and Deification*. Translated by Ioan Ionita and Robert Barringer. Brookline, MA: Holy Cross Orthodox Press, 2000.

————. *Life and Teachings of Gregory Palamas*. Sibiu, Romania: ?, 1938. (In Romanian: *Viața și Învățătura Sfântului Grigorie Palama*. Sibiu, Bucuresti: Scripta, 1938.)

————. "The World as Gift and Word." In *The Experience of God: Orthodox Dogmatic Theology, Vol. 2, The World: Creation and Deification*. Translated by Ioan Ionita and Robert Barringer, 21–63. Brookline, MA: Holy Cross Orthodox Press, 2000.

Stiernon, Daniel. "Bulletin sur le Palamisme." *Revue des Études Byzantines* 30 (1972) 231–341.

Tanev, Stoyan. "Actor Network vs Activity Theory: Dealing with the Asymmetry in Human-Technology Inter-Actions." In *Le Sujet de l'Acteur. An Anthropological Outlook on Actor-Network Theory*, edited by Georgi Kapriev et al., 65–85. Munich: Fink, 2014.

————. "ΕΝΕΡΓΕΙΑ vs ΣΟΦΙΑ: The Contribution of Fr. Georges Florovsky to the Rediscovery of the Orthodox Teaching on the Distinction between the Divine Essence and Energies." *International Journal of Orthodox Theology* 2 (2011) 15–71. http://orthodox-theology.com/media/PDF/IJOT1-2011/05-tanev-energeia-1.pdf.

————. "Essence and Energy: An Exploration in Orthodox Theology and Physics." *Logos: A Journal of Eastern Christian Studies* 50 (2009) 89–153.

————. "The Language of Orthodox Theology and Quantum Mechanics." In *Orthodox Theology and the Sciences*, edited by George D. Dragas et al., 292–329. Sofia: Sofia University Press & NewRome, 2016.

Tanev, Stoyan, et al. "How Do Value Co-creation Activities Relate to the Perception of Firms' Innovativeness?" *Journal of Innovation Economics* 1 (2011) 131–59.

————. "Value Co-creation as Part of an Integrative Vision for Innovation Management." *Technology Innovation Management Review*, December (2009): http://timreview.ca/article/309.

Taylor, Andrew. "The Dark Universe." In *On Space and Time*, edited by Shahn Majid, 1–55. Cambridge: Cambridge University Press, 2008.

Tchalakov, Ivan, and Georgi Kapriev. "The Limits of Causal Action: Actor-Network Theory Notion of Translation and Aristotle's Notion of Action." *Yearbook of the Institute for Advanced Studies on Science, Technology and Society* 47 (2005) 389–433.

Theobald, D. W. *The Concept of Energy*. London: Spon, 1966.

Timiadis, Emilianos. "Georges Florovsky 1893–1979." In *Ecumenical Pilgrims: Profiles of Pioneers in Christian Reconciliation*, edited by Ioan Bria and Dagmar Heller, 94–95. Geneva: World Council of Churches, 1995.

Tittel, Wolfgang, et al. "Violations of Bell Inequalities More Than 10km Apart." *Physical Review Letters* 81 (1998) 3565–66.

Tollefsen, Torstein. *Activity and Participation in Late Antique and Early Christian Thought*. Oxford: Oxford University Press, 2012.

————. *The Christocentric Cosmology of St. Maximus the Confessor*. Oxford: Oxford University Press, 2008.

Torrance, Alexis. "Personhood and Patristics in Orthodox Theology: Reassessing the Debate." *The Heythrop Journal* 52 (2011) 700–707.

Torrance, Alan J. *Persons in Communion: An Essay on Trinitarian Description and Human Participation*. Edinburgh: T. & T. Clark, 1996.

Torrance, Thomas. F. *The Christian Doctrine of God, One Being Three Persons.* Edinburgh: T. & T. Clark, 1996.

———. *Divine Meaning: Studies in Patristic Hermeneutics.* Edinburgh: T. & T. Clark, 1995.

———. *The Doctrine of Jesus Christ: Auburn Lectures 1938–39.* Reprint. Eugene, OR: Wipf & Stock, 2002.

———. "The Doctrine of the Holy Trinity in Gregory Nazianzen and John Calvin." In *Trinitarian Perspectives. Toward Doctrinal Agreement,* 21–40. Edinburgh: T. & T. Clark, 1994.

———. *Ground and Grammar of Theology.* Charlottesville, VA: University of Virginia Press, 1980.

———. "Karl Barth and the Latin Heresy." *Scottish Journal of Theology* 39 (1986) 461–82.

———. *Preaching Christ Today: The Gospel and Scientific Thinking.* Grand Rapids: Eerdmans, 1994.

———. *Reality and Scientific Theology.* Edinburgh: Scottish Academic Press, 1985.

———. *Space, Time and Incarnation.* 1969. Reprint. Edinburgh: T. & T. Clark, 1997.

———. *The Trinitarian Faith: The Evangelical Theology of the Ancient Catholic Church.* Edinburgh: T. & T. Clark, 1995.

———. *Theology in Reconciliation.* London: Geoffrey Chapman, 1975.

Valliere, Paul. *Modern Russian Theology: Bukharev, Soloviev, Bulgakov: Orthodox Theology in a New Key.* Edinburgh: T. & T. Clark, 2000.

Van Rossum, Joost. "Deification in Palamas and Aquinas." *St. Vladimir's Theological Quarterly* 47 (2003) 365–82.

———. "The *logoi* of Creation and the Divine 'Energies' in Maximus the Confessor and Gregory Palamas." *Studia Patristica* 27 (1993) 213–17.

———. "Vladimir Lossky et sa lecture de Grégoire Palamas." *Contacts* 229 (2010) 38–59.

———. "Паламизм и софиология." Христианская мысль 3 (2006) 62–66.

Vasiljevic, Bishop Maxim. *History, Truth, Holiness: Studies in Theological Ontology and Epistemology.* Alhambra, CA: Sebastian, 2011.

Vasileios, Archimandrite. *I Came that They May Have Life, and Have It Abundantly.* Montreal: Alexander, 2008.

Velimirovich, Nikolai. *The Universe as Symbols & Signs: An Essay on Mysticism in the Eastern Church.* South Canaan, PA: St. Tikhon's Seminary Press, 2010.

Ventis, Haralambos. *Toward Apophatic Theological Realism: An Orthodox Realistic Critique of Postmodernism with Special Attention to the Work of George Lindbeck.* PhD diss., Boston University, School of Theology, 2001.

Ware, Kallistos. "The Debate about Palamism," *Eastern Churches Review* 9 (1977) 45–63.

Wheeler, J. Craig. *Cosmic Catastrophes: Supernovae, Gamma-ray Bursts, and Adventures in Hyperspace.* 2nd ed. Cambridge: Cambridge University Press, 2007.

Wilczek, Frank. *The Lightness of Being: Mass, Ether, and the Unification of Forces.* New York: Basic, 2008.

Word, Kenneth. *The Quantum World: Quantum Physics for Everyone.* Cambridge: Harvard University Press, 2005.

Yannaras, Christos. Христос Янарас в разговор с Калин Янакиев, о. Николай Нешков и Георги Тенев. Християнство и Култура 3 (2003): http://hkultura.

com/db_text/2002_3_4_cristosjanaras.pdf. ("Christos Yannaras in a Conversation with Kalin Yanakiev, Fr. Nikolay Neshkov and Georgi Tenev." *Christianity and Culture* 3 (2003).)

———. "The Distinction between Essence and Energies and Its Importance for Theology," *St. Vladimir's Theological Quarterly* 19 (1975) 232–45.

———. *Elements of Faith. An Introduction to Orthodox Theology.* Edinburgh: T. & T. Clark, 1998.

———. *The Meaning of Reality: Essays on Existence and Communion, Eros and History.* Los Angeles: Sebastian & Indiktos, 2011.

———. *Person and Eros.* Brookline, MA: Holy Cross Orthodox Press, 2007.

———. *Postmodern Metaphysics.* Translated by Norman Russell. Brookline, MA: Holy Cross Orthodox Press, 2004.

Zeilinger, Anton. "Quantum Physics: Ontology or Epistemology?" In *Trinity and an Entangled World: Relationality in Physical Science and Theology*, edited by John Polkinghorne, 32–40. Grand Rapids: Eerdmans, 2010.

Zenkovsky, Vasily. V. *A History of Russian Philosophy*, Vol. 2. London: Routledge, 2003.

Zizioulas, John D. *Communion and Otherness: Further studies in Personhood and the Church.* Edited by Paul McPartlan. London: T. & T. Clark, 2006.

Аржаковски, Антуан. Журнал Путь (1925–1940). Поколение русских религиозных мыслителей в эмиграции. Киев: Феникс, 2000.

Беневич, Г. И., и Д. С. Бирюков, ред. *Антология восточно-христианской богословской мысли. Ортодоксия и гетеродоксия*, в 2-х томах, т. 2. Москва, Санкт-Петербург: Smaragdos Philocalias, 2009.

Бирюков, Д. С. "Давид Дисипат, его учение и место в паламитских спорах." In Дисипат, Монах Давид. Полемические сочинения. История и богословие паламитских споров. Перевод с древнегреч. Барзах, З. А., Волчкевич, А. И., Маркова, А. В., Поспелова, Д. А., Черноглазова, Д. А. Под общ. ред. А. И. Солопова, науч. ред. Д. С. Бирюков, сост. Д. А. Поспелов, 7–61. Москва: Святая гора Афон, Пустынь Новая Фиваида Афонского Русского Пантелеимонова монастыря, 2012.

Булатович, Антоний, Йеросхим. Апология веры во Имя Божие и во Имя Иисус. Москва: Путь, 1913. http://www.omolenko.com/imyaslavie/apologiya.htm.

Булгаков, С. Н. "Природа в философии Владимира Соловьева." Вопросы философии и психологии 5, 1910.

———. Философия имени. Paris: YMCA, 1953. French edition: Bulgakov, Père Serge. *La philosophie du Verbe et du nom.* Lausanne: L'age de l'homme, 1991.

———. Свет невечерний: Созерцания и умозрения. Москва: Путь, 1917.

Дисипат, Монах Давид. "Слово господина Давида Дисипата о богохульствах Варлаама и Акиндина, отправленое письмом господину Николаю Кавасиле." In Дисипат, Монах Давид. Полемические сочинения. История и богословие паламитских споров. Перевод с древнегреч. Барзах, З. А., Волчкевич, А. И., Маркова, А. В., Поспелова, Д. А., Черноглазова, Д. А. Под общ. ред. А. И. Солопова, науч. ред. Д. С. Бирюков, сост. Д. А. Поспелов, 48–56, 220–35 Москва: Святая гора Афон, Пустынь Новая Фиваида Афонского Русского Пантелеимонова монастыря, 2012. (Greek version of this work: *David Disypatou Logos Kata Barlaam Kai Akindynou Pros Nikolaon Kabasilan.* Thessalonikē: Kentron Vyzantinōn Ereunōn, 1973.)

Каприев, Георги. Византийска философия. Второ издание. София: Изток-Запад, 2011.

———. Максим Изповедник—Въведение в мисловната му система. София: Изток-Запад, 2010.

Кривошеин, Монах Василий. Аскетическое и богословское учение св. Григория Паламы. Сборник статей по археологии и византиноведению, издаваемый Институтом имени Н.П.Кондакова, VIII. Прага, 1936, 99–151.

Лосский, Владимир. "Спор о Софии." В: Лосский, Вл. Спор о Софии. Статьи разных лет. Москва: Издательство Свято-Владимирского Братства, 1996. *http://proroza.narod.ru/VLossky.htm.*

Майендорф., Иоанн, протопресвитер. Жизнь и труды́ святителя Григория Паламы́. *Введение в изучении.* Издание второе, исправленное и дополненное для Русского перевода. Перев. Г. Н. Начинкина. Санкт-Петербург: Византинороссика, 1997.

———. "Православное свидетельство в современном мире." В: Православие и современый мир. Минск, 1995.

———. "Тема 'Премудрости' в Восточноевропейской средневековой культуре и ее наследие." Пиотровский, Б. Б., ред. Литература и искусство в системе культуры, 244–52. Москва: Наука, 1988.

Медведев, И., В. Лурье/ Послесловие. В: Майендорф., Иоанн, , протопресвитер. Жизнь и труды́ святителя Григория Паламы́. *Введение в изучении.* Издание второе, исправленное и дополненное для Русского перевода. Перев. Г. Н. Начинкина, 327–73. Санкт-Петербург: Византинороссика, 1997.

Павлов, Павел. Богословието като Биография: Протойерей Георги Флоровски (1893–1979), *Био-Библиография.* София: Университетско издателство "Св. Климент Охридски," 2013.

Павлов, Павел, съст. Протойерей Георги Флоровски (1893–1979)—*IN MEMORIAM. Сборник с доклади от Годината на Флоровски.* София: International Center for Theological and Scientific Culture, 2012.

Павлюченков, Н. "Философия имени священика Павла Флоренского в контексте Имяславческой полемики начала XX в." *Вестник Православного Свято-Тихоновского гуманитарного университета. Серия 1: Богословие. Философия. Религиоведение* 2 (2008) 75–88.

Пентковски, А. М. "Письма Г.Флоровского С.Булгакову и С.Тышкевичу." Символ—Журнал христианской культуры при Славянской библиотеке в Париже 29 (1993) 199–216.

Рибалов, Светослав. Възвръщане към мистичния опит на отците. Учението за нетварните божествени енергии в гръцкото богословие на XX век. София: Синодално издателство, 2014.

Соловьёв, Владимир Сергеевич. Краткая повесть об антихристе. Рассказ, 1900.

Соколов, И. „Святой Григорий Палама, архиепископ Фессалоникийский, его труды и учение об исихии: По поводу исслед. Г. Х. Папамихаила, Ὁ ἅγιος Γρηγόριος Παλαμᾶς ἀρχιεπίσκοπος Θεσσαλονίκης ." ЖМНП (1913) № 4, 378–93; № 5, 159–86; № 6, 409–429; № 7, 114–39.

Софроний (Сахаров), архимандрит. Переписка с протоиереем Георгием Флоровским. Свято-Иоанно-Предтеченский монастырь, 2008.

Стоядинов, Мариян. Божията благодат. Велико Търново: Праксис, 2007.

————. "Естествено познание и богопознание в паламитското богословие." *Ars и scientia* през Средновековието: Сборник от научна конференция. Божилова, Нора, изд., 8–26 . Велико Търново: Издателство Одри, 2006.

Танев, Стоян. Ти, Който си навсякъде и всичко изпълваш. Същност и енергия в Православното богословие и във физиката. София: Университетско издателство "Св. Климент Охридски," 2013.

Флоровский, Г. В. "Тайна Фаворского Света." Сергиевские листки 3 (1935) 2–7.

————. „Тварь и тварьность." Православная мысль 1 (1928) 176–212 (English version: Florovsky, Georges. "Creation and Creaturehood." In *The Collected Works of Georges Florovsky III: Creation and Redemption*, 43–78. Belmont, MA: Nordland, 1976.)

Фраксис, Георгий. Диспут свт. Григория Паламы с Григорой философом— *Философские и богословские аспекты паламитских споров. Перевод с греч. Поспелов, Д. А. Бирюков, Д. С., редактор.* Святая гора Афон: Издание пустыни Новая Фиваида Афонского Русского Пантелеимонова монастыря, 2009.

Хоружий, Сергей. "Естественная теология в свете исихастского боговидения." *VOX* Философский журнал, Вьипуск 7, Декабрь, 2009. http://vox-journal.org/html/issues/vox7/44.

Христов, Иван. "Битие и съществуване в дискусията за метода между св. Григорий Палама и Варлаам." Хуманизъм, култура, религия, 37–48. София: Лик, 1996.

————. Византийското богословие през *XIV* век. Дискурсът за божествените енергии. София: Изток-Запад, 2016.

————. "Естествения разум и свръхестественото озарение в дебата между Варлаам и св. Григорий Палама." Критика и Хуманнизъм 1 (2001) 126–34.

Янарас, Христос. "Постмодерната актуалност на понятието личност." В: Кризата като Предизвикателство. София: Лик, 2002

Παπαμιχαήλ, Σ. Γ. Ὁ ἅγιος Γρηγόριος ὁ Παλαμᾶς, ἀρχιεπίσκοπος Θεσσαλονίκης. Πετρούπολις — Ἀλεξάνδρεια, 1911.

Made in the USA
Middletown, DE
03 June 2022

66655228R00156